Juneteenth 101

Popular Myths and Forgotten Facts

Third Edition - Updated July 2021

by

D. J. Norman-Cox

Printed in the United States of America

United States Copyright 2021—D. J. Norman-Cox

*In the body of truth,
facts are nutrients;
perceptions are parasites.*

Sept. 13, 1862

Hearsay began.

> On the 15th of September, Lincoln will issue a proclamation of general universal emancipation.

The Standard (Clarksville, Texas), page 1, column 3, September 13, 1862.

Nine days later, (September 22, 1862) President Lincoln issued the preliminary Proclamation of Emancipation.

June 3, 1865

Hearsay gave way to myths.

> There are no longer any slaves in the United States. All persons heretofore held as such became free by virtue of the Executive proclamation, of January 1, 1863, commonly known as the Emancipation Proclamation.

Excerpt from Maj. Gen. Herron's General Orders No. 20.
Published by Houston Tri-Weekly Telegraph. June 16, 1865.
Page 4, column 3. *Title of article:* Planters and Freedmen.

Sixteen days later, (June 19, 1865) Major General Gordon Granger issued a similar order.

"On June 18, 1865, when General Granger and 2,000 troops marched into Galveston..."

Psst... Them marching troops would'da drowned 'cause Galveston is an island. I ain't starting nothing; I'm just saying.

18th? Wait...what?

Yeah. And why was General G's first order from Galveston dated June 17th? Huh? Tell me.

Know this:

11	Slavery did not end on Juneteenth
16	The preliminary Emancipation Proclamation freed no one
20	Texas was not the last state to free enslaved Africans
24	The 13th Amendment became law *after* Juneteenth
31	The Emancipation Proclamation was a weapon of war
37	No state voluntarily complied with the Proclamation
40	Texans knew about the E. Proc. before June 19, 1865
66	Freedom was not delayed 30 months to harvest crops
74	Lincoln did not issue General Order No. 3
80	Ashton Villa is a tourism ploy
90	The Buffalo Soldiers did not exist in 1865
96	Reports of freedom celebrations are misleading
100	Juneteenth is the second oldest continuous freedom celebration
110	Early emancipation commemorations excluded women
116	Pennsylvania may have been first to officially honor emancipation

129	America national emancipation observances began in 1949
138	Lift Every Voice and Sing is not "an old slave song"
140	About John Brown's Body
144	The Rest of the Story
147	Juneteenth minutiae & trifles
154	Texas African American History Memorial
156	Fibbery, fables and foolishness
174	Who devised all this boo-boo?
176	Juneteenth specials: Commercializing emancipation is not new
186	More boo-boo talk: Bogus textbooks
188	Juneteenth bunk busters training manual
192	Juneteenth news vault
196	Before Juneteenth, stuff happened
200	After Juneteenth, more stuff happened
209	Juneteenth's had a sibling
210	The watermelon mess
216	Postscript: Accuracy Matters
220	Bibliography
232	Index

About this book

When America's newest holiday was created in mid-June 2021, news outlets offered explanations of what was being celebrated. Some got it right. Error-making was easy because there are two Juneteenth's - the national holiday celebrating slavery's end regard for date; and the Texas holiday that celebrates the beginning of militarily enforced emancipation in Texas. Both occur on June 19th.

Scholarly research of Texas emancipation events collectively called "Juneteenth" is plentiful, but celebrants who are not history scholars (a.k.a. the majority of Juneteenth revelers) remain steeped in emancipation myths. Unfortunately, thanks primarily to the internet, each year the volume of inaccurate information grows exponentially, increasing the validity of bogus folklore while obscuring reality.

It is this author's opinion that misinformation about Juneteenth oversimplifies the complexity of slavery's end, and harms our nation's continuous march toward becoming 'a more perfect union'. Essentially, measuring progress accurately is an onerous task when the starting point is nebulous.

Therein, the objective of this publication is to increase the relevance and appreciation of Juneteenth by confronting and hopefully eradicating inaccurate explanations of its origin.

Three questions spawned this study:
- 1) If no enslaved person in Texas knew about the Emancipation Proclamation, why did some hold Watch Night vigils?
- 2) How did news of the proclamation travel from Louisiana to New Mexico without passing through Texas?
- 3) If it took 2 1/2 years for news to reach Texas, how did General Granger's order induce a spontaneous statewide celebration?

Multiple news reports from 1862 through 1864 answered all three questions with one explanation: news of the Emancipation Proclamation was not late reaching Texas. That fact invalidates every explanation of *why* news was late. Simultaneously, it asks what really happened in Galveston on June 19, 1865.

No evidence has been found to suggest Juneteenth's popular myths were intentionally generated. Many inaccuracies addressed in this publication appear to be rooted in poorly worded explanations, and failure by Juneteenth champions to fact check. Ironically, the first fibber was the revered General Gordon Granger.

Juneteenth 101 is a survey of Juneteenth's most egregious myths. Castigating wrong-sayers is not its purpose. However, humor at the expense of a few "authorities" has been interjected to accommodate the book's target audience, they being: a) well-intentioned Juneteenth advocates pushing bogus information; b) the 'curious-but-not-enough-to-demand-accuracy'; and c) people oblivious and unconcerned about emancipation, but enjoy a occasional "ah-ha" moment.

The second edition increased the list of myths. The third edition is an update, and corrects details obtained from reputable sources later found to be incorrect.

Folklore addressed in this publication was culled from several hundred sources, including organizations responsible for coordinating Juneteenth celebrations; local, state and national government entities; news reports and social media commentaries.

Readers are encouraged to verify all assertions. The Library of Congress and records created in the nineteenth century are good starting points. Other resources are available, but beware, many are distorted perceptions posing as facts.

Juneteenth - Denver, Colorado

10

Myth #1

"Slavery in the United States ended on Juneteenth."

Countless reputable institutions and lessor known groups promote this hogwash. The statement contains two flagrant wrongs:

1) Slavery remained permissible in two non-rebellious states after June 19, 1865. (See page 21)
2) Military enforcement of emancipation in Texas was not a one-day effort. It *began* on June 19, 1865[1] The Texas General Land Office claims the campaign lasted six weeks.[3] Though no formal end date is observed, the reassignment date of the campaign's leader and driving force (Maj. Gen. Gordon Granger) marks a significant shift in the military's enforcement strategy. Granger was reassigned on July 19, 1865.[4] The Freedman's Bureau did not begin work in Texas until September 1865.

And If You're Wondering ...

The U.S. "military" arrived in Galveston on June 5th. That was when Captain Benjamin F. Sands of the U.S. Navy initiated military occupation of Texas.[2] The Army arrived June 16 - 19.

Decades after emancipation, formerly enslaved men and women recorded stories of freedom celebrations. Texas freedmen statewide, claimed freedom happened on June 19 1865. Their descriptions are not disputed, but the date is unlikely. General Order No. 3 was not distributed outside of Galveston County until *after* June 19th.

- Military records, public records and news reports do not verify Granger's third order was enforced anywhere other than Galveston on June 19th.
- Troops occupying Texas helped spread Granger's general orders statewide via distribution of handbills beginning in Houston on June 20th. (See page 106)
- Some newspapers received Order No. 3 via telegraph on June 19, 1865, but publication did not occur until their respective next issue dates, 1 to 7 days later.

Statewide emancipation was NOT a one day event. Resistance happened because...

Some newspapers reported the Emancipation Proclamation had been revoked.

From *The Standard* (Clarksville, Texas):

In the meantime, one of our exchanges tell us, "we see by the last mail that Gen. Herron, in his wise policy, has revoked the proclamation for the immediate emancipation of slaves." We hope so: it will be a great stride toward reason, and justice.[6]

&...

The potential for "compensated emancipation" existed.

In 1862, President Lincoln signed an Act requiring the government to pay slave owners up to $300 for each emancipated slave.[7] Later that year, just one month before signing the Emancipation Proclamation, President Lincoln's Annual Message to Congress proposed a resolution for Compensated Emancipation.[8] Though the proposal did not materialize, it was not forgotten by Texas slave owners resisting emancipation.

&...

Planters wanted to keep free labor until their crops were harvested.

This motive is frequently, but incorrectly mentioned as a reason why Texas slaves were not released on January 1, 1863. The scam did exist, but not until the 1865 growing season. (See page 66)

&...
Constitutionality of the proclamation was questioned.

Immediately after the proclamation was signed, scholars and attorneys began debating its legality. Arguments raged until ratification of the 13th Amendment made the proclamation moot.[9][10]

&...
A plan for gradual emancipation was floated.

Texans initially scoffed at gradual emancipation (i.e.: freedom granted according to age). However, after universal emancipation became reality in Texas some malcontents warmly embraced the idea[11][12][13] albeit without support from the Provisional Governor or news publishers.

&...
Confusion was rampant.

Emancipation instructions were clear, but some former slave owners required explicit elucidation. One owner shared his bewilderment publicly, writing in the Houston Tri-Weekly Bulletin:

> I have no cotton crop; two-thirds of my negroes are children, and useless to me - I am naturally attached to them, and them to me. I know I am their nearest and best friend, and I would gladly protect them, if permitted so to do; for this reason, and for their sakes, and if permitted to say so, for the sake of humanity. They desire to remain with me under any circumstances. The question is, "are they permitted to do so?"[14]

&...
Some heretics simply refused to obey the law.

Confederate sympathizers who stubbornly resisted emancipation *before* June 19th continued to do so *after* June 19th. Newspapers repeatedly published the general orders and the military posted bills statewide. Still, lawbreakers continued to enslave Black people after June 19, 1865.[15] (See page 202.)

TRANSLATION
by Somebody's Mama

"Next time somebody come talking about slavery ending everywhere on Juneteenth, you ought'a ask 'em to prove it. They can't, 'cause it ain't true. Never mind slavery keeping on in them other states. It take a plumb fool to believe news said in Galveston was heard across this whole state at the same time without no radio, no TV, no internet, no telephone. What kinna microphones did they have? How big were their speakers? Did they send pigeons? Was a telegraph sent to every brush harbor and household? That's just stupid."

MYTH #2

"Freedom began on October 22, 1862."

...said the multitude who did not adequately read either version of the Emancipation Proclamation.

Did y'all hear that?

Disgusting

Unspeakably wrong

No! No! No! No!

...forgive them...

Well—ah...

16

Juneteenth 101

Welcome to your circle of friends who believe now is always the best time to get some sense.

My sisters and brothers, the Preliminary Proclamation was only a threat which freed nobody.

It gave states in rebellion 100 days to stop fighting, or else!

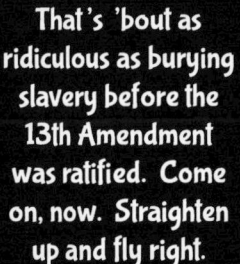

And if every slave holding state had stopped fighting, every state would have been exempted, Sweet Pea, not just five.

Don't get mad. All we're saying is, if October's proclamation had granted emancipation, there would've been no need for the one in January.

Might as well say slaves became freedmen on July 17, 1862. That's when Congress approved the 2nd Confiscation Act which said slaves in captured rebel territory "shall be forever free of their servitude and not again held as slaves." You knew that, right?

This myth exist thanks to cherry picking. You don't wanna be a cherry picker do you? When you read the whole thing instead of only the parts you like, the truth pops out.

That's 'bout as ridiculous as burying slavery before the 13th Amendment was ratified. Come on, now. Straighten up and fly right.

My daddy said nobody anywhere was freed by the proclamation in 1862. That means you don't know what you're talking about.

17

Juneteenth 101

When lawful slavery ended *(in Texas)*

Countless Juneteenth explanations claim enslaved Africans in Texas spent 2 1/2 years not knowing they were free. However, in October 1868, the Texas Supreme Court ruled lawful slavery in Texas did not end until June 19, 1865. The decision was necessary to settle lawsuits regarding the legality of slave sales occurring after Lincoln's Proclamation was formally issued and effective (January 1, 1863). One of the justices—Livingston Lindsay—wrote:

> *"The proclamation could not, proprio vigore, manumit the slaves. It required the power of the conquering forces. The liberation in Texas took effect from the date of the surrender of the insurgent forces, and the proclamation of that fact by the Commanding General, dated 19th June, 1865…Until this final surrender in Texas, the traffic in slaves was lawful."* [215]

Many dates are mentioned when discussing slavery's last day in Texas. The top four are:
- October 22, 1862 (that's just flat wrong),
- January 1, 1863 (when the operable Emancipation Proclamation was issued),
- June 19, 1865 (enforcement of the Proclamation began in Texas)
- December 6, 1865 (when the 13th Amendment ratified.)

The Texas Supreme Court chose June 19th.

Here's what happened. After Juneteenth, people who had previously purchased or rented slaves refused to pay their bills. So, lots of suing took place. To settle those suits, the court had to designate a first day of emancipation in Texas. They chose the day enforcement began. Anyone who bought a slave before that day had to pay their bill. Anyone who sold a slave after that day was out of luck. After that designation, emancipation celebrations moved to June 19.

Juneteenth - Denton, Texas

Myth #3

"Texas was the last state to end slavery."

Nope! Texas was the last state *"in rebellion"* to enforce the Emancipation Proclamation. Five slave-holding states were exempted from the proclamation.*

~ Enslaved people in Kentucky and Delaware were emancipated six months *after* Juneteenth.

~ Maryland's citizens approved statewide emancipation by popular vote: 30,174 in favor; 29,799 opposed. Freedom was declared on Nov 1, 1864.[16] (22 months after exemption.)

~ Missouri's legislature approved emancipation via ordinance to a new state constitution approved January 11, 1865.[17] (2 years after exemption.)

~ Tennessee was conquered before the proclamation was signed. Slaves there became freedmen on Oct. 24, 1864.

(Also, parts of Louisiana and Virginia were exempted. See page 22 for the complete roster of exempted locations.)

Juneteenth 101

People enslaved in the following locations were declared free by the Emancipation Proclamation:

- Alabama
- Arkansas
- Florida
- Georgia
- Parts of Louisiana
- Mississippi
- North Carolina
- South Carolina
- Texas
- Parts of Virginia

The Proclamation excluded people enslaved in the following locations.

- Delaware
- Kentucky
- Maryland
- Missouri
- Tennessee
- The Louisiana parishes of
    - Ascension
    - Assumption
    - Jefferson
    - Lafourche
    - Orleans, *(including the City of New Orleans)*
    - Plaquemines
    - St. Bernard
    - St. Charles
    - St. James
    - St. John
    - St. Mary
    - St. Martin
    - Terrebone
- The 48 Virginia counties that eventually became the state of West Virginia.
- The Virginia counties of:
    - Accomack
    - Berkley
    - Elizabeth City
    - Northampton
    - Norfolk
    - Princess Ann
    - York *(including the cities of Norfolk and Portsmouth)*

22

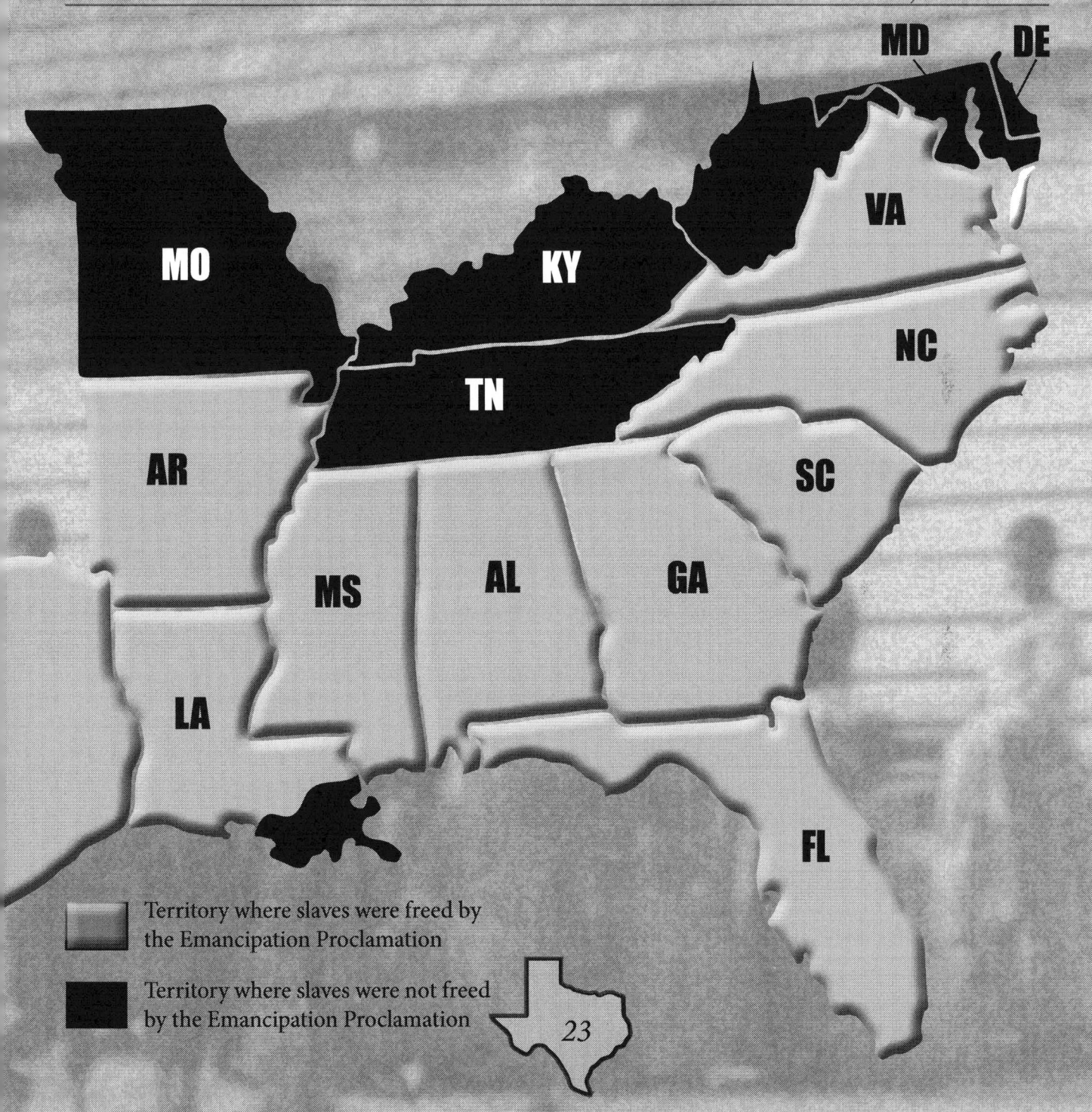

Juneteenth 101

MO | KY | MD | DE | VA | NC | TN | AR | SC | MS | AL | GA | LA | FL

Territory where slaves were freed by the Emancipation Proclamation

Territory where slaves were not freed by the Emancipation Proclamation

23

MYTH #4:

"The U. S. constitution was amended for the 13th time *before* Juneteenth."

TRUTH:

The 13th Amendment ended lawful slavery in the United States and its territories*, but it did not exist until Dec. 6, 1865. Prior to then, legislation that became the 13th amendment was merely a non-actionable "Congressional Joint Resolution" *proposing* a constitutional amendment.

- April 8, 1864 - The Senate passed the resolution.
- Jan. 31, 1865 - The House passed the resolution.
- Feb. 1, 1865 - President Lincoln signed the resolution.
- **Dec. 6, 1865** - The required number of state ratifications was secured.[18]
- *Dec. 18, 1865* - The U.S. Secretary of State certified the amendment's validity as part of the U.S. Constitution.[19]

Translation
Passing the resolution didn't mean jack 'til 3/4s of the states said, "okay, that's cool". That happened six months *after* Juneteenth.

Somebody's know-it-all barber

* See Mariana Islands, page 28

Juneteenth 101

13th Amendment to the U.S. Constitution

Section 1.
Neither slavery nor involuntary servitude, except as a punishment for crime whereof the party shall have been duly convicted, shall exist within the United States, or any place subject to their jurisdiction.

Section 2.
Congress shall have power to enforce this article by appropriate legislation.

TRANSLATION:

"No kind of slavery except for criminal punishment can exist in these United States. None I say, and again, I say none. Don't even think about it. Plus, Congress can rub some Act Right on whoever needs some. Oh, you doubt that? Well, go ahead and see if they can't."
Somebody's Pastor

See, what had happened was ...

a.k.a.

How Stuff Went Down

The House of Representatives when the 13th Amendment passed

- Apr. 12, '61   Fighting between the states jumped off after a bunch of political noise talking.
- Sept. 22, '62   Lincoln threatened to free enslaved Africans *IF* states didn't stop fighting, (i.e.: Preliminary Proclamation issued).
- Jan 1, '63   Lincoln's threat became real for unconquered states-in-rebellion that ignored him.
- Apr. 8, '64   The Senate passed a resolution proposing a 13th constitutional amendment.
- Jan 31, '65   The House of Reps. passed the proposed amendment. Now, 2/3s of the existing state legislatures had to approve the proposal before it could become effective.
- Feb 1, '65   Illinois became the first state to thumbs up the proposed 13th Amendment.
- Apr. 9, '65   After getting their butts whooped, the confederate army began surrendering in chunks.
- May 12, '65   A post-war battle broke out at Palmito Ranch, TX. The Union lost (big time). Confederates celebrated, but upon discovering their effort was fruitless, they pilfered supplies and ran home.
- June 2, '65   Confederate Gen. McGruder signed surrender docs near Galveston. 3 days later, Union troops initiated occupation of Galveston.
- June 19, '65   Major F. W. Emery signed three orders dictated by Gen. Granger. Order No. 3 enforced the Emancipation Proclamation.
- Aug. 20, '65   President Andrew Johnson proclaimed the Civil War was over.
- Dec. 6, '65   Georgia became the final state needed to ratify the proposed 13th amendment.
  - Dec. 18, '65   The U.S. Constitution was officially amended for the 13th time.

Juneteenth 101

Emancipation and slavery outlaw dates

In some U. S. states and territories, anti-slavery laws predate the emancipation dates listed. Such laws were selective and did not completely eradicate slavery in those jurisdictions. All dates listed indicate when emancipation was effective statewide or territory-wide.

Y'ALL CEASE AND DESIST

Alabama	September 22, 1865[20]
Alaska	* N/A
American Samoa	Feb. 20, 1929 On this day Congress ratified Samoa an American territory, subject to American law, including the 13th Amendment.
Arizona	February 24, 1863
Arkansas	March 14, 1864
California	November 13, 1849
Colorado	* August 1, 1876
Connecticut	1848
Delaware	December 18, 1865
Florida	January 1, 1863[21] *Enforced: May 20, 1865*
Georgia	January 1, 1863-1865
Guam	February 22, 1900[22]
Hawaii	* N/A
Idaho	* N/A
Illinois	^ April 1, 1848
Indiana	^ July 27, 1820
Iowa	September 3, 1857
Kansas	February 23, 1860
Kentucky	December 18, 1865
Louisiana	July 23, 1864
Maine	March 15, 1820
Mariana Islands	^^ March 24, 1976
Maryland	November 1, 1864
Massachusetts	July 8, 1783
Michigan	^ October 5, 1835

Minnesota	** October 13, 1857	Texas	June 19, 1865
Mississippi	December 6, 1865	Utah	February 19, 1862
	MS officially ratified the 13th Amendment Feb. 7, 2013.	Vermont	July 8, 1777
	Parts of MS observe May 8 as Emancipation Day ("8 O'May")	Virgin Islands	August 1, 1834
		Virginia	April 7, 1864
Missouri	January 11, 1865	Washington	* N/A
Montana	* N/A	Washington, D. C.	April 16, 1862
Nebraska	* N/A	West Virginia	February 3, 1865
Nevada	February 19, 1862	Wisconsin	^ May 29, 1848
New Hampshire	June 2, 1783	Wyoming	* February 26, 1821
	Persons born after 1783 were free. Persons born before 1783 remained slaves. Slavery eventually faded away without an emancipation plan.		*Admitted: July 10, 1890*
New Jersey	Feb 15, 1804		
	Law for gradual emancipation became effective.		
New Mexico	* N/A		
New York	July 4, 1827		
North Carolina	December 4, 1865		
North Dakota	* N/A		
Ohio	^ November 1802		
Oklahoma	* N/A		
Oregon	June 26, 1844		
	Admitted: Feb. 14, 1959		
Pennsylvania	March 1, 1780		
Puerto Rico	March 22, 1873		
Rhode Island	March 1, 1784		
South Carolina	Feb 18, 1865		
	(Charleston surrendered)		
South Dakota	* N/A		
Tennessee	February 22, 1865		

^ A 1787 ordinance outlawed slavery in the territory that would later become Illinois, Indiana, Michigan, Ohio, and Wisconsin. The dates listed for those states indicate when their respective state constitutions outlawed slavery. In Indiana, slavery continued into the late 1850s despite lawsuits emancipating individual slaves.[23]

* These states were admitted to the union after slavery had been outlawed by the Thirteenth Amendment. Some states approved anti-slavery laws while they were territories.

+ New York freed slaves in stages. The final group was freed in 1827.[24]

** Minnesota voters approved their constitution on this date. State legislators acted on the theory that statehood began when voters approved the constitution. Actual statehood began on May 11, 1858.[25]

^^ The Mariana Islands became a U.S. territory when legislation limiting applicability of federal law was signed by President Gerald Ford.[26] Servitude continued until 2017.[27]

Juneteenth 101

Juneteenth - Milwaukee, Wisconsin

Myth #5
(An endless squabble)

The Emancipation Proclamation's *foremost* purpose was to end slavery in the United States.

Lincoln's words:

"My paramount object in this struggle is to save the Union, and is not either to save or to destroy slavery. If I could save the Union without freeing any slave I would do it, and if I could save it by freeing all the slaves I would do it; and if I could save it by freeing some and leaving others alone I would also do that. What I do about slavery, and the colored race, I do because I believe it helps to save the Union..." [28]

TRANSLATION

He said, "I wanna win this war! I don't care who I gotta pray for, piss on or sleep with. That don't mean nothing to me. I just wanna win".

Abraham Lincoln's open letter
to the New York Tribune
August 23, 1862

The Emancipation Proclamation was a weapon of war
created to isolate and destabilize the confederacy.

Explanation

The Emancipation Proclamation assured the Civil War remained an American internal skirmish by making it domestically unwise for slave-free nations to join the war in support of the Confederacy. The Union might have lost the war had the Confederates acquired allies.[29]

AND THAT MEANS...?

TRANSLATION

It's like this. The folks in your house are starving 'cause your lazy self refuses to go make groceries. But! When ya' buddy on the corner calls asking you to grab some grub, you jumps ya' hungry butt up; and runs clean out the door. You drives 'im to everybody's lil' ol' raggedy buffet restaurant where you both eat two plates; maybe three...per stop! Guess what's gonna happen when you get home.

Somebody's spouse

An argument irrefutable:

If ending slavery was the proclamation's primary purpose, *all* slaves would have been included, not just the ones strategically convenient for warfare.

"Would that have been legal?"

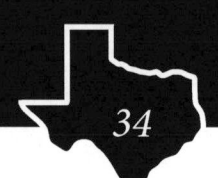

"Was the Boston Tea Party legal?"

Juneteenth - Tyler, Texas

35

Juneteenth - Atlanta, Georgia

ALWAYS REMEMBER
GIVE THANKS
JUNETEENTH

36

Myth #6

"All confederate states (other than Texas) complied with the Emancipation Proclamation."

Bull pie!

Somebody's working brain

FACT:

Only the chattel in territories specified in the Proclamation and *controlled by the Union Army* were freed. Chattel in territory controlled by the confederate army remained in bondage.

Juneteenth 101

That means...

- Slaves living in states covered by the Emancipation Proclamation were freed *IF* the Union Army controlled their location.

- Slaves living in areas controlled by the confederate army remained in bondage, but were free on paper.

- Slaves living in exempted places were luckless.

Speech bubble (man): This information isn't new.

Speech bubble (woman): It's new to me. And if you knew, why didn't you tell somebody?

Unlike some myths, the origin of this fallacy is easy to speculate.

Some of the former confederate states do not have a definitive date specifying when enforcement of the Emancipation Proclamation began or was completed. Enslaved people in those states were continuously freed as the Union Army gained territory. Therefore, in those states, enforcement began when the proclamation became effective, *and continued* until the war's end.

That fact has morphed into a false belief that all enslaved people in those states were freed on January 1, 1863.

More to consider:

(Some historians estimate 500,000 slaves skedaddled upon hearing a battle line was drawing closer. Many times that number remained in bondage.) + (After the preliminary proclamation was issued, the Texas slave population bulked up because owners in other states hid their slaves in Texas for safekeeping.) = **Slavery continued to exist *AFTER* Jan. 1, 1863.**

Juneteenth 101

The 1st Place Grand Champion Sho'nuf Biggest Lie:

40

"Texans didn't know about emancipation because..."

Origin unknown

"But if y'all find out who started that mess please let me know. I got something for 'em."

Somebody's Big Mama

MYTH #7.1

"It took 2 1/2 years for news of the proclamation to reach Texas."

THINK

If it took 30 months for news to travel from Washington, D. C to Atlanta, Texas (1,179 miles), it would have taken*:

- 3 months to reach Richmond, Virginia (120 mi.)
- 10.7 months to reach Charlotte, North Carolina (424 mi.)
- 12.3 months to reach Knoxville, Tennessee (487 mi.)
- 13.5 months to reach Charleston, South Carolina (532 mi.)
- 16.8 months to reach Atlanta, Georgia (661 mi.)
- 18.8 months to reach Birmingham, Alabama (742 mi.)
- 24.9 months to reach Jackson, Mississippi (979 mi.)
- 26.1 months to reach Pine Bluff, Arkansas (1,027 mi.)
- 27.8 months to reach Monroe, Louisiana (1,095 mi.)
- **and 20.7 *additional* months to travel across Texas (815 mi.)**

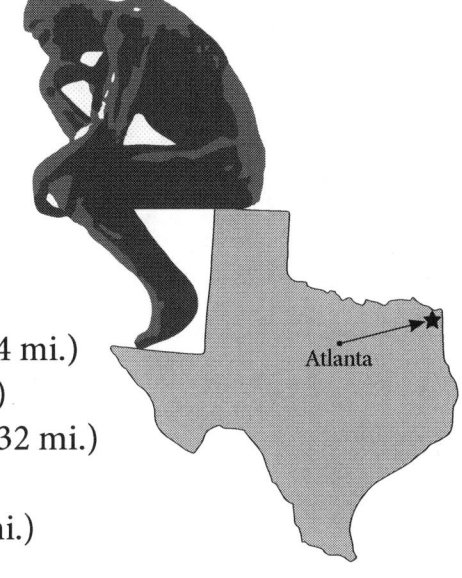

*All calculations were based on distances posted in www.google.com/maps

Food for Thought

A messenger moseying at only 2.15 miles per hr for 8 hrs per day could complete 4 round trips from Washington, D.C. to El Paso in 2 1/2 years, WALKING! That includes sixteen hours for rest or partying each day. A messenger on horseback trotting at 10 mph could make 14 round trips.

"Umm, did you know the distance from Atlanta, TX to Atlanta, GA is only 653 miles. But the distance from Atlanta, TX to El Paso is 815 miles?"

"What? Did you know El Paso, TX is closer to California than it is to Dallas?"

Juneteenth - Philadelphia, PA

44

MYTH #7.2

"...A lone rider on horseback carrying news of the Emancipation Proclamation was killed before he reached Texas."

Duh!

The proclamation was initially issued via telegraph. Everyone tapping the northern wire received the news.

Whereas, the Emancipation Proclamation was a military strategy, it was incumbent upon the Union Army to spread the word and enforce the strategy using all available resources.

Communication tools during the Civil War included couriers, the Military Telegraph Corps, the Signal Corps, newspapers and posting of handbills.

"Think about that, y'all. Any official courier of this weaponized information would have been a member of the Union Army. Texas was run by Confederates. Who was the guy bound for Texas supposed to tell?"

Somebody's classmate

The U.S. Telegraph Corp, lugging wires, poles and other equipment, followed Union troops to keep officers updated about war tactics.[30]

Distribution of the final Emancipation Proclamation began at 8 p.m., January 1, 1863, from the Telegraph Office of the War Department.[31]

TRUTH

Every explanation of why news was slow to reach Texas is false

because ...

Juneteenth 101

... the news was! not! late!

"Say wh–a–a–a–t?"

49

Juneteenth 101

Plus, they were warned.

https://texashistory.unt.edu/ark:/67531/metapth236437/m1/1

The entire preliminary Proclamation of Emancipation was published on the front page (col. 4) of the October 17, 1862 edition of Houston's newspaper, The Tri-weekly Telegraph. End of discussion.

50

"Close ya' mouth before bees fly in."

Juneteenth - Grambling, Louisiana

51

FACT:

Between September 1862 and December 1864 (inclusive), the Emancipation Proclamation was mentioned in at least 125 editions of Texas newspapers.

NOTE: There may have been many more. At 125, the writer of this book stopped counting.

Juneteenth 101

"But everyone knows slaves didn't buy newspapers."

Sweet Pea, everyone should also know when saying, "*they* didn't know about the Proclamation", '*they*' refers to slave owners, not the enslaved.

Yeah, teacher! Speak that truth. 'Cause what the slaves did or did not know didn't matter. Freeing themselves was called "running away."

> The Confederate Congress are endeavoring to arrange a retaliatory bill to the Lincoln emancipation proclamation.— The weight of talk appears to be in favor of hanging all officers who may fall into our hands after the 1st of January, 1863, until the proclamation is revoked. The weight, however, of influence is in favor of putting both officers and men at hard labor till the close of the war.

From: The Texas Almanac -- "Extra." (Austin, TX), Vol. 1, No. 6, Ed. 1, Oct. 23, 1862

Being a military strategy, spreading the word of emancipation was not a haphazard action. The excerpt above verifies Confederates discussed the matter insightfully, strategically and openly with effective reciprocation being their goal. It is unreasonable to believe confederate officers in Texas were excluded from such discussions for more than two years. Likewise, it is irrational to assume Texas officers did not discuss this urgent information with fellow statesmen.

A false but widely held belief is that enslaved Africans in Texas remained enslaved because they did not know they were free. The notion that better informed slaves could declare or litigate their freedom based on the say-so of their owner's enemy is wrongheaded and wholly ridiculous.

Numerous recordings by former Texas slaves verify they were not told about freedom until June 19th or after. Other documents verify some enslaved people were aware of the proclamation. Example: The ones that held secret Watch Night vigils. Informing slaves of the proclamation had no benefits for owners firmly opposed to emancipating their slaves. Yet, some may have done so. Prior to June 19, 1865, Sam Houston, former President of the Republic of Texas, reportedly read Lincoln's proclamation to his slaves, then freed them. That claim may be incorrect because his post-death estate included twelve slaves.[32]

In the words of historian Dr. Gregory Downs, Associate Professor of History at New York City College, *"Ending slavery was not simply a matter of issuing pronouncements. It was a matter of forcing rebels to obey the law."*[33]

> Speaking of the emancipation proclamation in one of his speeches, Lincoln is reported to have said:
> "What I did I did after very full deliberation, under a very heavy and solemn sense of responsibility. I can only trust in God I have made no mistake. I shall make no attempt on this occasion to sustain what I have done or said by comment. It is now for the country and the world to pass judgment on it and may be to take action upon it. I will say no more on this subject. In my position I am environed with difficulties."

The Tri-Weekly Telegraph (Houston) Nov. 10, 1862. Vol. 28, No. 102, Ed. 1.

> Washington correspondents all agree that Lincoln has resolved to stand by his Emancipation Proclamation, and will issue a supplementary proclamation on the 1st January, indicating states and parts of states in which slavery is forever outlawed.

The State Gazette. (Austin, TX), Jan. 14, 1863, Vol. 14, No. 24, Ed. 1,

> The resolution sustaining the President's Emancipation Proclamation, is as follows:
> "Resolved, That the Proclamation of the President, of the date of September 22d, 1862, is warranted by the constitution; that the policy of emancipation as indicated therein, is well adapted to hasten the restoration of peace; is well chosen as a war measure, and is an exercise of power with a proper regard to the rights of citizens and the perpetuity of a free Government."
> It passed by 78 to 51.

Below from: The Tri-Weekly Telegraph (Houston), Vol. 28, No. 130, Ed. 1, Jan. 14, 1863

54

Partial index of references to the Emancipation Proclamation published in Texas newspapers, September 1862 through December 1864.

The Bellville Countryman
(Bellville, TX)
   Sat., Jan. 17, 1863
      Vol. 3, No. 24, Ed. 1, p. 1, col. 3
   Sat., Feb. 7, 1863
      Vol. 3, No. 27, Ed. 1, p. 1, col. 3
   Sat., Feb. 21, 1863
      Vol. 3, No. 29, Ed. 1, p. 2, col. 2
   Sat., March 7, 1863
      Vol. 3, No. 31, Ed. 1, p. , col. & 2
   Sat., March 14, 1863
      Vol. 3, No. 32, Ed. 1, p 2, col. 2
   Sat., April 4, 1863
      Vol. 3, No. 35, Ed. 1, p. 1, col. 4
      Vol. 3, No. 35, Ed. 1, p. 2, col. 2
   Sat., May 30, 1863
      Vol. 3, No. 43, Ed. 1, p. 1, col. 2
   Sat., July 4, 1863
      Vol. 3, No. 48, Ed. 1, p. 1, col. 3
   Sat., Aug. 8, 1863
      Vol. 4, No. 3, Ed. 1, p. 1, col. 3
   Thur., Jan. 21, 1864
      Vol. 4, No. 22, Ed. 1, p. 2, col. 3
   Thur., March 17, 1864
      Vol. 4, No. 25, Ed. 1, p. 2, col. 1

Dallas Herald (Dallas, TX)
   Sat., Nov. 1, 1862
      Vol. 10, No. 49, Ed. 1, p. 1, col. 4
   Sat., Nov. 15, 1862
      Vol. 10, No. 51, Ed. 1
   Sat., Dec. 6, 1862
      Vol. 11, No. 2, Ed. 1, p. 2
   Sat., Dec. 13, 1862
      Vol. 11, No. 3, Ed. 1, p. 2, col. 2
   Wed., Dec. 31, 1862
      Vol. 11, No. 5, Ed. 1, p. col. 5
   Wed., Jan 21, 1863, p. 2, col. 2
      Vol. 11, No. 8, Ed. 1
   Wed., Jan. 28, 1863
      Vol. 11, No. 9, Ed. 1, p 2., col. 3 & 4
   Wed., Feb. 25, 1863
      Vol. 11, No. 13, Ed. 1, P. 2 , col. 2 & 3
   Sat., Oct. 1, 1864
      Vol. 12, No. 6, Ed. 1, p. 2

Henderson Times (Henderson, TX)
   Tues., Sept. 27, 1864
      Vol. 5, No. 35, Ed. 1, p. 2, col. 4

Houston Telegraph (Houston, TX)
   Fri., Nov. 7, 1862
      Ed. 1

Houston Tri-Weekly Telegraph
   Mon., Nov. 21, 1864
      Vol. 30, No. 172, Ed. 1

Fri., Dec. 23, 1864
    Vol. 30, No. 186, Ed. 1, P. 2, col. 4
Mon., Dec. 26, 1864
    Vol. 30, No. 187, Ed. 1, P. 1

The Ranchero (Corpus Christi, TX)
Thur., Feb. 5, 1863
    Vol. 2, No. 50, Ed. 1, p. 2, col. 3
Thur., Feb. 12, 1863
    Vol. 2, No. 51, Ed. 1, p. 2, col. 2
Thur., March 5, 1863
    Vol. 3, No. 2, Ed. 1, p. 2, col. 4

The Semi-Weekly News (San Antonio)
Mon., Jan. 26, 1863
    Vol. 2, No. 123, Ed. 1, p. 1, col. 4

The Standard (Clarksville, TX)
Sat., Sept. 13, 1862
    Vol. 19, No. 30, Ed. 1. p. 1, col. 3
Thur., Jan. 22, 1863
    Vol. 19, No. 42, Ed. 1, p. 2, col. 3
Sat., Jan. 31, 1863
    Vol. 19, No. 43, Ed. 1, p. 1, col. 3
Sat., Feb. 14, 1863
    Vol. 19, No. 45, Ed. 2, p. 2, col. 2 & 4
Sat., Sept. 3, 1864
    Vol. 20, No. 47, Ed. 1, p. 2, col. 3

The State Gazette (Austin, TX)
Wed., Dec. 10, 1862
    Vol. 14, No. 19, Ed. 1, p. 4., col. 2
Wed., Jan. 14, 1863
    Vol. 14, No. 24, Ed. 1, p. 1, col. 2

Thayer promises, if allowed to carry out his plan in its entirety, to bring Florida into the Union as a free State by the 1st. of February next. Texas and Virginia are already talked of as States to be subjected to the same process. This, like the proclamation of yesterday, will be another step in the path of a more vigorous policy, which the administration, in its proclamation of freedom, advertised that it should henceforth pursue.

The Texas Almanac -- "Extra." (Austin, TX), Oct. 30, 1862. Vol. 1, No. 9, Ed. 1

Of Lincoln's Emancipation Proclamation, the N. Y. World says:

We repeat our statement that the emancipation proclamation is a virtual confession of inability to conquer the south by fair fighting. It is a disgraceful acknowledgment of military weakness made by an administration that has wielded (allowance being made for the navy) open ports superior wealth, and mechanical skill, quadruple the military resources of the South, and finds itself over matched. There is not a more humiliating spectacle in history than this exhibition of moral abjectness. While the administration had hope of success by legitimate warfare, it never thought of emancipation.

    The Standard. (Clarksville, TX),
    Jan. 22, 1863. Page 2, col. 3

> We have been informed that a private letter, received in this city from Arkansas, states that a Kentucky regiment came over to our forces at Pine Bluff, and the writer says he saw them in camp, and conversed with several of them. He further adds that they stated to him there was great disaffection in the northern ranks, and that many of the western troops had threatened to withdraw at once from Lincoln's army unless the emancipation proclamation was at once repealed.

The State Gazette. (Austin, TX)
Feb. 11, 1863. Vol. 14, No. 28

> As an example of how Lincoln's proclamation is frightening our people, we publish the fact that at an auction sale of confiscated property in this city yesterday, the following prices were paid for slaves:
> Boy John, 24 years old, $3,025.00
> " Pick, 14 " " $2,850.00
> Woman and child......$2,500.00
> Woman and three children, from 1 to 5 years 4,850.00.
> We understand negroes are cheap in some parts of the Confederacy. If people will send them here, they can be sold at good prices.—*Telegraph.*

The Bellville Countryman
Feb. 21, 1863

Wed., Jan. 21, 1863
    Vol. 14, No. 25, Ed. 1, p. 1, col. 1
Wed., Feb. 11, 1863
    Vol. 14, No. 28, Ed. 1, p. 2, col. 1
Wed., June 17, 1863
    Vol. 14, No. 46, Ed. 1, p. 2, col. 4

The Texas Almanac -- "Extra" (Austin, TX)
Tues., Oct. 14, 1862
    Vol. 1, No. 2, Ed. 1
Thur., Oct. 23, 1862
    Vol. 1, No. 6, Ed. 1, p. 1, col. 1
Sat., Oct. 25, 1862
    Vol. 1, No. 7, Ed. 1, p. 1, col. 2
Thur., Oct. 30, 1862
    Vol. 1, No. 9, Ed. 1, p. 1, col. 2
Tues., Nov. 4, 1862
    Vol. 1, No. 11, Ed. 1, p. 1, col. 5
Sat., Nov. 8, 1862
    Vol. 1, No. 3, Ed. 1
Tues., Nov. 11, 1862
    Vol. 1, No. 14, Ed. 1, p. 1, col. 2
Sat., Dec. 6, 1862
    Vol. 1, No. 25, Ed. 1, p. 1, col. 2 & 3
Tues., Dec. 23, 1862
    Vol. 1, No. 32, Ed. 1, p. 1, col. 4
Thur., Feb. 5, 1863
    Vol. 1, No. 51, Ed. 1, p. 1, col. 1
Tues., March 10, 1863
    Vol. 1, No. 65, Ed. 1, p. 1, col. 3

The Tri-Weekly Telegraph (Houston)
Fri., Oct. 10, 1862
    Vol. 28, No. 89, Ed. 1, p. 1, col. 1

Mon., Oct. 13, 1862
    Vol. 28, No. 90, Ed. 1, p. 1, col. 1
Fri., Oct. 17, 1862
    Vol. 28, No. 92, Ed. 1, p. col. 4
Mon., Oct. 20, 1862
    Vol. 28, No. 93, Ed. 2, p. col. 1
Wed., Oct. 22, 1862
    Vol. 28, No. 94, Ed. 1, p. 1, col. 3
Fri., Oct. 24, 1862
    Vol. 28, No. 95, Ed. 1, p. 1, col. 1
    Vol. 28, No. 95, Ed. 1, p. 2, col. 1
Mon., Oct. 27, 1862
    Vol. 28, No. 96, Ed. 1, p. 2, col. 2
Wed., Oct. 29, 1862
    Vol. 28, No. 97, Ed. 1, p. 1, col. 2
    Vol. 28, No. 97, Ed. 2, p. 2, col. 1
Mon., Nov. 3, 1862
    Vol. 28, No. 99, Ed. 1, p. 1, col. 2
Fri., Nov. 7, 1862
    Vol. 28, No. 101, Ed. 1, p. 2, col. 2
Mon., Nov. 10, 1862
    Vol. 28, No. 102, Ed. 1, p. 2, col. 2
Wed., Nov. 12, 1862
    Vol. 28, No. 103, Ed. 1, p. 1, col. 4
Mon., Nov. 17, 1862
    Vol. 28, No. 105, Ed. 1, p. 1, col. 1 & 5
Wed., Nov. 19, 1862
    Vol. 28, No. 106, Ed. 1, p. 2, col. 2 & 3
Mon., Nov. 24, 1862
    Vol. 28, No. 108, Ed. 2, p. col. 1
Wed., Nov. 26, 1862
    Vol. 28, No. 109, Ed. 1, p. col. 1 & 3
Fri., Nov. 28, 1862
    Vol. 28, No. 110, Ed. 1, p. 1, col. 1

Mon., Dec. 1, 1862
    Vol. 28, No. 111, Ed. 1, p. col. 1
Wed., Dec. 3, 1862
    Vol. 28, No. 112, Ed. 1, p. 2, col. 5
Mon., Dec. 8, 1862
    Vol. 28, No. 114, Ed. 1, p. col.
Mon., Dec. 15, 1862
    Vol. 28, No. 117, Ed. 1, p. 1, col. 2
Mon., Dec. 22, 1862
    Vol. 28, No. 120, Ed. 1, p. 1, col. 5
Mon., Jan. 12, 1863
    Vol. 28, No. 129, Ed. 1, p. 1, col. 2
Wed., Jan. 14, 1863
    Vol. 28, No. 130, Ed. 1, p. 1, col. 3
Fri., Jan. 16, 1863
    Vol. 28, No. 131, Ed. 1, p. 2, col. 1
Wed., Jan. 21, 1863
    Vol. 28, No. 133, Ed. 1, p. 1, col. 2
Wed., Jan. 28, 1863
    Vol. 28, No. 136, Ed. 1, p. 1, col. 3
Wed., Feb. 4, 1863
    Vol. 28, No. 139, Ed. 1, p. 1, col. 3
Mon., Feb. 16, 1863
    Vol. 28, No. 144, Ed. 1, p. 1, col. 3
Fri., Feb. 27, 1863
    Vol. 28, No. 149, Ed. 1, p. 1, col. 1
Fri., March 6, 1863
    Vol. 28, No. 152, Ed. 1, p. 1, col. 2
Mon., March 23, 1863
    Vol. 29, No. 3, Ed. 1, p. 2, col. 4
Fri., April 3, 1863
    Vol. 29, No. 8, Ed. 1, p. 1, col. 4
Fri., May 1, 1863
    Vol. 29, No. 20, Ed. 1, p. 2, col. 2

Fri., May 15, 1863
    Vol. 29, No. 26, Ed. 1, p. 1, col. 5
Wed., June 10, 1863
    Vol. 29, No. 37, Ed. 1, p. 2, col. 2
Mon., June 22, 1863
    Vol. 29, No. 42, Ed. 1, p. 2, col. 3
Fri., June 26, 1863
    Vol. 29, No. 44, Ed. 1, p. 1, col. 2
Wed., July 15, 1863
    Vol. 29, No. 52, Ed. 1, p. 1, col. 5
Fri., Aug. 14, 1863
    Vol. 29, No. 63, Ed. 1, p. 1, col. 2
Fri., Sept. 25, 1863
    Vol. 29, No. 81, Ed. 1, p. 1, col. 2
Tues., Oct. 5, 1863
    Vol. 29, No. 85, Ed. 1, p. 1, col. 1
Wed., Oct. 7, 1863
    Vol. 29, No. 86, Ed. 1, p. 1, col. 4
Wed., Oct. 14, 1863
    Vol. 29, No. 89, Ed. 1, p. 1, col. 2
Fri., Nov. 20, 1863
    Vol. 29, No. 105, Ed. 1, p. 2, col. 2
Wed., Nov., 25, 1863
    Vol. 29, No. 107, Ed. 1, p. 1, col. 3
Fri. Dec. 11, 1863
    Vol. 29, No. 114, Ed. 1, p. 2, col. 4
Mon., Dec. 21, 1863
    Vol. 29, No. 118, Ed. 1, p. 1, col. 2
Wed., Dec. 23, 1863
    Vol. 29, No. 119, Ed. 1, p. 2, col. 3
Mon., Jan. 4, 1864
    Vol. 29, No. 124, Ed. 1, p. 2, col. 2 & 3
Thur., Jan. 14, 1864
    Vol. 29, No. 128, Ed. 1, p. 1, col. 4
Wed., Jan. 20, 1864
    Vol. 29, No. 131, Ed. 1, p. 1, col. 4
Fri., Jan. 29, 1864
    Vol. 29, No. 135, Ed. 1, p. 2, col. 2

The Weekly Telegraph (Houston, Texas)
Wed., Oct. 8, 1862
    Vol. 28, No. 30, Ed. 1 p. col. 4
Wed., Oct. 15, 1862
    Vol. 28, No. 31, Ed. 1, p. 1, col. 2 & 3
Wed., Oct. 22, 1862
    Vol. 28, No. 32, Ed. 1, p. 2, col. 1, 3 & 6
Wed., Oct. 29, 1862
    Vol. 28, No. 33, Ed. 1, p. 1, col. 1
    Vol. 28, No. 33, Ed. 1, p. 2, col. 1
Wed., Nov. 5, 1862
    Vol. 28, No. 34, Ed. 1, p. 1, col. 2
    Vol. 28, No. 34, Ed. 1, p. 2, col. 2
Wed., Nov. 12, 1862
    Vol. 28, No. 35, Ed. 1, p. 1, col. 2
    Vol. 28, No. 35, Ed. 1, p. 2, col. 5 & 6
Wed., Nov. 19, 1862
    Vol. 28, No. 36, Ed. 1, p. 1, col. 3
    Vol. 28, No. 36, Ed. 1, p. 2, col. 2 & 6
Wed., Dec. 3, 1862
    Vol. 28, No. 38, Ed. 1, p. 1, col. 2, 3 & 4
Wed., Dec. 10, 1862
    Vol. 28, No. 39, Ed. 1, p. 2, col. 7
Wed., Dec. 24, 1862
    Vol. 28, No. 41, Ed. 1, p. 1, col. 1
Wed., Jan. 14, 1863
    Vol. 28, No. 44, Ed. 1, p. 1, col. 2 & 3
Wed., Jan. 28, 1863
    Vol. 28, No. 46, Ed. 1, p. 1, col. 1

> In my judgment Mr. Lincoln's proclamation is a very innocent and ridiculous affair, though its supposed innocence is no fault of his. He issues a proclamation with the great seal of the U. S. affixed thereto, and with Abraham Lincoln written in large capitals at the bottom, declaring that on account of the continued and persevering resistance of the rebels to all law and order, and their pertinacious disregard of all constitutional obligations—that "on and after the 1st day of January 1863, all slaves holden in such rebellious States shall be forever free," etc. Well, now, what does all this fanfarnade amount to ? Simply nothing at all.

Houston Telegraph Supplement
Nov. 7, 1862, page 1, column 2

This clip from the Tri-Weekly Telegraph captures what Texans thought of the Proclamation.

Wed., Feb. 11, 1863
    Vol. 28, No. 48, Ed. 1, p. 2, col. 6
Wed., March 4, 1863
    Vol. 28, No. 51, Ed. 1, p. 1, col. 1
Wed., March 11, 1863
    Vol. 28, No. 52, Ed. 1, p. 1, col. 3
Wed., March 18, 1863
    Vol. 29, No. 1, Ed. 1, p. 2, col. 4
Tues., June 9, 1863
    Vol. 29, No. 13, Ed. 1, p. 2, col. 3
Tues., June 30, 1863
    Vol. 29, No. 16, Ed. 1, p. 1, col. 3
Tues., Oct. 6, 1863
    Vol. 29, No. 28, Ed. 1, p. 1, col. 3
Tues., Oct. 13, 1863
    Vol. 29, No. 29, Ed. 1, p. 1, col. 2
Tues., Oct. 20, 1863
    Vol. 29, No. 30, Ed. 1, p. 1, col. 2
Tues., Dec. 8, 1863
    Vol. 29, No. 37, Ed. 1, p. 2, col. 6

And Another thing...

It is often said that the Battle at Palmito Ranch (a.k.a. the so-called "Last Battle of the Civil War") occurred because the Texas Confederate Army did not know the war had ended.

Historian Richard Gardiner argues the Palmito Ranch battle was "a *post-war* encounter between Federals and ex-Confederate outlaws."[34]

A letter written by a Texas confederate soldier confirms the writer's awareness that the war had ended before the fight, but his comrades were determined to continue fighting. They feared becoming subordinate to freedmen if they lost.[35]

Tues., Dec. 15, 1863
    Vol. 29, No. 38, Ed. 1, p. 2, col. 5
Tues., Dec. 29, 1863
    Vol. 29, No. 40, Ed. 1, p. 2, col. 4
Tues., Jan. 19, 1864
    Vol. 29, No. 43, Ed. 1, p. 1, col. 5
Tues., Feb. 16, 1864
    Vol. 29, No. 47, Ed. 1, p. 1, col. 1

* * *

Ha! Bet you thought the list was complete. It was not. Nor does the list end here. This is simply where the author stopped searching.

When searching pre-1865 newspapers for news about the Emancipation Proclamation, use alternate names such as "Universal Emancipation", "Lincoln's Proclamation" etc.

"On the part of the Government, I retract nothing heretofore said as to slavery. I repeat the declaration made a year ago, and that while I remain in my present position I shall not attempt to retract or modify the Emancipation Proclamation …"

Abraham Lincoln

The Houston Tri-Weekly Telegraph
Dec. 23, 1864, Vol. 30, No. 186, Ed. 1

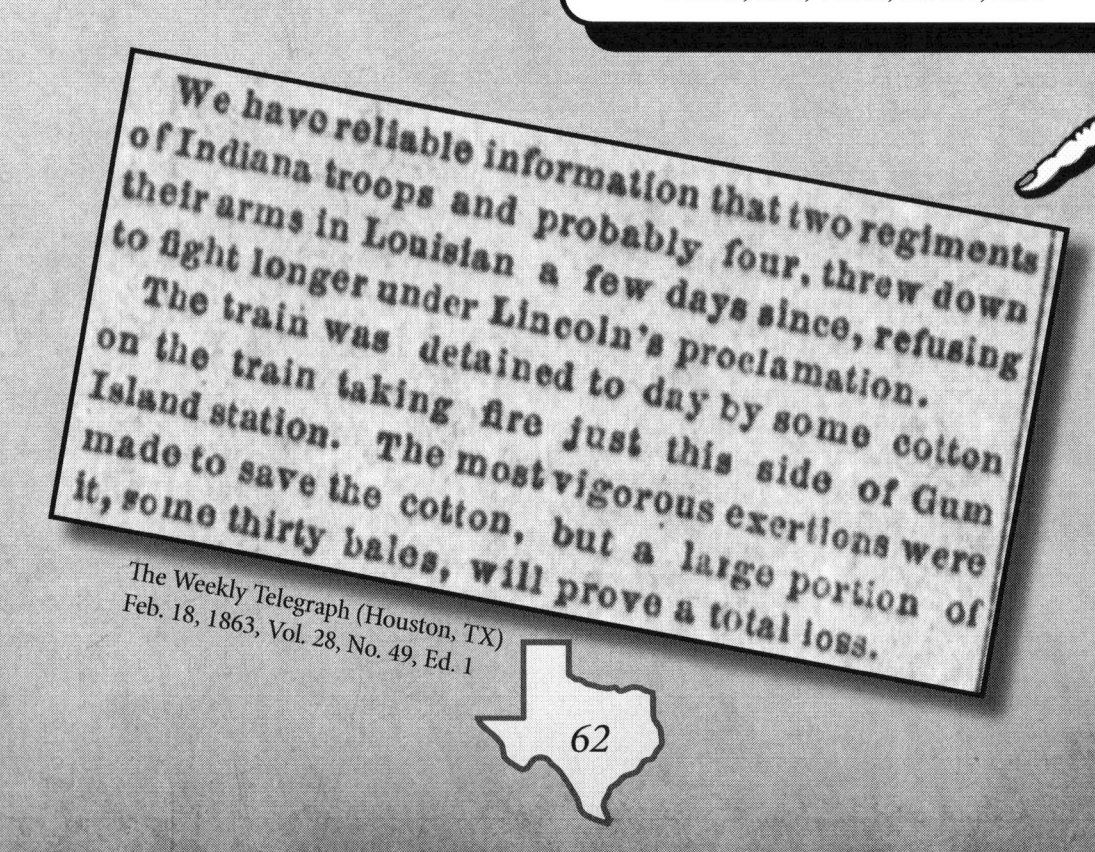

> We have reliable information that two regiments of Indiana troops and probably four, threw down their arms in Louisiana a few days since, refusing to fight longer under Lincoln's proclamation. The train was detained to day by some cotton on the train taking fire just this side of Gum Island station. The most vigorous exertions were made to save the cotton, but a large portion of it, some thirty bales, will prove a total loss.

The Weekly Telegraph (Houston, TX)
Feb. 18, 1863, Vol. 28, No. 49, Ed. 1

FAKE NEWS!

A good search for references to the Emancipation Proclamation in Texas newspapers will uncover enough false news to raise the possibility of an intentional misinformation campaign. Similarities between slanted news of the mid-1860s and questionable news of the 2016 United States Presidential election are eerily uncanny.

The term "fake news" was not in vogue during the 1860s. However, networks of suspicious reports existed. Newspapers frequently posted reports published by their like-minded peers. In Texas, most papers were confederate-leaning. In turn, reprints often advocated northern states' disdain for the proclamation, Lincoln's dismay, and the proclamation's eminent demise.

It is often said that unlearned history repeats itself. If so, contemporary 'true news seekers' should be encouraged by this parallel. If a campaign of false emancipation news existed during the mid-1860s', hindsight clearly shows said campaign did not produce the results its perpetrators likely desired.

Something to ponder:
Is misleading information about emancipation still harmful? If so, how so, and who is responsible for combating it?

> A private letter from the front, states that Lincoln has rescinded his emancipation proclamation.
> JUNO.

(From): The Standard. (Clarksville, TX), Vol. 20, No. 47, Ed. 1, Sept. 3, 1864

Juneteenth 101

Question:

If Texans knew, why were slaves not freed?

Answers:

Three of the most significant reasons.

1) Under the Texas State Constitution of 1861, emancipation was illegal. "No citizen, or other person residing in this State shall have power by deed, or will, … to emancipate his slave or slaves."[36]

2) Lincoln was President of the United States. When Texas succeeded from the Union, Lincoln became their enemy. Any instructions he issued were not worth diddily squat.

3) Texans believed the confederates would win the war which would have made Lincoln's proclamation moot.

MYTH #8

"Texans knew about the proclamation, but freedom was delayed to harvest crops."

Y-e-a-h, but ...

This popular belief
is not plausible
b-e-c-a-u-s-e
no crop requires 2 1/2 years to grow. This reason would apply only to the 1865 growing season.
H-o-w-e-v-e-r,...

An 1865 editorial published by a Galveston newspaper *(right)* affirms that Texas planters hoped to maintain free slave labor until the end of harvesting. The writer refers to General Order No. 3 as "a sudden change," but not new news.

The strategy would have impacted only the people enslaved on farms and plantations. It did not address the fate of people who worked as domestics or tradesmen performing non-agricultural jobs.

> A few month's delay would have saved some millions of dollars to the planters in the incoming crops, by securing the promising harvest; and some thousands of lives that the sudden change exposes to all the ills of the hot and sickly season. But few changes of laborers will occur in this county until December. By simply refusing to hire Negroes from other plantations, the whole matter resolves itself at once into the rules that all must remain where they are and labor as they have heretofore done, or starve!
>
> It is curious to see the motley race as they appear when congregated as freedmen. Some twenty who concluded to enjoy liberty, left their homes and congregated at a man's farm near Washington; some were dressed gaudily; some coarsely, some with shoes and some without, while several of the youths of fifteen were parading about as naked as Adam before his introduction to miss Eve. To that complexion will it come at last, however wisely planters may shape affairs with the present. The adult Negro is but a grown child, and in our warm climate, nakedness, idleness, beggary, theft and every species of crime and distress await certain developments as an inevitable result of an experiment the most gigantic and hazardous ever attempted on civilized or half civilized humanity.

Reprinted from Flake's Daily Bulletin.
Vol. 1, No. 28, Ed. 1
July 18, 1865

TRANSLATION

This unnamed pundit is telling planters how to get around General Granger's order. He claims financial losses would not have happened if Granger had waited to emancipate the slaves after the crops were in (December). Even so, a diabolic vindication was concocted. He urged planters to hire only their former slaves, assuming that would force freedmen back to where they formerly worked or they would starve.

Somebody's dinner guest

Juneteenth 101

Juneteenth - Buffalo, New York

69

MYTH #9

"Texans didn't know the Civil War was over until June 19th."

Juneteenth 101

For this to be true, the following clues had to be ignored:

5. *(Spring 1865)* Texas was suddenly consumed by lawlessness.[64]

   "That's kinda vague. Crime often happens in waves. Next."

4. *(April/May 1865)* Texas confederate soldiers vacated their posts en masse and returned home.

   "So what? People jump in and out of the army everyday."

3. *(May 1865)* Texas newspapers reported the war's end and published the surrender agreements.

   "Yeah? Well lots of people couldn't read. They didn't know what was happening 'round the country."

2. *(June 2, 1865)* Confederate Generals signed terms of surrender aboard the U.S.S. Fort Jackson *in Galveston Bay.*

   "That happened way out in the Gulf. Who saw it?"

1. *(June 5, 1865)* Two Union Naval ships docked in Galveston. Capt. B. F. Sand gave a brief public statement to a crowd gathered at the Mayor's Office. Afterwards, Union officers and ex-confederates went to the U.S. Customs Office and raised the national flag. (Page 72)

Well, um... See, um...

"Would any of that have happened if Texans thought the war was still going?"

"But folks keep saying, Texans didn't know."

"Saying stuff doesn't require knowing stuff."

Juneteenth 101

Synopsis
U.S. Naval ships docked in Galveston on June 5, 1865 to begin occupation of the island. That happened fourteen days before Major General Gordon Granger's arrival. A peaceful transfer of governmental authority was successfully executed.

Galveston's historic U.S. Customs House was built in 1861. At 11:00 AM, June 5, 1865, a flag raising ceremony affirming the Civil War's end and the Union Army's victory was held at this site.

BY TELEGRAPH.

Special to the Daily Telegraph.

GALVESTON, June 5, 1865.

Galveston Taken Possession of by the U. S. Naval Forces.

Flake's Bulletin has the following:

At ten o'clock this morning two vessels of the U. S. blockading fleet, entered the harbor. Capt. Sands commanding the fleet landed in company with several other officers at Central wharf, and was received by Major Von Harten Confederate commissioner, proceeded to the Mayor's office, where the party was introduced by Major Von Harten, to His Honor the Mayor. Captain Sands addressed a few words to the assembled people in substance as follows:

The Mayor after introducing Captain Sands to the people, stated that the Captain had to raise the national flag over the Custom House He hoped that the people would on this occasion behave orderly as they have always done before.

Capt. Sands remarked that he came as the friend of the people, not as an enemy. That this country had been happily reunited, and that he would give the people all the protection required. He was glad to see the people receive him with so much order and decorum. He was not afraid of the people, he had come ashore without a guard and without arms, except his side arms which he was wearing in respect to h s Honor the Mayor.

After these remarks, the U. S. officers, accompanied by the Mayor and Major Von Harten, proceeded to the Custom House and raised on that building the U. S. flag at 11 A. M.

A large number of people were present; all of them behaved in the most orderly manner and as became good citizens.

At 11:30 A. M., Capt. Sands had the flag taken down again and proceeded back on board his fleet.

Capt. Sands informed our Mayor that his fleet would go in and out of Galveston harbor often until the land forces should arrive, which were expected in a few days, when the fleet would depart from these waters. Whilst here, Capt. Sands offered to send in papers and do anything to oblige the people. He offered to furnish the city authorities any number of men necessary to preserve order in the city, which offer was declined by the Mayor because the present police force of the city is sufficient for all purposes.

Capt. Sands stated that Confederate soldiers now here, will have an opportunity to return to other States as soon as the parole officers arrive. **

This report was originally published on the afternoon of June 5, 1865 in Flake's Bulletin, a Galveston newspaper. The report was distributed by telegraph to other newspapers. Below is a partial list Texas publications that reprinted the report prior to June 19, 1865.

The Tri-Weekly Telegraph
Houston, Texas
June 7, 1865. (Page 3, column 2)

Flake's Tri-Weekly Bulletin.
Galveston, Texas
June 8, 1865 (Page 1, column 4)

Texas State Gazette
Austin, Texas
June 9, 1865. (Page 2, column 3)

The Bellville Countryman
Bellville, Texas
June 10, 1865 (Page 1, column 4)

Dallas Herald
Dallas, Texas
June 15, 1865. (Page 2, column 3)

NOTE:
"Captain Sands" was Benjamin F. Sands, Captain of the U.S.S. Carnelia.

MYTH #9.1

"President Abraham Lincoln issued General Orders No. 3."

One version of this hoax claims Lincoln tried unsuccessfully to personally deliver news of emancipation to Texas. The tale does not clarify when that happened.

FACT:

President Lincoln was assassinated two months before instructions that became General Orders No. 3 were copied by Gen. Philip Sheridan*;[37] altered and ordered by Gen. Gordon Granger; and issued *[signed]* by Major F. W. Emery, A. A. Gen.[38]

* NOTE: General Sheridan's instructions to General Granger were copied from orders previously issued by Major General Francis J. Herron in Shreveport, LA on June 3, 1865. General Herron's emancipation order circulated in Texas prior to June 19, 1865. (See pages 78-79.)

General Order No. 3

The people of Texas are informed that, in accordance with a proclamation from the Executive of the United States, all slaves are free. This involves an absolute equality of personal rights and rights of property, between former masters and slaves and the connection heretofore existing between them, becomes that between employer and hired labor. The Freedmen are advised to remain at their present homes and work for wages. They are informed that they will not be allowed to collect at military posts; and they will not be supported in idleness either there or elsewhere.

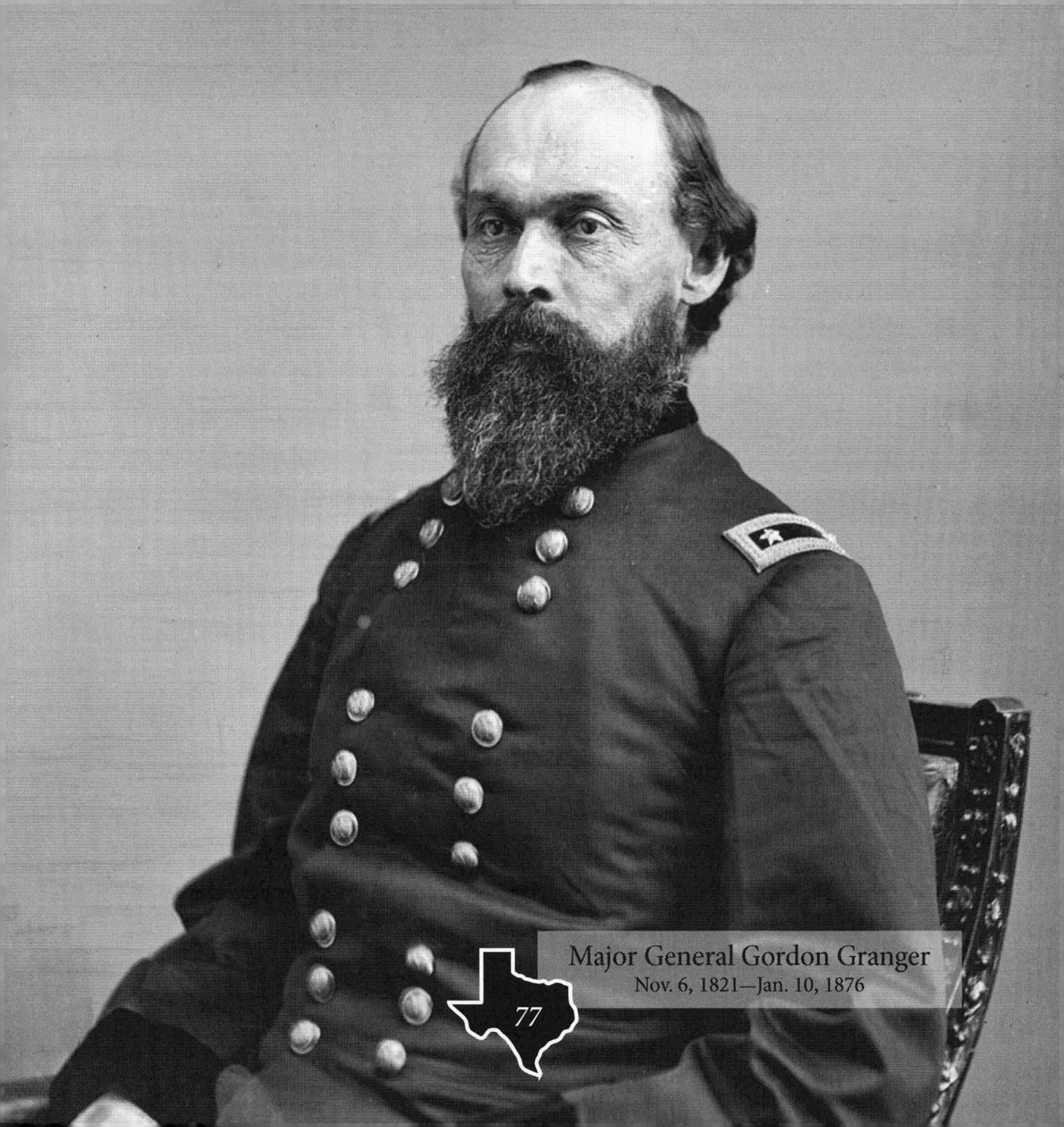

Major General Gordon Granger
Nov. 6, 1821—Jan. 10, 1876

77

GENERAL ORDERS #3

PHACTS!

- Maj. Gen. Sheridan is credited with writing the instructions that became Granger's General Order #3. However, Sheridan's instructions parallel orders issued by Maj Gen. Herron ten days earlier (June 3, 1865.) At least two Texas newspapers published Herron's order on June 16th, three days prior to Granger's arrival.
- General Granger signed orders 1 and 2, but not 3, 4 and 5. Major Emory signed 3, 4 and 5, but not 1 and 2.
- The words "by order of General Gordon Granger" appear only on Orders 3, 4 and 5.

Dude, you feel a hypothesis jumpin off, up in here?

Most indubitably, I'm thinking Granger penned Orders 3, 4, and 5, but Emory made 'em public.

Affirmative. And check this. Granger was Emory's boss. If Granger had announced No. 3 himself, Emory's signature would not be necessary. Emory signed it 'cause he was Granger's spokesperson.

Right! I don't think Granger was talking in third person. I think the words "by order of General Granger," mean "Granger told me to tell y'all." I dare ya to prove Emory wasn't the one who announced and posted G. O. 3 on Granger's behalf.

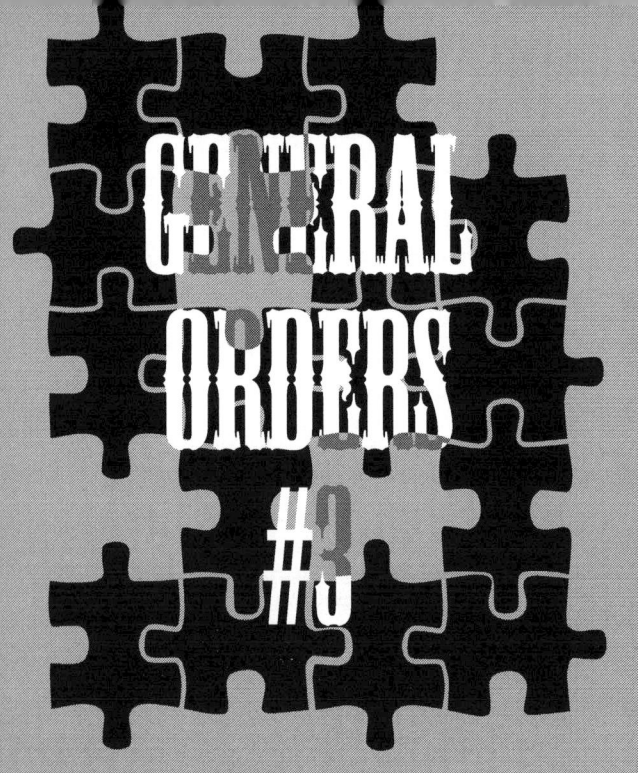

(Sheridan's orders to Granger)
June 13, 1865

On your arrival at Galveston assume command of all troops in the State of Texas; carry out the conditions of the surrender of General Kirby Smith to Major-General Canby; notify the people of Texas that in accordance with the existing proclamation from the Executive of the United States "all slaves are free;" advise all such freedmen that they must remain at home; that they will not be allowed to collect at military posts, and will not be supported in idleness. Notify the people of Texas that all acts of the Governor and Legislature of Texas since the ordinance of secession are illegitimate. Take such steps as in your judgment are most conducive to the restoration of law and order and return of the State to her true allegiance to the United States government,

P. H. Sheridan, Major-General, Commanding.

Epilogue

General Granger was a middle man. Multiple versions of General Orders #3 can be traced to orders from Maj. Gen. Francis Herron. All versions contain the same mistake. They claim the E. Proc. freed all slaves in the United States. It did not.

A Huge Deal

One the most frequently repeated myths about Juneteenth is that General Granger originated news of emancipation to Texans on June 19, 1865, via his General Orders No. 3. However, the clip *(at right)* refutes that.

Clip source: June 17, 1865 issue of *The Standard*, page 2, column 3, Clarksville, Texas. The clip is an excerpt from General Orders No. 2, issued by Lieut. Col. S. G. Van Anda, in Nachitoches, Louisiana, June 6, 1865. Van Anda's order originated from instructions issued by Major General Herron on June 3, 1865.

See General Orders No. 20. War of the Rebellion, Volume XL - Part 3. 1892. (Vol. 40, Chap. 52) page 749.

> By the Proclamation of the President of the United States "Slavery no longer Exists." All men, white or black, are free, and all attempts to restrict, or subvert the Proclamation of Emancipation, will be considered a violation of the laws of the United States.
>
> But persons heretofore held as slaves must learn that they must earn their bread by the sweat of their brow—that they will not be supported in idleness by the Government, nor will they be allowed to congregate about the Military Posts. At the same time the United States Government will exact competent wages from all persons employing "Freedmen" in their service, and the crops will be held for the services rendered.

Comparison

Granger: **The people of Texas are informed that, in accordance with a proclamation from the Executive of the United States,**
Van Alda: By the Proclamation of the President of the United States.

Granger: **all slaves are free.**
Van Alda: "slavery no longer exists." All men, white or black, are free,

Granger: **This involves an absolute equality of personal rights and rights of property between former masters and slaves, and the connection heretofore existing between them becomes that between employer and hired labor.**
Van Alda: and all attempts to restrict, or subvert the Proclamation of Emancipation will be considered a violation of the laws of the United States.

Granger: **The freedmen**
Van Alda: But persons heretofore held as slaves

Granger: **are advised to remain quietly at their present homes and work for wages.**
Van Alda: must learn that they must earn their bread by the sweat of their brow

Granger: **They are informed that they will not be allowed to collect at military post.**
Van Alda: nor will they be allowed to congregate at the military posts.

Granger: **And that they will not be supported in idleness either there or elsewhere.**
Van Alda: they will not be supported in idleness by the government

Van Aldi, Orders #2 (LA)
Granger, Orders #3 (TX)

MYTH #10

"General Order No. 3 was first read from a balcony at Ashton Villa."

REAL TALK

Ashton Villa was built by J. M. Brown, a Galveston tycoon who supported the Confederate Army. Prior to the first Battle of Galveston, the home was headquarters for the Confederate Army. The Union Army moved in after winning the first Battle of Galveston in October 1862. The Confederates moved back in after recapturing Galveston on January 1, 1863.[39] The Union's brief occupation of the house is a likely root of the implausible belief that General Granger resided there in 1865, as guest of its ex-confederate owner.

General Orders No. 3 was issued from "Headquarters District of Texas - Galveston" located in the Osterman Building, not Ashton Villa.

"We have turned newspapers from the day inside out looking for a direct relation between Granger, General Order No. 3 and Ashton Villa to no avail."[40]

Jami Durham, Historian
Galveston Historical Foundation

"There is no contemporary evidence that the Juneteenth order was read at Ashton Villa or any other public place in Galveston in 1865."[41]

Ed Cotham, Guest Columnist
The Daily News - Galveston County

• •

Yet, an enigma lurks within this truth.

Granger's first General Order from his Galveston headquarters was issued on June 17th.[42] Granger arrived in Galveston on June 19th.

Juneteenth 101

"Augh man. Does anybody see the words "Ashton Villa" on this directory?"

(Right) From Flakes Daily Bulletin July 4, 1865.

"My mama said some, but not all of General Granger's orders were signed by a subordinate. What is that? And what was the purpose of the signatures?"

"Oo! I know. When somebody does the telling, a subordinate does the doing."

"Maybe, that's who really read Order No. 3."

MILITARY DIRECTORY.

GALVESTON CITY.

Major-Gen'l Gordon Granger, commanding District of Texas—Office: Osterman's building, corner Straud and 22d streets.

Major F. W. Emery, A. A. General—Office: Osterman's building.

Lieutenant-Colonel J. C. Palfrey, Assist't Insp'r General—Office: Osterman's building.

Lieut't-Colonel R. G. Laughlin, Provost Marshal General—Office: Custom House.

Lieutenant-Colonel F. G. Noyes, Chief Commissary Subsistence—Office: Nichol's building, Strand.

Lieutenant-Colonel C. B. White, Surgeon, Medical Director—Office: Osterman's building.

Capt. G. W. Fox, Chief of Artillery—Office: Nichol's building.

Capt. S. Howell, Chief of Ordnance—Office: Hendley's building, Strand.

Lieutenant J. L. Baker, Commissary of Musters —Office: Nichol's building.

Major W. L. Avery, Aide-de-Camp—Office: Osterman's building.

Captain C. S. Sargent, Aide-de-Camp—Office: Osterman's building.

Colonel F. W. Moore and staff, commanding 3d Brigade, 2d Division, 13th Army Corps, and Post—Office: Hendley's building.

Captain Harry Beard, Assistant Provost Marshal—Office: Custom House.

Captain G. E. Atwood, Assistant Quarter Master, Transportation and Depot Q. M.—Office: Kuhn's building, Strand.

Captain S. A. Cobb, Depot Commissary—Office: Merchant's Press, Strand.

Lieutenant G. W. Carey, Acting Assistant Post Quarter Master—Office: Kuhn's building.

82

Juneteenth 101

Houston Tri-Weekly Telegraph
February 1, 1864.

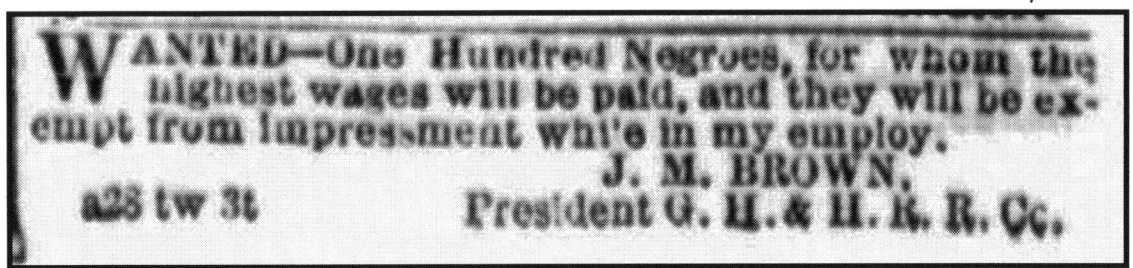

> WANTED—One Hundred Negroes, for whom the highest wages will be paid, and they will be exempt from impressment while in my employ.
> J. M. BROWN,
> a28 tw 3t   President G. H. & H. R. R. Co.

"Sweet Pea, look at this want ad from the owner of Ashton Villa."

"Look at where he said, "*for* whom", not "*to* whom." What you think, that mean?"

"Oh my goodness, wonder where they found that, Baby?"

"It mean the money went to the masters. The workers probably didn't see one dime. And the part that says, "exempt from impressment," that mean once he rents 'em, they can't be pulled away for other work."

"Oo, Sweetie, you right. Now, do you really think somebody who was okay with this kind of behavior would open his home to let a bunch of Union officers sleep there and eat up his suppers for six weeks? He didn't even know those people."

"And he didn't let 'em in his house, I don't care what nobody say."

83

What Texans Expected to happen

Gen. Sheridan will come to Texas by way of Galveston, with a considerable force, in a few days. Gen. Canby, and after him Gen. Sheridan, gave the assurance that the negroes in Texas would be required to stay at home on the plantations and work for their masters as heretofore until their status can be definitely settled. It was the plan of operations to send an overwhelming force, numbering 150,000 mounted men, to overrun Texas. For this purpose the troops had been ordered to Kentucky, Tennessee and Ohio, portions of the West to be mounted. In consequence of the representations made to Gen. Sheridan, a much less number of troops will be sent, but enough to garrison strongly some interior points and the Mexican frontier, and whatever may be necessary to insure the tranquility and security of the State.

We are under the impression, from the remarks of Col. Smith, that no black troops will be raised in the State, as it is the determination of the Federal authorities that all negroes in Texas shall be employed as agriculturalists.

What Happened

Each year, the historic happenings in Galveston, Texas on June 19, 1865 are fervently recounted with imaginative eloquence. Reality was less varnished. The following timetable was assembled from post-civil war records of the U.S. Army and news reports published before, during or after June 19, 1865.

∗ ∗ ∗

June 13, 1865
Maj. Gen. P. H. Sheridan assigned Maj. Gen. Gordon Granger to command all troops in Texas, upon arrival at Galveston. Specific instructions were given regarding emancipation.[37]

June 14, 1865
Four Union transport ships left Mobile, AL (Rice, Exact, Corinthian, Clinton). Gen. Granger, his staff[43] and 2,050 soldiers were on-board. Three ships went to New Orleans for supplies. (page 95)

June 16, 1865
U.S.S. Corinthian arrived in Galveston creating a spectacle among Galveston's citizens.[44][45][46]

June 17, 1865
- The Rice, Exact and Clinton left New Orleans. Upon leaving, the Rice ran aground and remained there until the tide lifted it the next day. (page 94)
- Maj. Gen. Godfrey Weitzel and staff arrived in New Orleans aboard the U.S.S. Crescent along with four other army transports (ship names unknown).[47]
- From New Orleans, Gen. Granger issued General Order No. 1, announcing his command of Texas troops.[42]

June 18, 1865
- Gen. Weitzel and staff left New Orleans. Gen. Granger accompanied him.[48][49]
- The Clinton, Exact, Rice and a supply ship arrived in Galveston.[43][50][51] Note: Present day explanations of Juneteenth claim either 1,800 or 2,000 troops arrived *with* Gen. Granger. This study found evidence that 2,050 troops arrived *before* Gen. Granger.
- An unspecified number of sailors were already at Galveston, but remained aboard naval vessels in the harbor.[52]

June 19, 1865
- Five ships (Nightingale, Prometheus, Montauk, Wilmington, and William Kennedy) unexpectedly arrived in Galveston adding potentially 2,648 "colored troops" to the assembly. (Approximately 1,725 were aboard the first three ships, excluding officers. The 4th and 5th ships carried an aggregate of 923 troops).[53][54] (page 95)
- Generals Granger and Weitzel arrived in Galveston aboard the U.S.S. Crescent.[55]
- From Texas Army Headquarters Galveston, Major F. W. Emery issued General Orders No. 3, 4 and 5 by order of Gen. Gordon Granger.[38] The three orders plus Orders No. 1 and 2 were telegraphed to newspapers where telegraphs were possible.

June 20, 1865
Granger's troops began disbursement, traveling first to Houston by train.[56][57] Galveston's Flake's Daily Bulletin was first to publish all five of Granger's orders. Texas newspapers outside of Galveston began publishing them the next day.

∗ ∗ ∗

This photo was taken by a photographer standing in front of Galveston's Osterman Building (not pictured) where Order #3 was issued. *(Courtesy: Galveston Historical Foundation)*

The Fine Print
Contradictions, Explanations and Clarifications

1. When did Granger arrive in Galveston?

Gen. Granger and his troops left Alabama on the same day. His troops arrived in Galveston, June 16th through 18th. Granger arrived on June 19th, as validated by two messages. First, from Galveston, Granger sent a message to Maj. Gen. Philip Sheridan dated June 19, 1865. It begins, "I arrived here this morning."[53] Second, Houston's Tri-Weekly Telegraph received a report from their Galveston agent dated June 19th. The message reads, "Generals Granger and Weitzel have arrived ..."[55]

2. When and where was General Order No. 1 issued?

The Official Record of the Union Army identifies June 17, 1865 as the issue date of General Order No. 1.[42] Gen. Granger was in New Orleans on June 17th.

The order appeared in Texas newspapers starting June 20, 1865. In Galveston's newspapers the order was dated June 17. In all other Texas newspapers, the order was dated June 19, 1865.

Newspapers published in other states offered this summery of the order: "Granger...takes command of all the troops in Texas."[58][59] The same summery published by the Wheeling Daily Intelligencer (Wheeling, WV) credited a June 17, 1865 telegraph from New Orleans as the source.[60]

Galveston's Tri-Weekly Bulletin published a special edition on Sunday, June 18th. Order #1 was not included.

3. What army transport ships were involved?

Reports are inconsistent. A definitive list of ships used for this campaign was not located by this study. Most news reports claim Weitzel and Granger traveled on the Crescent.

Multiple reports identify one ship as the Rise. A history book written by men who were aboard that vessel recorded its name as U.S.S. John K. Rice.

Conflicting definitions of the word 'arrival' produced conflicting arrival dates. In some publications, 'arrival' refers to dates when ships docked in Galveston, no matter when they arrived off the sandbar. Some publications defined arrival as dates when ships reached Galveston, even if they were unable to dock.

4. Who issued Granger's general orders?

Gen. Granger is credited with personally issuing General Orders No. 1 - 5. However, only General Orders 1 and 2 were issued directly by Gen. Granger. Orders 3 - 5 were signed by Major and Assistance Adjutant General F. W. Emery, and include the phrase: "*by order of Major General Granger,*" which means, 'Granger told me to tell y'all'.

5. What else did General Granger do on June 19th?

Enforcement of the Emancipation Proclamation was the most historic action undertaken on June 19, 1865, but a lengthy list of issues commanded Gen. Granger's attention that day. In additional to issuing orders, Gen. Granger:
- initiated the release and transport of prisoners from the state penitentiary to Galveston.
- planned the immediate distribution of troops—a process that began the next morning.
- generated a supply acquisition plan for the subsistence of troops, statewide.
- initiated plans for military defense against the intense robbery and plundering occurring around the state.

These significant matters were in addition to the mundane tasks of establishing operations; resolving the dilemma of the unexpected "Colored troops"; and preparing for statewide distribution of his five General Orders.

The gravity and urgency of the four tasks mentioned above significantly depreciate the spectacle of a hastily assembled public meeting called solely to announce five comparatively diminutive general orders: No. 1 announced Granger was in charge of the entire state (*not locally urgent news*); No. 2 named his eleven member staff (*trivia*); No. 3 affirmed the emancipation of enslaved Africans (*a commonly known fact addressed in Galveston's newspapers long before Granger's arrival*); No. 4 declared confederate laws and officers illegitimate (*old news*); and No. 5 announced where to sell cotton (*a minor detail for distribution by subordinates*).

6. Did a public reading of the General Orders occur?

A. Some historians contend the orders were read in multiple locations. A historian at Galveston's Preservation Resource Center said, "[After the first reading, Granger's] staff marched to the 1861 Custom House, where they were read again. From the Custom House, Granger's staff marched to the courthouse on 21st and read them all again before another reading at Reedy Chapel, known then as the Colored Church on Broadway."[42]

Evidence of this route was requested from the Galveston Historical Foundation, but not received as of publication date. This theory raises the question, why would anyone be at the "Colored Church" during work hours on a Monday?

Fort Worth, Texas resident and prominent Juneteenth backer, Mrs. Opal Lee, advocates the announcement was posted at the church, granting review by freedmen as needed.

B. Other historians also contend the orders were posted without a reading, arguing they were too insignificant. An 1865 editorial published in a Washington Co. newspaper and reprinted in the July 19, 1865 edition of Flake's Weekly Bulletin contradicts this theory. It suggest either multiple readings occurred or most of the attendees were Black.

> "The order issued by General Granger on his first landing at Galveston, was generally read to the Negroes."[10]

To assess the trivialness of these orders, consider the gravity of Granger's previously mentioned tasks. Juxtapose that on him parading around town unannounced, declaring, I'm the leader; here is my team; and, where to sell cotton.

C. The most popular belief is that Gen. Granger personally read his orders at what amounts to a town hall gathering in the front yard of someone's private residence, i.e., Ashton Villa. This theory has numerous flaws. It is implausible that townsfolk would have gathered at someone's private home without invitation or mandate, especially freedmen. Inarguably, commingling confederate men and women with freedmen was wholly inconsistent with race relations and social mores of 1865. Records of such grandstanding do not exist.

The crowd being "generally Negroes" further decreases the probability they were invited to the home of one of Galveston's most prominent ex-confederates. But that is conjecture. This is not: Order No. 3 was issued from Headquarters District of Texas, housed in the Osterman Building, not Ashton Villa. The official State of Texas historical marker acknowledging Juneteenth is located there, not at Ashton Villa.

Though all three theories are refutable, each may harbor a sliver of truth. (a) Multiple readings of (b) a posted flyer may have occurred (c) at Granger's headquarters for whomever requested such.

7. Was Granger's Order No. 3 Texas' first official enforcement notification?

Not necessarily. The Houston Tri-Weekly Telegraph published this statement from General Herron on June 16th. A similar statement report was published in a North Texas paper on June 17th.

> "There are no longer any slaves in the United States. All persons heretofore held as such became free by virtue of the Executive proclamation, of January 1, 1863, commonly known as the Emancipation Proclamation."[61]

Nine days earlier, Whites were given instructions.

> "Negroes must be made to comprehend what their new condition will be. They must be taught that freedom is not license. They must be made to understand that the same power that sets them free compels them to work for their living and for the support of that power."[62]

Other Considerations

Undeniably, June 19, 1865 was a historic day in Texas, but emancipation was not the military's only duty. After the war's end, Texas plunged into civil chaos. Theft and violence were rampant. Military intervention was necessary to restore civility.[63]

> "The lawlessness and absolute robbery which has pervaded much of the country between here and the Rio Grande has been of much greater magnitude than what was at first supposed,... Large bands of jay-hawkers infest the country, watch the roads, and plunder indiscriminately."[64]

Texas Gov. Pendleton Murrah, a staunch confederate, abetted resistance to emancipation and Union authority. But knowing federal occupation was eminent, he escaped to Mexico where he died a few months later. After Murrah's desertion, pillaging and mayhem increased. Looters raided the state treasury; judges and sheriffs implemented their own laws; etc. Into such havoc, enslaved Africans in Texas were released on June 19, 1865.

Meet Major General Gordon Granger*
November 6, 1821 - January 10, 1876

Birth place: Wayne County, New York
Died (age 54):   Santa Fe, New Mexico
Buried: Lexington, Kentucky

FAMILY:
- Parents: Oldest child of Gaius Granger and Catherine Taylor.
- Siblings: Emeline and Catherine Granger
  When Gordon was three years old, his mother died at age 25, one month after the birth of her third child. Gaius remarried (Sara or Sally Emery) and fathered ten more children.
- Wife: Maria Letcher. Granger married at age 46.
- Children: Gordon Granger II and Ellen Gordon Granger

EDUCATION:
- Primer School - Joy, New York.
- High School - Lyons, New York
- College - U.S. Military Academy at West Point
  Graduated in 1845, 7th from the bottom of his class.

WORK EXPERIENCE
- One room school teacher - at age 17 and 18.
- Military Officer - from college graduation until his death.

MILITARY PROMOTIONS
- Mexican-American War: Brevet 2nd Lieutenant through 1st Lieut.
- Civil War: 1st Lieutenant through Major General.

* [65]

OTHER FACTS

Also at West Point during Granger's tenure were Ulysses S. Grant (future U.S. President) and Thomas J. Jackson - aka Confederate General Stonewall Jackson. Granger's contemporaries called Granger [a man of] indomitable courage, a true soldier, a formidable combat soldier, cantankerous, rough and uncouth. A classmate (General T. J. Wood) said, "Wrong and injustice ever excited his indignation, and he never hesitated to give utterance to it. At the core of his heart was tender and gentle; and his tender sympathy ever went out toward misfortune, sorrow and suffering."[66]

Juneteenth 101

Juneteenth - Phoenix, Arizona

89

Myth #11
40% Wrong & 60% Incorrect

"The Buffalo Soldiers accompanied Major General Granger."

This bogusness may be rooted in the false belief that all African American soldiers in the 1800s were called Buffalo Soldiers. However ...

(Fact:)

... originally, that moniker applied only to the 9th and 10th Cavalry of the United States Army—formed Sept. 21, 1866, fourteen months *after* Maj. Gen. Granger's General Order No. 3 was issued. Eventually, the name also included the 24th Infantry and 25th Infantry Regiments.

F.Y.I.:
A battle in Texas fought one month before Juneteenth included Missouri's 62nd Colored Infantry Regiment.[67][68] *Black sailors participated in the Union's naval blockade of Galveston until the war's end.*[69] *Troops from the 25th Corps were in Galveston on June 19th*   (See "Arriving June 19th" on page 95)

Juneteenth 101

Here's the real deal ...

On June 19, 1865, five Army ships transporting part of the 25th Union Army Corps (Colored soldiers/White Officers) stopped in Galveston.[70] They were headed to Brazos Santiago.

Earlier that morning, five other ships arrived in Galveston. They were the 3rd Brigade, 2nd Division of the 25th Union Army Corps (more Colored soldiers/White Officers). Gen. Granger, traveling with the second group, documented his bafflement over the first contingent's unexpected presence.

What had happened was ...

After learning the confederacy lost, Texans went buck wild. Former state government officials became lawless criminals.[71] Gen. Grant—refusing to put up with that foolishness—sent a cajillion troops to settle things down. Black soldiers of the 25th Union Army Corps were part of that effort.[72][73] White members of the 25th were sent elsewhere. Initially, many Black troops refused to go. They thought plans were afoot to: a) trick them into colonizing a new territory; b) sell them; and c) force them into working on cotton plantations to pay the national debt.[74][75][76]

June 9th -- The 3rd Brigade, 2nd Div. left Ft. Morgan, AL., heading to Brazos Santiago, TX. A pit stop was taken at "the mouth of the Mississippi" (a.k.a. New Orleans).

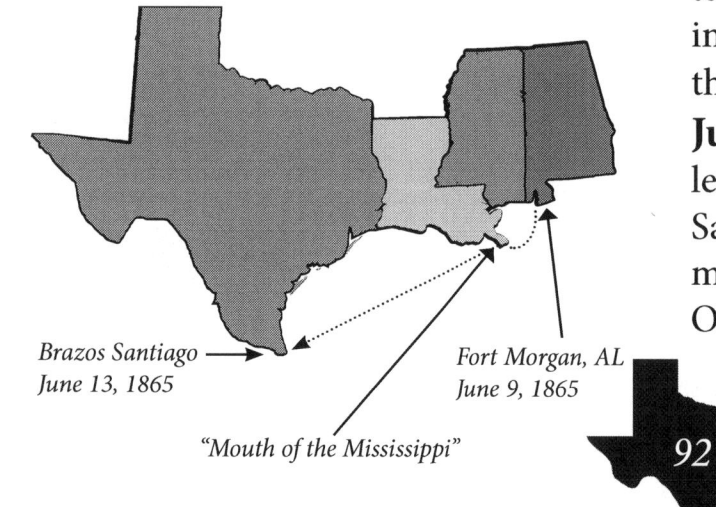

June 13 -- They arrived at Brazos Santiago, but could not disembark. Two days later they were ordered to

Brazos Santiago — June 13, 1865

"Mouth of the Mississippi"

Fort Morgan, AL June 9, 1865

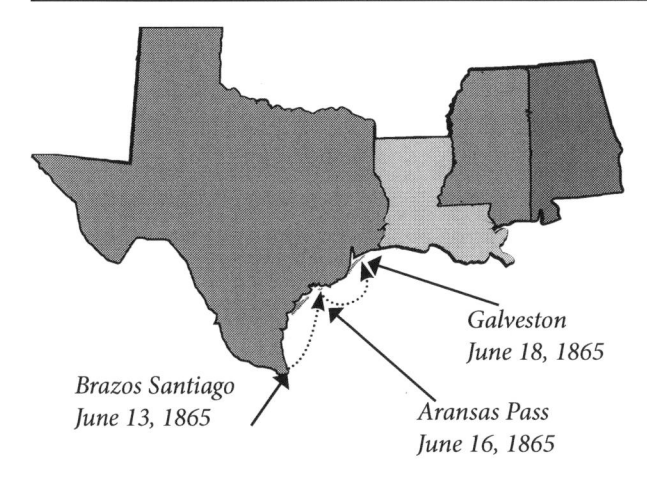

action against one white officer.[76] What they were celebrating is unknown. Being Union soldiers, emancipation was not news to them.

June 21 -- They headed back to Brazos Santiago.[77]

* * *

The Official Record does not mention this division or any other troops assisting with the announcement of Granger's General Orders in Galveston. One news report states the military rounded up Galveston's freedmen, but that happened *after* they had received news of freedom.

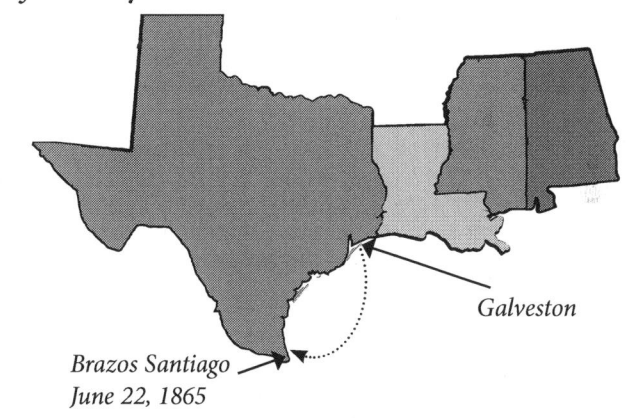

Galveston
June 18, 1865

Brazos Santiago
June 13, 1865

Aransas Pass
June 16, 1865

Aransas Pass (a few stout hollers from Corpus Christi).

June 16 -- They arrived at Aransas Bar, but could not disembark because the tide was too low for ships to cross the sandbar. Running short on coal and water for their steamboats, they left Aransas Pass and headed to Galveston.

June 18 -- They arrived at the Galveston sandbar.

June 19 -- They docked and began loading supplies. Celebratory frolicking on the beach resulted in disciplinary

Galveston

Brazos Santiago
June 22, 1865

"Wait. Hold up. There were about 2,650 Black soldiers, plus four extra shiploads present? So why don't history books count them among the troops who were in Galveston with Granger. Yeah, they weren't supposed to be there, but why does that matter? They were there, so count 'em! No, they didn't participate in the initial news release, but did anybody? What? You think 2,050 white troops stood outside the Osterman building watching someone tack Granger's orders to a wall?"

Excerpt from
History of the Eighty-Third Ohio Volunteer Infantry
by T. B. Marshall

On June 12th, the dreaded marching orders came, to embark for Galveston. We sent the baggage to the wharf and at 5 P. M. on the 13th, the propeller, "John K. Rice," left the dock with the Eighty-Third on board. Just as we were passing the last row of piles, the vessel ran aground and there we stuck until the tide floated us off which was not until eight in the morning of the 14th, and we steamed out past Fort Morgan at noon.

We were soon out of sight of land, and the prow of vessel headed directly towards a heavy rain storm which we struck about the middle of the afternoon.

We could see several rain storms all around but our pilot did not seem to care very much about his passengers, as he drove right ahead as if it was all sunshine and a level road and we were going to a picnic. The sea became rougher and rougher; the vessel pitched and tossed about like a tub and it was not very long until about all the regiment was lined up along the rail—but a veil of reticence will be drawn over this scene, only remarking that the fish in that part of God's domain certainly did not lack for material with which to build up flesh and bones, especially bones.

On June 16th, we sighted the harbor of Galveston and reached the entrance about the middle of the afternoon, too late for a pilot to come out and take us in over the bar and into the smooth waters of the bay. Our anchor was dropped, and we were left to the mercy of the winds and waves all night and not only the next day, but well along into the 18th before a pilot came to our relief. By that time nearly every one had suffered so much from sea sickness that we were almost too weak to walk, but we did manage to get off the boat. Quietness soon restored us and in a few hours we were able to discard our sea legs, and walk without wabbling.

Our first camping place was in the public square where we put up our shelter tents. It was a decidedly hot place. At noon, one with an ordinary brim hat on, would cast but a round shadow as he stood in the sun. Some citizens were kind enough to tell our officers they would have us all sick if they did not take us out of that square and from under those low shelter tents.

We were then separated into divisions and quartered in abandoned dwellings and hotels. Companies E and K and the band occupied the Island City House. This was a large hotel with wide porches to each story, covering the full length of the building and facing the gulf. These were about the best quarters of any as we had the full benefit of the sea breeze. Other companies had other commodious quarters and taking it on the whole, we were very well cared for in this tropical land.

When we landed, we found that markets were regularly kept up, and on going through them were surprised to see nothing but gold and silver as the medium of exchange, Confederate money having been repudiated. It did not take long, however, for this hard money to disappear and Uncle Sam's money to take its place, and be just as eagerly accepted.

The city itself was a place of great interest to us. Every house had a paling fence in front, and through the interstices grew the luxuriant oleanders with their wealth of blossoms. Another peculiarity was the manner in which the water supply was kept. It was too near the salt water to have wells, as by digging it soon became brackish, and the only way was in the use of cisterns. These were from fifteen to thirty feet in diameter and sunk in the ground only about two feet, and then built up some five feet with cement, making them something like seven feet in depth. During the rainy season these cisterns were filled and covered sometimes with a good, tight, substantial cover. Others were covered by a lot of boards of any and all kinds, the water being visible in most any place.

Sometimes these cisterns were built underneath the houses and this helped to keep the water cooler besides keeping out a lot of dust and dirt. Those out of doors cisterns were magnificent places for the breeding of mosquitoes, and said bugs utilized it to their "bills" content.

The shore of the Gulf was about a half a mile away and it proved to be one of the finest bathing beaches that is on any coast, anywhere, and extended for miles. The water shoaled gradually, so that one could grade the depth that best suited, from six inches to as many feet as wanted. There were three bars along the beach, each one deeper and spaced some distance apart, so it was a perfectly safe proposition to bathe whenever inclination prompted. During the entire time we remained in Galveston, there was not a single life lost among the many thousands of bathers, and from five hundred to as many thousands could be seen at almost any time.

The movement of so many tried and disciplined troops to Texas, having apparently accomplished its object, there was no further necessity for postponing our final discharge.[78]

The following guests were present when General Granger initiated enforcement of the Emancipation Proclamation in Galveston, Texas:

Arriving June 16th aboard the U.S.S. Corinthian
- 114th Regiment, Ohio Infantry, 13th Army Corps. 400 troops commanded by Col. John H. Kelly.[45]

Arriving June 17th aboard the U.S.S. Clinton
- Gen. Gordon Granger's staff.
- 34th Iowa Inf. Regiment commanded by Col. George W. Clark
- 83rd Ohio Volunteer Inf. Regiment, 3rd Brigade, 2nd Div., 13th Army Corps, commanded by Col. Frederick W. Moore. (800 troops combined).[43]

Arriving June 17th aboard the U.S.S. Exact
- Part of the 94th Illinois regiment. 250 troops commanded by Capt. J. B. Okeson[sic].[43]

Arriving June 18th aboard the U.S.S. John K. Rice.
- 83rd Ohio Volunteer Regiment. 600 troops commanded by Lieut.-Col. William H. Baldwin.[43]

Arriving June 19th
- aboard the U.S.S. Montauk, Nightingale, and Prometheus:
- 28th Ind. Colored Inf. 896 troops.* Com. Thomas Logan.[79]
- 31st NY Colored Inf. 829 troops.* Com. Henry Ward.[81]

- aboard the USS Wilmington, and U.S.S. William Kennedy
- 29th Illinois Colored Infantry. 450 troops *(Wilmington)*; and 473 troops *(William Kennedy)*. Commanded by Clark E. Royce.[80]

- aboard the U.S.S. Crescent
- Generals Granger and Weitzel and Weitzel's staff.

Also arriving: five transports carrying Weitzel's troops, bound for Indianola.[82]

* See Notes, page 230.

MYTH #12

"General Granger's announcement produced immediate celebrations
- statewide -
replete with barbecue, singing and joyous revelry."

FACTS & DEDUCTIONS

- Since the announcement of Granger's third order outside of Galveston began on June 20th, there was no reason for enslaved people outside of Galveston to celebrate on June 19, 1865.

- Militarily enforced emancipation in Texas was an on-going operation. Most enslaved people were freed in late June and early July. But reportedly, some people remained in bondage for several years after June 19, 1865.

- Celebrating freedom was dangerous, especially given the state's unruly condition. Angry former owners blamed freedmen for their emancipation. Reports of violence against exuberant freedmen were plentiful.

- State law prevented slaves from owning property, including poultry and live stock.[83] Former slave owners did not provide celebratory victuals. Without food or venues, barbecues were unlikely.

**Attention Freedmen:
Due to Southernitus and Texasology, all jollification, rejoicing and hullabaloo must stop until ... eventually.**

Descriptions of Juneteenth's origin commonly include reports of joyous celebrations in Galveston on June 19, 1865. The source: Decades after emancipation, freedmen recorded their memories. One reportedly said, "Everybody went wild..." Whether that happened or not, one fact is undeniable: frenzied merriment induced by General Order No. 3 did not last long.

On the same day that General Order No. 3 was issued, General Granger's troops rounded up Galveston's joyful freedmen and interrogated each of them.

Those who identified their previous owners were forced to return "home" and work. Those who did not identify their previous owners were placed into servitude on military ships.

They were instructed to remain there until officials from the Freedmen's Bureau arrived to help them secure contracts. Two months passed before Freedmen's Bureau officials arrived.

Meanwhile, "freed" men and women were not allowed to gather in public places, travel without permission from their "employers", or quit their jobs for any reason. These rules were issued by General Granger.

Clippings from Houston and Austin papers capture the limits of emancipation and suggest the window for celebration was only a few hours.

(#1)

"About fifty negroes were this morning, taken by the Federals and sent under guard to work on the steamers, to cut wood, and act as laborers generally."

(above) "About fifty negroes were this morning, taken by the Federals and sent under guard to work on the steamers to cut wood, and act as laborers generally."
From: Received from Galveston, June 19, 1865 at 7 PM.
Published June 28, 1865, page 1, col. 1
The Weekly State Gazette (Austin, TX)

(#2)

We hear that the Federal authorities at Galveston are bringing the negroes to common sense in a summary manner. They call them up, one by one, and ask who they belong to. Those who tell the truth are sent home at once, while those who acknowledge no home or master are put to work on the streets, and on other labor, under the control of the military authorities.

Untitled news article
June 21, 1865, page 2, col. 4
Houston Tri-Weekly Telegraph

An Austin newspaper reported Galveston's freedmen were forced into labor the same morning General Order No. 3 was issued *(image #1)*. Houston's paper explained what transpired. *(Image #2)*

Three days after Juneteenth, a military officer advised Galveston's Mayor to pass a city ordinance allowing "hired servants" to be imprisoned if they left their "employers."[84] That same day, a new General Order #3 was issued in Houston by Colonel Clark. It threatened to arrest unemployed freedmen and force them into unpaid labor *(image #3)*. Given that option, freedmen had no choice but to accept whatever agreement their former owners offered, preceding arrival of the Freedmen's Bureau.

June 26, Granger circulated an order preventing "persons formerly slaves" from traveling on public thoroughfares without passes or permits from their employers (a.k.a. their former owners) All Texas newspapers were required to publish the circular for one month.[85]

(#3)

HEADQUARTERS, POST OF HOUSTON,
June 22d, 1865.
GENERAL ORDERS, No. 3.
The freedmen in and around the city of Houston are hereby directed to remain for the time being with their former owners. They are assured that by so doing they forfeit none of their rights of freedom. An agent of the government, whose business it is to superintend the making of contracts between the freedmen and those who desire to employ them, is expected here soon. In the meantime the freedmen are advised to be patient and industrious.
No encouragement or protection will be given to those who abandon their present homes for the purpose of idleness. If found in this city without employment or visible means of support, they will be put to labor cleaning the streets, without compensation.
The Provost Marshal is charged with the execution of this order. By order of
Colonel G. W. CLARK.
CHAS. F LOSHE. Post Adjutant. ju23 dtf

General Orders, No. 3 (Col. Clark)
Issued June 22, 1865. Published June 23, 1865 in the Houston Tri-Weekly Telegraph page 4, column 5.

MYTH #13

"Juneteenth is America's oldest continuous celebration of emancipation."

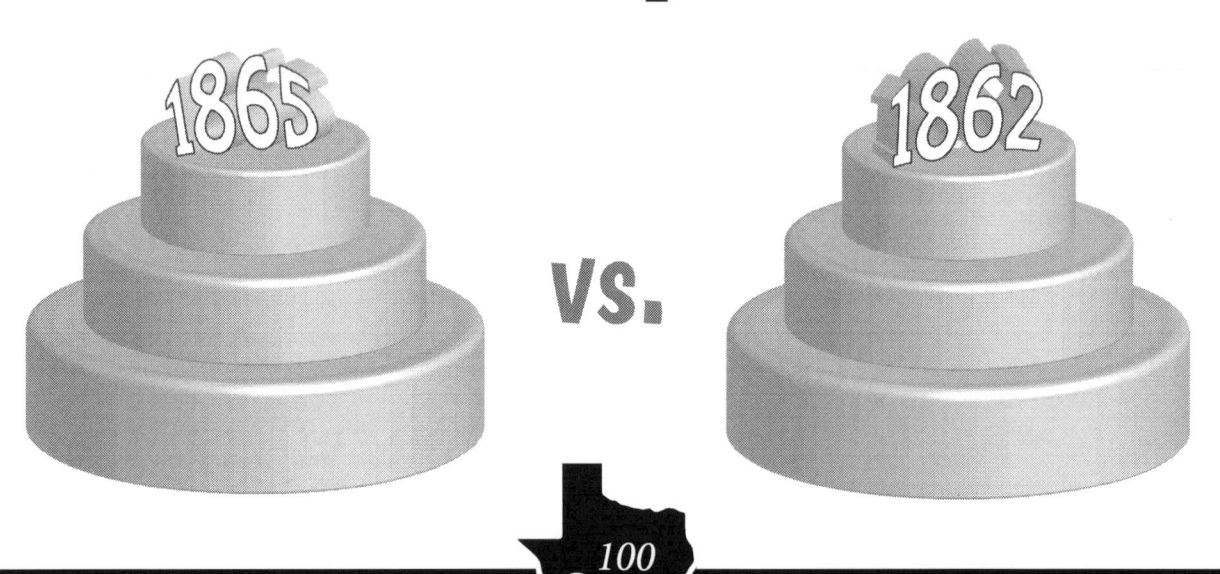

1865 vs. 1862

100

No!

The original celebration of emancipation began *before* emancipation was realized. Some called it,

Freedom's Eve

Historical purists argue the New Year's Eve vigil celebrated annually by predominately African American churches is a Christian practice that began in Europe[86] in the early 1700s. Celebrants called that event, "Watch Night". Right or wrong, that tenet neither negates or discounts the fact that congregations of abolitionists and pockets of enslaved people held vigils awaiting the Proclamation's effectiveness on the night of December 31, 1862. In fact, the pre-existence of Watch Night plausibly explains how a national emancipation vigil could originate in secret. Essentially, a pre-existing vigil was hijacked.

Regardless of when the Christian renewal component started, the emancipation component, starting 1862—now a cultural pillar of African American churches—predates Juneteenth's origin by three years.

And...

Charlotte, South Carolina's annual Emancipation Day event began January 1, 1866.

The First Commemorative Jubilee

A description of Galveston's first commemoration of emancipation is recorded in the January 2, 1866 edition of *Flake's Daily Bulletin*, a Galveston newspaper. The celebration occurred on New Year's day, 1866, six months after the issuance of General Order #3 and third anniversary of the Emancipation Proclamation.[87] A second celebration occurred on June 19, 1866. The moniker "Juneteenth" was not included. Both days were called "Freedom Day."

The first celebration began with what was labeled an *"orderly and creditable procession"* through town. Between 800 - 1,000 people participated. After the procession, a program was held at Galveston's church for the now 'freedmen', known as The Colored Church on Broadway. That building and the land it sat on were purchased by white Methodist Episcopals in 1848. The facility would have been their only public gathering place since law prevented slaves from owning property, and six months was not enough time for freedmen to purchase additional communal property.

The following year (1867), the church affiliated with the African Methodist Episcopal (A.M.E.) denomination. Eventually, its name changed to Reedy Chapel A.M.E. Church in honor of it's second pastor, Rev. Houston Reedy. Reedy Chapel is still thriving in its original location. Its current building (pictured right) was constructed in 1885 after a citywide fire destroyed the original building.[88]

During the first Freedom Day program, the Emancipation Proclamation and General Order No. 3 were read. Speeches were made and the popular military marching song *John Brown's Body* was performed (see page 140). Reedy Chapel A.M.E., which boast of being "The (A.M.E.) Mother Church of Texas" still proudly hosts annual Juneteenth festivities.

This location is often cited as one of four locations where General Order No. 3 was originally read. If that happened, the number of freedmen present for the reading, if any, is questionable. The realities of slavery make it highly implausible that enslaved Christians could assemble at will during a workday.

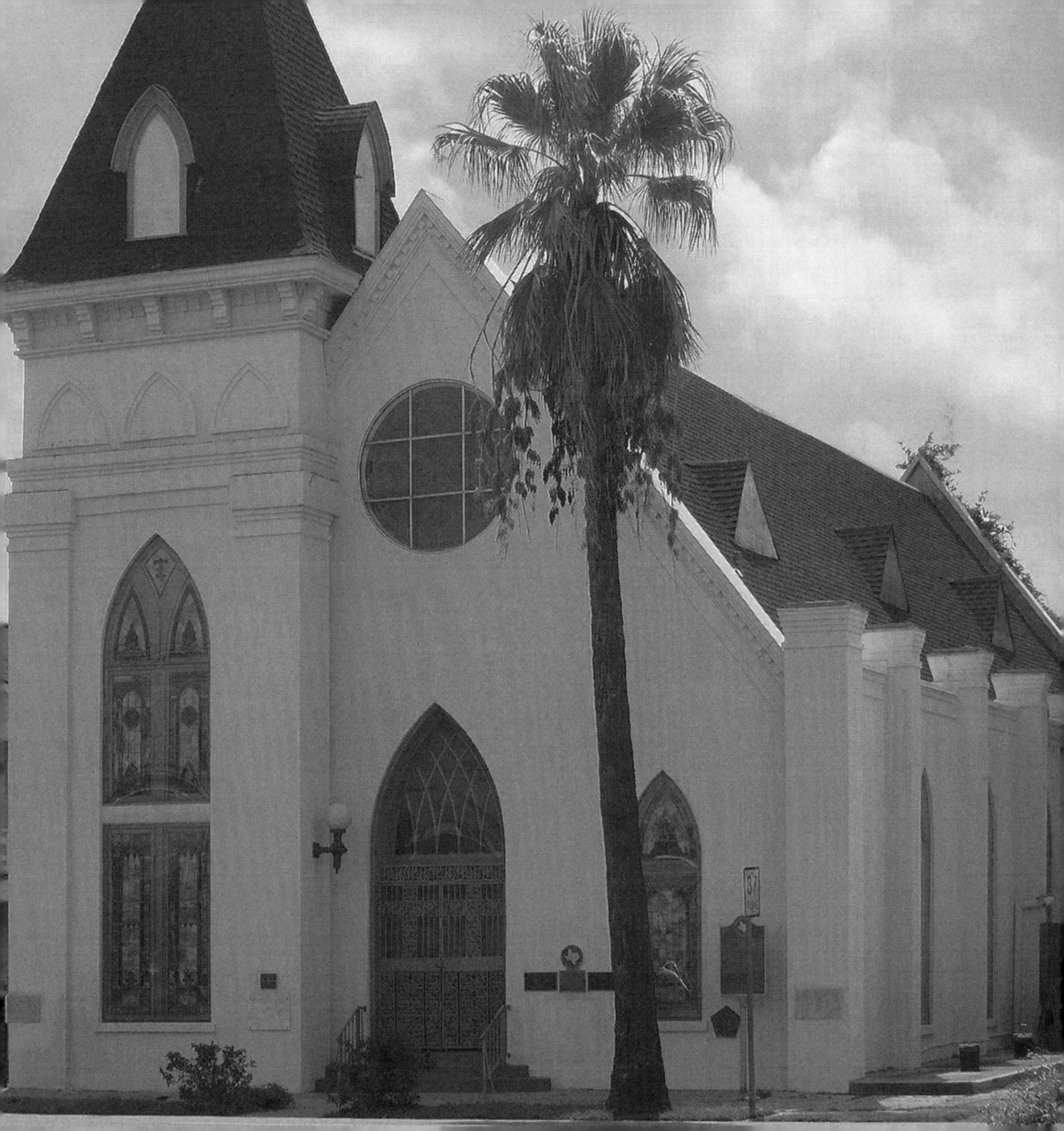
37

Summary

The first public celebration of emancipation was promoted via an advertisement in Flake's Daily Bulletin, a newspaper in Galveston. The second commemorative celebration was held six months later, on June 19, 1866. Emancipation celebrations in June have been held annually, thereafter.

EMANCIPATION CELEBRATION
—BY—
COLORED PERSONS.

All colored persons residing in Galveston, are invited to attend on New Year's Morning, at 10 o'clock, at the Public Square, to celebrate the abolition of slavery. Addresses will be delivered by Alex. Pearce Howard Cavenaugh, and the Rev. Daniel Gregory. All colored people, and their friends, are invited to attend. United States officers are especially desired to be present. de31

Advertisement from Flake's Daily Bulletin, December 31, 1865. [78]

Happy Emancipation Day!

June **20th**, 1866

& 21st, 22nd, 23rd, etc.

The first celebration of emancipation in several communities occurred on the anniversary of dates when those communities were freed. Example: Enslaved Africans in Houston were freed on June 20, 1865. In turn, Houston's first celebration occurred on June 20, 1866. The Houston Tri-Weekly Bulletin published a plea for Whites to act civilly during the celebration.

Statewide celebrations soon consolidated onto June 19th. Eventually, the word "Juneteenth" emerged. The earliest appearance of "Juneteenth" in print was found in the June 19, 1891 edition of the Brenham Weekly Banner. (page 107)

THE CELEBRATION OF THE ANNIVERSARY OF THEIR FREEDOM BY THE BLACKS,

Takes place to-day. There will be a grand barbecue.

We earnestly trust that nothing will be done by the inconsiderate or ill-disposed to interrupt or mar the merry-making of the freedmen. Throughout the war, up to the last hour, the negroes were faithful and dutiful to their masters. That they are now freedmen is not their act, and whatever may be thought of emancipation, it is none of their doing. That many freedmen should be indolent, some insolent, and some thievish when the restraints and moral support of their former condition was thrown off, was to be expected. He that cannot throw the mantle of charity and forbearance over these, has little of the kindlier feelings of our nature in his composition. The freedmen believe their emancipation a great good—it is natural they should wish to celebrate it. Let them enjoy its celebration unmolested. We believe, and justly too, that we, their old masters, are still the best friends the negroes have; let us prove it on this and on all occasions. Generosity and kindness to inferiors is a Southern virtue.

June + 'teenth

(Transcription)

The celebration of the anniversary of their freedom by the Blacks, takes place to-day. There will be a grand barbecue.

    We earnestly trust that nothing will be done by the inconsiderate or ill-disposed to interrupt or mar the merrymaking of the freedmen. Throughout the war, up to the last hour, the Negroes were faithful and dutiful to their masters. That they are now freedmen is not their act, and whatever may be thought of emancipation, it is none of their doing. That many freedmen should be indolent, some insolent, and some thievish when the restraints and moral support of their former condition was thrown off, was to be expected. He that cannot throw the mantle of charity and forbearance over these, had little of the kindlier feelings of our nature in his composition. The freedmen believe their emancipation a great good - it is natural they should want to celebrate it. Let them enjoy its celebration unmolested. We believe, and justly too, that we, their old masters, are still the best friends the Negroes have; let us prove it on this and on all occasions. Generosity and kindness to inferiors is a Southern virtue.

Houston Tri-Weekly Bulletin
June 20, 1866, page 2

The excerpt below is the earliest appearance of the word "Juneteenth" in surviving 19th century newspapers. Misspelling words (ex: "siliibration") was a typical method newspapers regularly used to mock Freedom Day celebrants.

> The second day of the emancipation celebration at the Fair grounds in this city Saturday was better attended than the first day, in fact the most interesting features of the celebration were reserved for Saturday evening when they had some races and other prize contests which drew a large crowd. There was not so many colored people in the city as usual on Saturday evening, all of them, very near, being out at the "Juneteenth siliibration."

June 15, 1891,
Brenham Daily Banner

Juneteenth - San Francisco, CA

108

SPEECH OF THE HON. RICHARD NELSON ON THE ANNIVERSARY CELEBRATION OF EMANCIPATION JUNE 19, 1871

Fellow Citizens:

I feel the weight of the honor conferred upon me by the kind partiality of my friends, in selecting me to speak to you on the anniversary of the birthday of our freedom, and while I feel sensibly indeed, that my feeble abilities are over-taxed I shall not shrink from the task, well knowing, that the same kindred spirit which animates my heart on this occasion thrills with ecstasy each throbbing heart within the sound of my voice, and that the same partiality which called me here will protect me from too severe a criticism, in this new field of labor and of love.

Had I been called upon to plow the field, to plant, to toil, to labor under the direction of some master, such would have been an old familiar, calling. But to be called upon to speak to you of that bright boon, so brilliantly foreshadowed in the Declaration of Independence, "that all men are created with the equal right of life, to liberty and the pursuit of happiness, and that such rights are unalienable;" I am filled with wonder and amazement that my race was so long denied the boon so boldly proclaimed as belonging to all creation alike. Ninety-five years ago American Independence was declared, and five years ago that sweet sound reached our ears in the Proclamation, we this day celebrate as one of Emancipation from slavery.

Memory itself must forever punish us if we can forget that blessed boon so dearly brought, yet so freely given. It is not saying too much when we as a race, declare our never-ceasing gratitude to that noble Union Army that plucked us as brands from the burning and made us free. All hail the Proclamation of Emancipation.

My fellow freemen, why do we linger round the sacred thought that life is only worth itself when possessed in freedom? Because it is the birthright of every sacred element of mankind. Without freedom man is not man, he is but a thing, an animal, a slave.

But in this land now we are realizing the full inspiration that animated the fathers when they penned the Declaration of Independence near one hundred years ago

Let us this day renew our love of that spirit which came hovering over our heads in the words of our Declaration of Freedom from the head and heart of that God-given inspiration, of that martyred, now Sainted President Abraham Lincoln, who ushered in this, to us, millennium of a perfect freedom in the Proclamation that severed the fetters which bound our manhood to the iron wheel of despotism. Let us revere the name of Abraham Lincoln, and teach our children to honor his memory, as the white man's father taught his children to revere the name of the beloved Washington. He is to us, what Washington is to our white brethren. He gave to them liberty and freedom, and Abraham Lincoln gave to us the same. Let us not forget either to honor always that noble soldiery who sent forth with life in hand and death in the van to win our freedom. I never see a Union Soldier that I do not want to grasp him by the hand, and say I thank you for an honest heart. But I am to tedious, I will close with a call for three cheers for freedom and equal rights to all, and I say all honor to the Proclamation Day. May we live many years to celebrate the anniversaries as they come and go, each one lending a brighter ray to freedom's cause. Remembering, that on the day through this now land of perfect liberty, near four millions of our race are this hour holding a jubilee and a thanksgiving as a rich tribute and a boon to Freedom's cause.[89]

Richard Nelson,

Editor's note: Richard Nelson was publisher of The Representative, one of Texas' earliest African American owned newspapers.

Females!

"Oh, no they didn't."

110

"Oh, yes they did."

The Representative, a Black-owned newspaper published in Galveston during the 1870's exposed the exclusion of freed women from the sixth commemoration of "Freedom Day."

"The ladies were somewhat displeased because they could not express their love of liberty by marching also. But when they attain to the blessings of female suffrage, this matter will be decided."[90]

Note: The January 2, 1866 edition of *Flake's Journal* (Galveston), claimed women and children participated in the first commemoration procession. That suggest exclusion of women evolved as the commemoration developed.

111

Well, why?

Early emancipation celebrations were rallies to teach men about politics and voting rights.[91] Women could not vote, therefore, their participation would have been ineffectual. In 1920, the 19th Amendment granted women's suffrage. By then, Jim Crow was acting a plumb fool. Poll taxes and the Texas All White Democratic Primary vote-blocked Black women and men as often as possible.
[92][93]

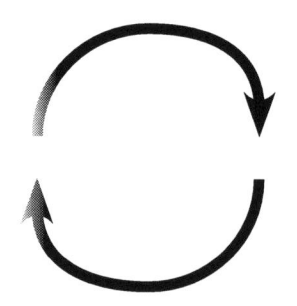

What you serve, you eat
Believe it or not, back in 1869, four of the ten Black men serving as delegates to the Texas Constitutional Convention voted against suffrage for women. One year later, reconstruction ended in Texas and Black men lost their political power.
Somebody's windbag sister-in-law

Juneteenth - Las Vegas, Nevada

113

Juneteenth 101

Current Commemorations

For the Texas State Historical Association, historian Teresa Palomo Acosta wrote:

"The first broader celebrations of Juneteenth were used as political rallies and to teach freed African Americans about their voting rights. Within a short time, however, Juneteenth was marked by festivities throughout the state, some of which were organized by official Juneteenth committees."[94]

Contemporary Juneteenth celebrations are held in every state. Members of the United States military have transported the observance to numerous nations.

Here is a list of Juneteenth celebration activities reported by communities worldwide.

Art exhibitions
    African weaving lessons
    Children's art competitions
    Coloring contests
    Photography exhibits
Car shows
Commemorative memorabilia sales
    Annual commemorative books
    Commemorative t-shirts
Community service activities
    Blood drives
    Clothing drives
    Community service award presentations
    Food drives
    Health fairs
    Job fairs
    Voter registration drives
    Voter awareness events
Dances
    Teen dances
    Outdoor dances
    Fundraising balls and galas
Displays
Economic empowerment workshops
Family reunions
Fashion shows
Film festivals
Flag design competitions
Food events

Juneteenth 101

- Banquets / luncheons
- Barbecue competitions
- Cake and pastry competitions
- Fish frys
- Picnics
- Soul food tastings and competitions
- Fund raisers
- Games
    - Bingo tournaments
    - Carnivals
    - Children's games and activities
    - Pool tournaments
    - Spade/domino tournaments
- Historical re-enactments
    - Emancipation Proclamation readings
    - General Order #3 readings
- Historical tours
- Juneteenth flag raisings
- Literary events
    - Book signings / book sells
    - Poetry readings
    - Story telling
    - Writing competitions
- Marching band competitions
- Motorcycle club rides
- Musical events
    - African drumming performances
    - Gospel / spiritual concerts
    - Jazz concerts
    - Rap / hip-hop concerts
- Pageants
    - Miss. / Mr. Juneteenth
    - Little Miss. / Mr. Juneteenth
- Parades, marches, freedom walks
- Quilt Shows
- Religious events
    - Praise dance performances
    - Prayer breakfasts
- Scholarship competitions
- Speaking events
    - Historical lectures
    - Oratory competitions
    - Seminars
- Sporting Events
    - Baseball tournaments
    - Basketball tournaments
    - Bowling tournaments
    - Fun runs
    - Golf tournaments
    - Rodeos
- Step shows
- Sunrise libations
- Talent shows
- Theatrical productions
- Trail rides
- Trivia contests
- Underground Railroad events
- Vendors

115

Semi-MYTH #14

"Texas was first to officially commemorate emancipation."

~ ~ ~

Maybe. Maybe not. Texas was the first state to create *an official state holiday* in recognition of emancipation ('79). Official state commemorations in other forms existed elsewhere prior to 1979. That includes gubernatorial proclamations and legislative resolutions commemorating emancipation.

During the 1940's, at least two Pennsylvania governors signed state proclamations celebrating emancipation. Before that, according to Texas Gov. J. V. Allred, Texas governors issued annual proclamations honoring emancipation. Representatives of the Texas State Library could not locate those proclamations. However, Gov. Allred's entire 1938 commemorative proclamation was published in The Houston Informer *(page 117)*.

Did the governor of any state other than Pennsylvania and Texas issue an "official" proclamation or resolution commemorating emancipation? Maybe. Maybe not. Assuming they did not do so appears to be the general consensus, but that popular idea seems to be based solely on speculation.

To All to Whom These Presents Shall Come:

Whereas, the Negroes in the State of Texas observe June 19 as the official day for the celebration of Emancipation from slavery; and

Whereas, June 19, 1865, was the date when General Robert S. Granger, who had command of the Military District of Texas, issued a proclamation notifying the Negroes of Texas that they were free; and

Whereas, since that time, Texas Negroes have observed this day with suitable holiday ceremony, except during such years when the day comes on a Sunday; when the Governor of the State is asked to proclaim the following day as the holiday of State observance by Negroes; and

> Whereas, June 19, 1938, this year falls on Sunday;

Now, Therefore, I, James V. Allred, Governor of the State of Texas, do set aside and proclaim the day of June 20, 1938, as the date of observance of Emancipation Day in Texas, and do urge all members of the Negro race in Texas to observe the day in a manner appropriate to the importance to them.

In Testimony whereof, I have hereunto signed my name officially and caused the Seal of State to be impressed here at Austin, this 25th day of May, A.D. 1938

J. V. Allred

Governor of Texas

Source: "Juneteenth Texas: Essays in African American Folklore" by Louis Abernathy, former Professor of History at University of North Texas.

IN THE NAME AND BY AUTHORITY OF THE

COMMONWEALTH OF PENNSYLVANIA
GOVERNOR'S OFFICE
HARRISBURG

PROCLAMATION
NATIONAL FREEDOM DAY - FEBRUARY 1, 1945

The Thirteenth Amendment to the Consitution of the United States stands forth as a beacon of enlightenment to guide all who love liberty and are united in the present struggle to save the world from enslavement by the forces of cruel aggression.

It was that brief statement written into the fundamental law of our land which gave new force and vigor to the inspired words of the Declaration of Independence "that all men are created equal."

Eighty years have passed since President Lincoln, on February 1, 1865, signed the Resolution of Congress submitting the Thirteenth Amendment to the States for ratification. It is proper and fitting that this memorable date be observed each year to perpetuate and honor an epochal step in human progress.

Now, therefore, I, Edward Martin, Governor of the Commonwealth of Pennsylvania, do hereby designate and proclaim Thursday, February 1, 1945, as National Freedom Day. I urge that this day be observed with appropriate ceremonies in all parts of the Commonwealth of Pennsylvania.

                                        GIVEN under my hand and the Great Seal of the State, at the City of Harrisburg, this thirty-first day of January, in the year of our Lord one thousand nine hundred and forty-five, and of the Commonwealth the one hundred and sixty-ninth.

Edward Martin

By GRAVES AND HOLMES H.S.R. No. ___

R E S O L U T I O N

WHEREAS, On June 19, 1865, Major General Gordon Granger, representing the United States Government, landed at Galveston and issued a general order from the President of the United States and declared that all slaves were free; and

WHEREAS, On June 19, 1865, Black people in Texas rejoiced in joining fellow Blacks across the nation who were freed January 1, 1865; and

WHEREAS, From that day, which is fully six and one-half months after the Emancipation Proclamation of President Abraham Lincoln came into force, Black people in Texas were recognized to be an integral part of our State's social, political, and economic structure; and

WHEREAS, The Black people in the State of Texas continue to make increasing contributions to the development and culture of the State of Texas; and

WHEREAS, Blacks serve in many high offices and capacities in Texas, including the State Legislature, where they have made distinctive contributions to the legislative process and in the service of all their constituency; now, therefore, be it

RESOLVED, That the House of Representatives of the 62nd Legislature, 3rd Called Session, honor the Black people of Texas for their contributions to the State; and, be it further

RESOLVED, That the House of Representatives recognize "Juneteenth" as an annual holiday of significance to all Texans and, particularly, to the Blacks of Texas, for whom this date symbolizes freedom from slavery.

Address by Representative Al Edwards to the Texas 66th Legislature after passage of H.B. 1016 which created Texas Emancipation Day

Mr. Speaker and members of the House, I rise today on a matter of personal privilege. I want to answer to common assertion. Millions of blacks, and whites, in Texas do not celebrate June 19 as Emancipation Day out of ignorance nor did the 66th Legislature pass my House Bill 1016 just to give the state another holiday since most members have a number of black constituents.

June 19, 1865, was the date on which slaves in Texas were actually freed. General Gordon Granger landed at Galveston, proclaimed himself military governor and freed the slaves. You and I know and most Texas blacks know that Lincoln issued the Emancipation Proclamation on January 1, 1863. We also know that it freed no slave in Texas until June 19, 1865.

By passing my House Bill 1016, the legislature was not just engaging in politics. The members were not just throwing a cheap bone to their black constituents. The legislature was giving official recognition to a uniquely Texas holiday that has been celebrated for 115 years. These celebrations commemorate an event that was good for all of Texas and indeed the whole nation. Slavery was a burden on the entire society. Its existence paralyzed politics for decades. Slavery dehumanized slave and master alike. It is right that we joyfully celebrate the demise of the "Peculiar Institution" with picnics, music, conferences, and thanksgiving to God.

I want you to know that it would be impossible for me to let this session come to an end without calling to your attention the fact that the 66th Legislature has made one of the greatest accomplishments in the history of Texas and the nation in helping e to make June 19 a state holiday in Texas. There have been a great number of what I, and I am sure you, consider to be bad bills, but I want all of you to know that house Bill 1016 can never be labeled as a totally bad bill. I want all of you to know that you can always be proud of the fact that you were actually a part of and were responsible for another great historical landmark in Texas. I also want you to know that Texas is the first and only state in the nation to make this date a state holiday. I am sure other states will try to follow out leadership.

The bill is now on the Government's desk and I am confident that he will sign it.

If I had failed in having these remarks entered into the record, then I would have failed in my responsibilities as a legislator. It is important that it be made clear what the legislature's intent was in passing this measure. It is important for future generations to understand that this effort was not a cheap political trick, complete devoid of meaning, but rather that it was an expression of the respect we have for a great date I the struggle for all men's freedom and of the hope which we hold for the future.

I would like to thank all of you for your help in passing his legislation. I would especially like to thank the Speaker for his help and his fast gavel.

Mr. Speaker and members, I thank you for this opportunity to make these remarks and may God bless you and your future endeavors, and for standing up and being real men and women.[95]

Juneteenth State Recognition Legislation

This registry includes effective, approval or enrollment dates of state legislation recognizing Juneteenth as of June 30, 2021.

Alabama - June 7, 2011
"...we hereby recognize the historical significance and importance of June 19, 1865, and, by copy of this resolution, we extend our best wishes to the participants in the celebration of Juneteenth on June 19, 2011."[96]

Alaska - April 11, 2001
"Juneteenth Day is established on the third Saturday in June each year to commemorate the abolition of slavery throughout the United States and its territories in 1865. The governor shall issue a proclamation to commemorate the day. On Juneteenth Day, citizens of the state are urged to reflect on the suffering endured by early African-Americans and to appreciate the unique freedom and equality enjoyed by all state citizens today."[97]

Arizona - March 17, 2016
"June 19, in each year, shall be observed as Juneteenth Day. Juneteenth Day is not a legal holiday."[98]

Arkansas - April 13, 2005
"The third Saturday in June shall be known as Juneteenth Independence Day to commemorate the end of over two hundred (200) years of slavery in the United States of America and to demonstrate racial reconciliation and healing from the legacy of slavery. Juneteenth Independence Day shall not be a legal holiday but shall be a memorial day to be commemorated by the issuance of an appropriate proclamation by the Governor."[99]

California - July 31, 2003
"The Governor shall proclaim the third Saturday in June of each year to be known as "Juneteenth National Freedom Day: A day of observance," to urge all Californians in celebrating this day to honor and reflect on the significant roles that African-Americans have played in the history of the United States and how African-Americans have enriched society through their steadfast commitment to promoting freedom, brotherhood, and equality."[100]

Colorado - April 9, 2004
"Be It Resolved by the House of Representatives of the Sixty-fourth General Assembly of the State of Colorado, the Senate concurring herein: That we, the members of the Colorado General Assembly, designate Saturday, June 19, 2004, and the third Saturday in June in each year thereafter, as Juneteenth in the state of Colorado, and encourage Coloradans to reflect on the value of freedom."[101]

Connecticut - June 3, 2003 *(Effective date)*
"The Governor shall proclaim the Saturday that is closest to June nineteenth of each year to be Juneteenth Independence Day in recognition of the formal emancipation of enslaved African-Americans pursuant to General Order No. 3 of June 19, 1865, in Galveston, Texas. Suitable exercises shall be held in the State Capitol and elsewhere as the Governor designates for the observance of the day."[102]

Delaware - Feb. 18, 2000

"The following day shall be commemorated in this State by appropriate ceremonies: The third Saturday of June, known as Juneteenth National Freedom Day."[103]

District of Columbia - June 3, 2003 (Enrolled)
"It is the sense of the Council to recognize June 19th as "Juneteenth National Freedom Day," to support the campaign to recognize "Juneteenth National Freedom Day" as a national holiday, and to encourage participation of all citizens in the annual Washington Juneteenth National Holiday Observance on the National Mall in Washington, D.C., during the week of the 19th of June.[104]

Florida - May 30, 1991
"June 19th of each year is hereby designated "Juneteenth Day" to commemorate the traditional observance of the day the slaves in Florida were notified of the Emancipation Proclamation. The Governor may issue annually a proclamation designating June 19th as Juneteenth Day and calling on public officials, schools, private organizations, and all citizens to honor the historic significance of the day.[105]

Georgia - Feb. 16, 2011
"Be it resolved by the Senate that the members of this body hereby recognize "Juneteenth Celebration Day" in remembrance of those who received the exultant news of their freedom and as a memorial to all those who suffered from the cruelties of slavery, and encourage ceremonies, celebrations, and other activities to be held in their honor. Be it further resolved that the Secretary of the Senate is authorized and directed to transmit an appropriate copy of this resolution to the National Juneteenth Observance Foundation."[106]

Hawaii - June 16, 2021
"June 19 of each year shall be known and designated as Juneteenth to commemorate the end of slavery in the United States and in honor and recognition of the significant roles and contributions of African Americans in the history of the United States. Juneteenth is not and shall not be construed to be a state holiday." [220]

Idaho - Feb. 28, 2001
"Be it resolved by the members of the First Regular Session of the Fifty-sixth Idaho Legislature, the Senate and the House of Representatives concurring therein, that June 16, 2001, and the third Saturday of June of every year thereafter be designated as "Juneteenth National Freedom Day" and that appropriate ceremonies and presentations be conducted during that day to honor Idahoans of African descent.[107]

Illinois - January 1, 2004 (effective)
"Juneteenth National Freedom Day. The third Saturday in June of each year is designated as Juneteenth National Freedom Day to commemorate the abolition of slavery throughout the United States and its territories in 1865. Juneteenth National Freedom Day may be observed with suitable observances and exercises by civic groups and the public, and citizens of the State are urged to reflect on the suffering endured by early African-Americans and to celebrate the unique freedom and equality enjoyed by all State citizens today.[108]

Indiana - February 9, 2010
"Be it resolved...: That the Indiana General Assembly celebrating the Emancipation Proclamation and urging the establishment of June 19th as Juneteenth National Freedom Day urges the establishment of June 19th as Juneteenth National Freedom Day to acknowledge the freedom of all people regardless of their race, creed, religion, or nationality. That the Indiana General Assembly urges the establishment of June 19th as Juneteenth National

Freedom Day to provide an opportunity for the people of the United States to learn more about the past and to better understand the experiences that have shaped our nation. That the Indiana General Assembly urges the establishment of June 19th as Juneteenth National Freedom Day to acknowledge that the end of slavery is an important and enriching part of the history and heritage of the United States and our history should be regarded as a means for understanding the past and solving the challenges of the future."[109]

Iowa - April 11, 2002

"The governor of this state is hereby authorized and requested to issue annually a proclamation designating the third Saturday in June as Juneteenth National Freedom Day and to encourage all governmental entities, civic organizations, schools, and institutions of higher education in the state to observe the day in a manner that emphasizes the meaning and importance of the emancipation proclamation that ended slavery in the United States and to recognize and celebrate the importance of this day to every person who cherishes liberty and equality for all people."[110]

Kansas - April 2, 2007

"Be it resolved by the Senate of the State of Kansas: That we support the National Juneteenth Holiday Campaign and encourage participation by all citizens in observance of Juneteenth National Freedom Day[111]

Kentucky - June 20, 2005

"The nineteenth of June each year shall be observed in Kentucky as "Juneteenth National Freedom Day." The Governor shall proclaim June 19 of each year as "Juneteenth National Freedom Day" and will encourage all Kentuckians celebrating this day to honor and reflect on the significant roles that African-Americans have played in the history of the United States[112]

Louisiana - August 15, 2003 (effective date)

"Juneteenth Day has long been recognized as a special day of celebration for the freedom of African Americans. As such, since 1865 the day has been celebrated as the day African Americans received the news of the signing of the Emancipation Proclamation. The celebration of this day has grown into a special day celebrating this freedom as well as a day of learning, sharing, and giving respect to the history, culture, and achievements of African Americans. The third Saturday in June is recognized and designated as Juneteenth Day throughout the state of Louisiana, in honor of the day African Americans celebrate as Emancipation Day."[113]

Maine - April 25, 2011

"The Governor shall annually issue a proclamation designating the 3rd Saturday in June as Juneteenth Independence Day to commemorate the day freedom was proclaimed to all slaves in the South by Union General Gordon Granger in 1865, 2 1/2 years after the Emancipation Proclamation was signed.[114]

Maryland - June 1, 2014 (effective)

"The Governor annually shall proclaim June 19 as Juneteenth National Freedom Day."[115]

Massachusetts - June 16, 2007

"The governor shall annually issue a proclamation setting apart the nineteenth of June as Juneteenth Independence Day, to be observed on the Sunday that is closest to June 19th of each year, in recognition of June 19, 1865 when Union General Gordon Granger announced freedom for all slaves in the Southwestern United States and in recognition of the end of slavery in the United States as well as the significant contributions, individuals of

African decent have made to the commonwealth and to the United States and recommending that said day be observed in an appropriate manner by the people.[116]

Michigan - June 17, 2005

"The legislature further observes that congress passed the thirteenth amendment to the United States constitution on January 31, 1865, abolishing slavery throughout the United States and its territories. In the following months, spontaneous celebrations erupted throughout the country whenever African-Americans learned of their freedom. News of the amendment reached the states at different times, and it was not until June 19, 1865 that the message of freedom reached the slaves in the western states. In honor of this great moment in the history of our nation, the legislature declares that the third Saturday in June of each year shall be known as "Juneteenth National Freedom Day." The legislature encourages individuals, educational institutions, and social, community, religious, labor, and business organizations to pause on Juneteenth National Freedom Day and reflect upon the strong survival instinct of the African-American slaves and the excitement and great joy with which African-Americans first celebrated the abolition of slavery.[117]

Minnesota - March 27, 1996

"June 19 is designated Juneteenth in recognition of the historical pronouncement of the abolition of slavery on June 19, 1865, when the Emancipation Proclamation was said to have been first publicly read in Texas. The governor may take any action necessary to promote and encourage the observance of Juneteenth and public schools may offer instruction and programs on the occasion.[118]

Mississippi - March 29, 2010

"Be it resolved by the Senate of the State of Mississippi, the House of Representatives concurring therein, that we do hereby recognize June 19 as "Juneteenth Freedom Day" in recognition and commemoration of June 19, 1865, as the date of the communication to former slaves of African descent of the fact that slavery had ended in America, and as a day when the ideals of liberty and justice for all citizens is celebrated. We acknowledge that this day is a day of commemoration, recognition and observation and not to be recognized as a legal holiday.[119]

Missouri - August 28, 2003

"June nineteenth, known as Juneteenth, of each year shall be known and is designated as "Emancipation Day" to provide an opportunity for the people of Missouri to reflect upon the United States of America's passion for freedom as exemplified in the Constitution of the United States, the Bill of Rights, and the Emancipation Proclamation, and to reflect upon the significance and particularity of the Emancipation Proclamation and its role in ending slavery in the United States. To celebrate that Juneteenth commemorates the spirit and quest of African-American freedom emphasizing education, art, and intellectual achievement, through reflection, rejoicing, and manifestation of a more substantive economic and just citizenry, the people of the state, offices of government, and all educational, commercial, political, civic, religious, and fraternal organizations in the state are requested to devote some part of the day to remember the proclamation that began the full realization for all people in the United States of the self-evident truth, as stated in the Declaration of Independence of the United States, that all men are created equal, by: Celebrating the abolishment of slavery, accomplished by ratification of the thirteenth amendment to the Constitution of the United States, as the former slaves celebrated on June 19, 1865, upon learning the message of freedom from Major General Gordon Granger of the Union Army in Galveston, Texas, which celebration, known as "Juneteenth", is the oldest known celebration of the ending of slavery; and reaffirming their commitment to achieving equal justice and opportunity for all citizens.[120]

Montana - October 1, 2017

"The third Saturday in June is designated as Juneteenth national Freedom Day to commemorate African-American emancipation from slavery, to celebrate the freedom won by people in many countries, and to rededicate ourselves to the cause of liberty.[121]

Nebraska - April 7, 2009

"...That the Legislature recognizes June 19 as Juneteenth National Freedom Day and encourages celebration of this day to honor and reflect on the significant roles that African-Americans have played in the history of the United States. That the Legislature acknowledges how African-Americans have enriched society through their steadfast commitment to promoting freedom, brotherhood, and equality.[122]

Nevada - May 12, 2011

"The Governor shall annually proclaim June 19 to be "Juneteenth Day" in the State of Nevada to commemorate the abolition of slavery in the United States. The proclamation must call upon the news media, educators and appropriate governmental officers to bring to the attention of Nevada's residents the historical significance of the day when the last slaves in the United States were emancipated and the significant contributions of African-Americans to the State.[123]

New Hampshire - June 19, 2019

"The governor shall annually issue a proclamation calling for the proper observance of June 19 as Juneteenth and shall call on the citizens of New Hampshire to observe the day with appropriate ceremonies and activities commemorating the abolition of slavery.[124]

New Jersey - April 5, 2004

"The third Saturday in June of each year is hereby designated as "Juneteenth Independence Day" in New Jersey to commemorate and celebrate the emancipation of African-Americans and foster respect for all cultures.[125]

New Mexico - May 17, 2006

"The "Juneteenth Freedom Day" is created. It shall be commemorated on the third Saturday in June of each year and be observed by reflecting on the history of African-American slavery in the United States; the experience of Africans brought to the United States in a five- to twelve-week journey across the Atlantic, the deaths of thousands of Africans who died in inhuman conditions of passage; the abuse of African-American slaves, including whipping, castration, branding and rape; the importance of the Thirteenth Amendment of the United States constitution abolishing slavery throughout the United States and its territories; and the significance of June 19, 1865, the day on which the message of freedom and abolition reached the western states; and recognizing the importance of Americans of African descent as American citizens and New Mexico residents.[126]

New York - July 16, 2004

"The following days shall be days of commemoration in each year: June nineteenth, to be known as "Juneteenth Freedom Day."[127]

North Carolina - August 2, 2009

"When Juneteenth National Freedom Day or a substantially similar holiday becomes a nationally recognized holiday, the General Assembly shall recognize the nineteenth day of June each year as Juneteenth National Freedom Day, to commemorate the end of slavery in the United States and to demonstrate racial reconciliation and healing from the legacy of slavery.[128]

NOTE: *The nationally recognized similar holiday existed prior to this bill. See page 130.*

North Dakota - April 12, 2021

"Juneteenth. To commemorate the ending of slavery in the United States, the nineteenth of June of each year is designated and established as Juneteenth for the state of North Dakota. [221]

Ohio - April, 7, 2009

"The nineteenth day of June is designated as "Juneteenth National Freedom Day" to acknowledge the freedom, history, and culture that June 19, 1865, the day on which the last slaves in the United States were set free in Texas, has come to symbolize."[129]

Oklahoma - April 27, 1994

"The third Saturday in June of each year is hereby declared an official holiday, to be known as Juneteenth National Freedom Day."[130]

Oregon - June 19, 2001

"We, the members of the Seventy-first Legislative Assembly, do hereby declare Juneteenth, June 19 of each year, to be a day for celebration statewide of the dignity and freedom of all citizens.[131]

Pennsylvania - June 19, 2019

"June 19 is designated as "Juneteenth National Freedom Day" in this Commonwealth."[132]

Rhode Island - Feb. 2013

"This Senate of the State of Rhode Island and Providence Plantations hereby urges the citizens of the State of Rhode Island to recognize the historical significance of Juneteenth Independence Day and to observe Juneteenth National Freedom Day on June 19th; and be it further resolved that this Senate supports the annual celebration of Juneteenth National Freedom Day in order to provide an opportunity for the people of the state to learn more about our country's past and to better understand the experiences that have shaped our nation..."[133]

South Carolina - May 14, 2008

"The nineteenth day of June of each year is designated as "Juneteenth Celebration of Freedom Day" to commemorate and reflect on the freedom of African Americans and their contributions to this State and nation."[134]

Tennessee - April 30, 2007

"...We hereby designate June 19, 2007, as "Juneteenth Day" in Tennessee, and in support of the National Juneteenth Holiday Campaign, we encourage all Tennesseans to join in the celebration of this special day of national observance. Be it further resolved, that it is the sense of this General Assembly that the nineteenth day of each June thereafter should be observed as "Juneteenth Day" in Tennessee. Be it further resolved, that an appropriate copy of this resolution be prepared for presentation with this final clause omitted from such copy."[135]

Texas - January 1, 1980 (effective date)

"The 19th day of June is designated "Emancipation Day in Texas" in honor of the emancipation of the slaves in Texas on June 19, 1865.[136]

Utah - May 10, 2016

"The following days shall be commemorated annually: ... Juneteenth Freedom Day, on the third Saturday in June, in honor of Union General Gordon Granger proclaiming the freedom of all slaves on June 19, 1865, in Galveston, Texas;[137]

Vermont - Feb 27, 2008
"The third Saturday of the month of June is designated as "Juneteenth National Freedom Day."[138]

Virginia - Feb 22, 2007
"Resolved by the House of Delegates, That the third Saturday of June, in 2007 and in each succeeding year, be designated as "Juneteenth" Freedom Day in Virginia; and, be it resolved further, that the House of Delegates recognize the pain caused by the enslavement of generations of African Americans in Virginia, and call for reconciliation among all Virginians; and, be it resolved further, that the Governor call upon the people of the Commonwealth to reflect upon the significant roles and many contributions of African Americans to Virginia and the nation throughout history and today, and to celebrate this day with appropriate activities and events that honor this rich legacy..."[139]

Washington - July 22, 2007
"The legislature declares that the following days are recognized as provided in this subsection, but may not be considered legal holidays for any purpose: ... The nineteenth day of June, recognized as Juneteenth, a day of remembrance for the day the slaves learned of their freedom."[140]

West Virginia - 2008 (exact date undetermined)
"Resolved by the House of Delegates: That the House of Delegates hereby designates June 19, as "Juneteenth" a day of reflection and renewal, a day to honor and respect the sufferings of slavery, a day to acknowledge the evils of slavery and its aftermath, a day to think about that moment in time when the enslaved in Galveston, Texas received word of their freedom, a day for people of all races, nationality and ethnic background to join together to support and participate in "Juneteenth"; and, be it further resolved, That the House of Delegates invites all members of the West Virginia Legislature and all citizens of the great State of West Virginia to join it on every June 19th in recognizing and celebrating that historical event of 1865 in Galveston, Texas, known as "Juneteenth."[141]

Wisconsin - December 16, 2009
"Legal Holidays: ... June 19, which shall be the day of observation for Juneteenth Day.[142]

Wyoming - July 1, 2003
"In celebration of the end of slavery in the United States proclaimed by Major General Gordon Granger on June 19, 1865 more than two and one-half (2½) years after the Emancipation Proclamation was issued by President Abraham Lincoln, and in recognition of those who died and sacrificed to achieve the end of slavery, the Juneteenth holiday is established. The Juneteenth holiday shall be celebrated each year with appropriate activities on the third Saturday of June. This section shall not affect commercial paper, the making or execution of written agreements or judicial proceedings, or authorize public schools, business or state and local government offices to close.[143]

State not listed:
South Dakota's Governor issued a gubernatorial proclamation after President Biden signed the holiday into law.

Juneteenth - San Diego, California

As of this book's original publication year (2018), forty-seven* states and the District of Columbia had officially recognized Juneteenth. However, celebrations were held in all fifty states. The celebratory photographs appearing in this publication reveal the expansiveness and national scope of Juneteenth celebrations.

* This number includes North Carolina. Conditions for recognition set by the North Carolina legislature had already been met when the legislation was signed.

The March to a National Juneteenth Holiday

112TH Congress, 2D Session,
Senate Joint Resolution 45

IN THE SENATE OF THE UNITED STATES
JUNE 19, 2012

Mrs. Hutchison (for herself, Mr. Levin, Mr. Cornyn, Mr. Cardin, Ms. Landrieu, Mr. Brown of Ohio, Mrs. Boxer, Ms. Stabenow, Mr. Harkin, Mr. Begich, Mr. Durbin, Mr. Warner, Mr. Webb, Mr. Nelson of Florida, and Mr. Akaka) introduced the following joint resolution; which was read twice and referred to the Committee on the Judiciary.

JOINT RESOLUTION

Amending title 36, United States Code, to designate June 19 as "Juneteenth Independence Day."

Whereas news of the end of slavery did not reach the frontier of the United States, and in particular the Southwestern States, for more than 2½ years after President Abraham Lincoln issued the Emancipation Proclamation on January 1, 1863, and months after the conclusion of the Civil War;

Whereas, on June 19, 1865, Union soldiers led by Major General Gordon Granger arrived in Galveston, Texas, with news that the Civil War had ended and that the slaves were free;

Whereas African Americans who had been slaves in the Southwest celebrated June 19, commonly known as "Juneteenth Independence Day", as the anniversary of their emancipation;

Whereas African Americans from the Southwest continue the tradition of celebrating Juneteenth Independence Day as inspiration and encouragement for future generations;

Whereas for more than 145 years, Juneteenth Independence Day celebrations have honored African-American freedom while encouraging self-development and respect for all cultures; and

Whereas the faith and strength of character demonstrated by former slaves remain an example for all people of the United States, regardless of their background, religion, or race: Now, therefore, be it

Resolved by the Senate and House of Representatives of the United States of America in Congress assembled,
SECTION 1. DESIGNATION OF JUNE 19 AS JUNETEENTH INDEPENDENCE DAY.
(a) In General.—Chapter 1 of title 36, United States Code, is amended by adding at the end the following:
"§ 145. Juneteenth Independence Day
"(a) Designation.—June 19 is Juneteenth Independence Day.
"(b) Proclamation.—The President is requested to issue each year a proclamation calling on State and local governments and the people of the United States to observe Juneteenth Independence Day with appropriate ceremonies, programs, and activities."[144]

> Y'all, this bill went to that Judiciary Committee and don't you know them folks let it die. Ain't that a shame?
> *Somebody's nosy neighbor*

NATIONAL FREEDOM DAY

America's original national emancipation-related observance.

Est. 1948

[CHAPTER 755]

June 30, 1948
[S. J. Res. 37]
[Public Law 842]

National Freedom Day.

13 Stat. 567.

JOINT RESOLUTION

Requesting the President to proclaim February 1 as National Freedom Day.

Resolved by the Senate and House of Representatives of the United States of America in Congress assembled, That the President of the United States is authorized to issue a proclamation designating the 1st day of February of each year as National Freedom Day for the purpose of commemorating the signing by President Abraham Lincoln, on February 1, 1865, of the joint resolution adopted by the Senate and the House of Representatives of the United States, proposing the thirteenth amendment to the Constitution of the United States of America.

Approved June 30, 1948.

Law Library of Congress, Statues at Large, 80th Congress, Session 2. Chapter 755

130

National Freedom Day, observed February 1, is a non-paid American holiday celebrating emancipation and honoring the day President Abraham Lincoln endorsed the Congressional Joint Resolution that eventually became the 13th Amendment.[145]

The first observation in 1942 was a grassroots show of patriotism, gratitude and national pride initiated by Ret. Major Richard R. Wright, Sr., an octogenarian freedman and resident of Philadelphia, Pennsylvania. The celebration quickly gained popularity, particularly in the northeastern states.

Major Wright personally conducted a multi-year campaign to gain national recognition of the celebration. He died eleven months before President Truman signed Presidential Proclamation #2824 declaring Freedom Day a national holiday.

Wright left no explanation of why Lincoln's signing date was celebrated rather than the amendment's ratification date. That concern is important because Lincoln's signature was superfluous and did not enhance the resolution's legality.

Twenty-four states include the words 'National Freedom Day' in the name of their respective June 19th recognition legislation. No state acknowledges this national observance on their roster of state holidays or special recognition days.

United States Code, 2017 Edition

Title 36	Patriotic and National Observances, Ceremonies, and Organizations
Subtitle I	Patriotic and National Observances and Ceremonies
Part A	Observances and Ceremonies
Chapter 1	Patriotic and National Observances

§124. National Freedom Day

The President may issue each year a proclamation designating February 1 as National Freedom Day to commemorate the signing by Abraham Lincoln on February 1, 1865, of the joint resolution adopted by the Senate and the House of Representatives that proposed the 13th amendment to the Constitution.

(Pub. L. 105–225, Aug. 12, 1998, 112 Stat. 1259.)
Historical and Revision Notes
Source (U.S. Code)   Source (Statutes at Large)
124   36:156.   June 30, 1948, ch. 755, 62 Stat. 1150.

# Presidential Proclamation 2824
National Freedom Day

Whereas, near the end of the tragic conflict between the Northern and Southern States, the Congress adopted a joint resolution proposing an amendment to the Constitution which would outlaw slavery in the United States and in every place subject to its jurisdiction; and

Whereas the resolution was signed by President Lincoln on February 1, 1865, and thereafter led to the adoption of the Thirteenth Amendment to the constitution; and

Whereas that Amendment is a corner stone in the foundation of our American traditions, and the signing of the resolution is a landmark in the Nation's effort to fulfill the principles of freedom and justice proclaimed in the first ten amendments to the Constitution; and

Whereas, by a joint resolution approved June 30, 1948 (62 Stat. 1150), the Congress authorized the President to proclaim the first day of February of each year as National Freedom Day in commemoration of the signing of the resolution of February 1, 1865; and

Whereas the Government and people of the United States wholeheartedly support the Universal Declaration of Human Rights approved by the General Assembly of the United Nations on December 10, 1948, which declares that "recognition of the inherent dignity and of the equal and inalienable rights of all members of the human family is the foundation of freedom, justice and peace in the world":

Now, Therefore, I, Harry S. Truman, President of the United States of America, do hereby designate February 1, 1949, and each succeeding February 1, as National Freedom Day; and I call upon the people of the United States to pause on that day in solemn contemplation of the glorious blessings of freedom which we humbly and thankfully enjoy.[146]

TRANSLATION

Looka here. Back in '42, folks in Baltimore started celebrating emancipation on Feb. 1. Why they chose that day is muddy, 'cause the only thing happened on that day was Lincoln unnecessarily put his signature on a recommendation. That's all it was—just a recommendation. His signature made a bunch of people feel happy, but his blessing didn't mean squat. Two thirds of the states had to ratify the resolution before it became a real amendment.

So, seems like the people in Baltimore should've been celebrating the actual ratification date. Anyway, after a few years of local celebrations, the man who started it all (an 80–year–old freedman) went to Congress and got 'em to pass a resolution naming Feb. 1 "National Freedom Day." Congress approved his request on June 1, '48 and they put it in the National Code on June 30. After that, President Truman wrote a proclamation declaring February 1, National Freedom Day, annually. Since then. no President has signed a similar proclamation. They could do it if they want to because the congressional resolution is still in effect.

The reason why Presidents can get away with not doing anything is 'cause the law says, "the President MAY sign ..." Meaning, Congress gave the presidents permission to do something if they were in the mood. Apparently, none of 'em have been in the mood. Anyway, it don't matter if they do or don't 'cause Truman's proclamation said, "...and each succeeding February 1..." In a few places, Freedom Day is still celebrated.

Now, here's a complication. Go back and look at what the North Carolina legislature approved (page 126). Given that a congressional resolution already existed when North Carolina wrote their stuff, seems like the word "busted" should be used.

Somebody's Uncle Bubba

Juneteenth 101

Thursday, June 17, 2021
President Joseph Biden signed into law:

S. 475, the "Juneteenth National Independence Day Act,"

What is Juneteenth?

The answer depends upon one's location. Juneteenth National Independence Day is a symbolic celebration of emancipation, no matter when or where it occurred. Whereas, slavery in America ended in December 1865, claiming Juneteenth marks the day slavery ended in the U.S. is solidly wrong.

Samuel Collins III, co-founder of the Juneteenth Legacy Project likens the national holiday to Memorial Day. He explained, "Memorial Day symbolically honors everyone who died while in service regardless of when or where. Likewise, emancipation occurred on multiple dates. Juneteenth symbolically honors all of them." [146A]

In Texas, Juneteenth enjoys two definitions. On June 19th, the state celebrates twin holidays that have the same name. Oddly, to better understand this quandary, consider similar celebrations in other locations.

Example: Florida.

On May 20th, Florida observes Emancipation Day - a celebration of emancipation *in that state*. On June 19th, Florida observes Juneteenth - a celebration of emancipation *nationwide*.

Likewise, Washington, D.C. celebrates local emancipation on April 16, and national emancipation on June 19.

In Texas, June 19th encompasses both the national holiday, and Emancipation Day, a state holiday acknowledging the day Union soldiers began enforcement of universal emancipation in Texas. 49 states and Washington, D.C. acknowledged Juneteenth prior to the national holiday, but only in Texas did emancipation begin on June 19th.

Ironically, Texas is the only state that does not include the word "Juneteenth" in its state recognition legislation.

Juneteenth National

Birth of a Holiday - A Very Condensed Chronology

1994 -- Rev. Ronald Myers, Sr., founded the National Juneteenth Observance Foundation (NJOF.) The organization's primary goal was to make Juneteenth a national non-paid day of observance. Prior to NJOF's formation, two states (Texas and Florida) had officially recognized June 19th. Twenty-seven years later, NJOF's goal was surpassed by the creation of an unconditional national holiday.

-- A legislative template for the creation of state recognitions was written and made available to interested Juneteenth proponents. Oklahoma was first to successfully implement the effort.

1995 -- Rep. Barbara-Rose Collins introduced a House Joint Resolution recognizing "the true day of independence for African Americans."

1997 -- Bills encouraging observance of Juneteenth Independence Day passed in the House and Senate. The first congressional observance of Juneteenth occurred in the rotunda of the Russell Senate Office Building.

1999 -- A Juneteenth observance was held at the National Mall.

2000 -- By this year's end, Juneteenth was officially recognized in 5 states.

2007 -- By this year's end, 26 states and the District of Columbia had recognized Juneteenth.

2009 -- A campaign was launch to promote issuance of a Juneteenth postage stamp.

2014 -- By the end of this year, 42 states and D.C. had recognized Juneteenth.

2015 -- NJOF distributed a resolution promoting "Juneteenth National Freedom Day." Organizations nationwide were encouraged to endorse the resolution and send copies to the White House.

2020 -- Resolutions to create a national holiday honoring Juneteenth were introduced in the House and Senate. The Senate's bill was blocked. The House passed its bill.

2021 -- The holiday bill was reintroduced in both chambers.

-- (June 15) Hours before the Senate passed SB 475 unanimously, Hawaii became the 49th state to recognize Juneteenth.

-- (June 16) The House passed its bill.

-- (June 17) President Biden signed SB 475, creating the twelfth national holiday.

-- (June 19) The first celebration of Juneteenth National Independence Day occurred.

-- After Juneteenth became a national holiday, South Dakota became the last state to acknowledge the commemoration.

Between 1995 through 2021 inclusive, 37 congressional resolutions were introduced. See pages 167-172 for the complete list.

Independence Day

Why June 19th?

Numerous dates could have been chosen to celebrate slavery's end. All deferred to Juneteenth, prompting the quandary, "*Why?*" Twenty-three advocates and officials involved with the creation of this holiday were asked, "Why did June 19th become the preferred day for a national celebration of emancipation?" Only three responses were received. None addressed the question. The three replies received provided popular but incorrect information about Juneteeth's origin.

The lack of responses strongly support an unattractive probability, i.e.: to reduce political resistance, accuracy deferred to popularity.

- Prior to becoming a national holiday, Juneteenth was celebrated in countless communities nationwide, making it substantially more popular than other emancipation observances.
- Even states that emancipated slaves after Texas, embraced Juneteenth.
- Arguably, the false, but commonly held belief that Texas was last to emancipate slaves was a driving force behind Juneteenth's popularity.

Other dates that could have been used:
7/17/62   Confiscation Act of 1862 passed.
10/22/62   Universal emancipation threatened.
1/1/63   Emancipation Proclamation issued.
4/9/65   End of the Civil War.
12/6/65   Ratification of the 13th Amendment.
(varied)   Emancipation dates of other states.

Falsetivities, falselergrams

Since 1866, news reports of June 19th commemorations have been controversial. Example: Houston's earliest report was an editorial asking White people to tolerate the celebration. (See pg. 101)

In 2021, inaccurate explanations of Juneteenth increased exponentially. Possibly, the birth of a new national holiday happened so swiftly, there simply wasn't time for reporters to worry about checking facts.

Misinformation is not unique to Juneteenth. Other holidays are coated with falsehoods. Example: The holiday now called "President's Day" is still officially titled "Washington's Birthday." Lincoln's birthday never was a official national holiday though many states acknowledged it. Some still do, but not the federal government.

Begin the Money Grab!

In recent decades, t-shirts were the major product sold honoring Juneteenth. Typically, sales occurred at vendor booths during Juneteenth celebrations and on the internet. Beginning June 2021, virtual stores flooded the net with all things Juneteenth, including yard signs, table cloths, photo backdrops, balloons, napkins, etc. Though the sudden commercialization of Juneteenth was off-putting, it was not new. During the early 1900's, Juneteenth specials included car sales, clothing, groceries, even apartment rental discounts. (See pgs 176-185.)

MYTH #15

"Freedmen traditionally performed Lift Every Voice and Sing at early emancipation ceremonies."

FACT:

It is standard practice among contemporary celebrations to include a performance of "Lift Every Voice and Sing."

However,

The lyrics now called "The Black National Anthem" were first recited publicly on Feb. 12, 1900, in Florida.[147]

By then, Juneteenth was 34 years old.

John Brown's Body

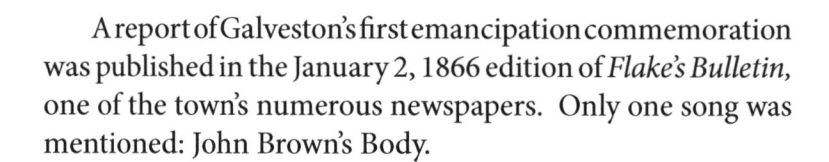

A report of Galveston's first emancipation commemoration was published in the January 2, 1866 edition of *Flake's Bulletin*, one of the town's numerous newspapers. Only one song was mentioned: John Brown's Body.

'John Brown's Body' was a military marching song that originated with soldiers of the 12th Regiment Massachusetts Volunteer Infantry in 1861. It quickly became the most popular anthem of Union soldiers.[148] Numerous variations existed, most with some of the original lyrics plus additional lyrics written by whomever was performing.

There is no way to know what version was performed in Galveston, but the more probable version were lyrics attributed to the First Arkansas Colored Regiment.

While visiting relatives near Washington, D. C., poet Julia Ward Howe heard Union soldiers singing this song. Like several others, Ms. Howe preserved the melody, but crafted her own lyrics. Her adaptation became the American classic titled: Battle Hymn of the Republic.[149]

(Lyrics of the First Arkansas Colored Regiment)

Oh, we're the bully soldiers of the "First of Arkansas,"
We are fighting for the Union, we are fighting for the law,
We can hit a Rebel further than a white man ever saw,
      As we go marching on.
        (Chorus)
        Glory, glory hallelujah.
        Glory, glory hallelujah.
        Glory, glory hallelujah.
      As we go marching on.

See, there above the center, where the flag is waving bright,
We are going out of slavery; we're bound for freedom's light;
We mean to show Jeff Davis how the Africans can fight,
      As we go marching on! (Chorus)

We have done with hoeing cotton, we have done with hoeing corn,
We are colored Yankee soldiers, now, as sure as you are born;
When the masters hear us yelling, they'll think it's Gabriel's horn,
      As we go marching on. (Chorus)

They will have to pay us wages, the wages of their sin,
They will have to bow their foreheads to their colored kith and kin,
They will have to give us house-room, or the roof shall tumble in!
      As we go marching on. (Chorus)

We heard the Proclamation, master hush it as he will,
The bird he sing it to us, hopping' on the cotton hill,
And the possum up the gum tree, he couldn't keep it still,
      As he went climbing on. (Chorus)

They said, "Now colored brethren, you shall be forever free,
From the first of January, Eighteen hundred sixty-three."
We heard it in the river going rushing to the sea,
      As it went sounding on. (Chorus)

Father Abraham has spoken and the message has been sent,
The prison doors he opened, and out the pris'ners went,
To join the sable army of "African descent,"
      As we go marching on. (Chorus)

Then fall in, colored brethren, you'd better do it soon,
Don't you hear the drum a-beating the Yankee Doodle tune?
We are with you now this morning, we'll be far away at noon,
      As we go marching on. (Chorus)

~~~

(William W. Patton's Lyrics)

    John Brown's body lies a-mouldering in the grave,
    John Brown's body lies a-mouldering in the grave,
    John Brown's body lies a-mouldering in the grave,
        But his soul goes marching on.
        (Chorus)
        Glory, glory, hallelujah,
        Glory, glory, hallelujah,
        Glory, glory, hallelujah,
        His soul goes marching on.

    He's gone to be a soldier in the Army of the Lord,
    He's gone to be a soldier in the Army of the Lord,
    He's gone to be a soldier in the Army of the Lord,
        His soul goes marching on.

    John Brown's knapsack is strapped upon his back,
    John Brown's knapsack is strapped upon his back,
    John Brown's knapsack is strapped upon his back,
        His soul goes marching on.

    John Brown died that the slaves might be free,
    John Brown died that the slaves might be free,
    John Brown died that the slaves might be free,
        His soul goes marching on.

    The stars above in Heaven now are looking kindly down,
    The stars above in Heaven now are looking kindly down,
    The stars above in Heaven now are looking kindly down,
        His soul goes marching on.

Juneteenth 101

Additional verses by other songsters

(Originator unknown)

His pet lambs will meet him on the way;
His pet lambs will meet him on the way;
His pet lambs will meet him on the way;
They go marching on!
    (Chorus)

They will hang Jeff Davis to a sour apple tree!
They will hang Jeff Davis to a sour apple tree!
They will hang Jeff Davis to a sour apple tree!
As they march along!
    (Chorus)

Now, three rousing cheers for the Union;
Now, three rousing cheers for the Union;
Now, three rousing cheers for the Union;
As we are marching on!
    (Chorus)

Version by William Weston Patton

Old John Brown's body lies moldering in the grave,
While weep the sons of bondage
    whom he ventured all to save;
But tho he lost his life while struggling for the slave,
His soul is marching on.
    (Chorus)

John Brown was a hero, undaunted, true and brave,
And Kansas knows his valor
    when he fought her rights to save;
Now, tho the grass grows green above his grave,
His soul is marching on.
    (Chorus)

He captured Harper's Ferry, with his nineteen men so few,
And frightened "Old Virginny"
    till she trembled thru and thru;
They hung him for a traitor, they themselves the traitor crew,
But his soul is marching on.
    (Chorus)

John Brown was John the Baptist of the Christ we are to see,
Christ who of the bondmen shall the Liberator be,
And soon thru out the Sunny South
    the slaves shall all be free,
For his soul is marching on.
    (Chorus)

The conflict that he heralded he looks from heaven to view,
On the army of the Union with its flag red, white and blue.
And heaven shall ring with anthems
    o'er the deed they mean to do,
For his soul is marching on.
    (Chorus)

Ye soldiers of Freedom, then strike, while strike ye may,
The death blow of oppression in a better time and way,
For the dawn of old John Brown has brightened into day,
And his soul is marching on.
    (Chorus)

Juneteenth 101

Juneteenth - Spokane, Washington

143

Juneteenth 101

The Rest of the Story

When the preliminary Emancipation Proclamation was issued (Sept. 22, 1862), Galveston and all parts of Texas were controlled by the Confederate Army. Nineteen days later (October 4, 1862), the Union Army launched the first Battle of Galveston—an effort to control Texas' most important port during the war years.

After successfully capturing Galveston Island and bay, the Union Army could not free the slaves because the preliminary proclamation was merely an ultimatum. Confederate states had until January 1, 1863 to meet the conditions necessary to avoid emancipation (i.e., quit fighting). Also, prior to the first battle, most if not all of Galveston's slaves had been removed from the island by owners fearing an attack.

On Watch Night (December 31, 1862), the Confederates launched an attack against Union soldiers occupying the island and Union naval ships in the bay. This time, the Confederates won. The defeated Union Army evacuated Galveston and Galveston Bay on January 1, 1863—the exact day slaves may have become freedmen.

For the remainder of the war, Galveston was Confederate territory. Hence, the slaves of Galveston remained in bondage.

On June 5, 1865, the Union military began occupation of Texas. Fourteen days later (June 19th), General Granger arrived to bring order to Texas in preparation for its readmission to the Union. Though the proclamation was a war weapon, it was law and remained intact after the war. Therefore, Granger's law enforcement mission included enforcing the proclamation.

Food for Thought:

1) If Galveston's slaves had been freed, where would they have gone? There were no secured paths through Texas to Union held territory. No reports have been found indicating ships were available to evacuate them.

2) Emancipation was openly discussed in Galveston. Prior to Jan. 1, 1865, slaves could have learned of impending freedom from numerous sources including Union troops.

144

Destruction of the Westfield

Drawing of the Union warship Westfield being destroyed January 1, 1863, after running aground in Galveston Bay. Rather than let the ship fall into Confederate hands, the crew abandoned ship and a charge was set, which prematurely exploded before everyone had reached safety, killing all the crew members, including Captain Renshaw, in two lifeboats just setting off from the Westfield.

Origin: Harper's pictorial history of the Civil War / Alfred H. Guernsey and Henry M. Alden. The Puritan Press Co., c1894, v. 2, p. 422. (Library of Congress Prints and Photographs Division)

Juneteenth - Memphis, Tennessee

146

Juneteenth minutiae & trifles

A Most Peculiar Partnership

The Texas legislative bill that created Emancipation Day contains this language:

> The nineteenth day of January shall be known as "Confederate Heroes Day" in honor of Jefferson Davis, Robert E. Lee and other Confederate heroes. The 19th of June is designated "Emancipation Day in Texas" in honor of the emancipation of the slaves in Texas on June 19, 1865.[136]

CONGRATUALATIONS!

June 19, 1898, Ms. Pearlie Telford was crowned Goddess of Liberty at the Brenham, Texas Juneteenth celebration.[150] *Woo-hoo!*

PARTY TIME

June 19, 1876, The Texas House of Representatives took a recess of fifteen minutes while the emancipation procession was passing through the capital grounds. After recess, the House adjourned, "so that members who desire to do so may be permitted to attend the anniversary celebration now progressing."[151]

ON JUNETEENTH, TEXAS FREED THE (CONVICTS)

June 19, 1865: Gen. Granger's staff sent a letter to the Texas state prison releasing all Negroes captured from the U.S. forces and everyone arrested resulting from a Texas' law requiring imprisonment of all free persons of color.[152]

June 19, 1925: In keeping with her reputation for generously granting pardons, Texas Gov. Miriam "Ma" Ferguson commemorated Juneteenth by pardoning forty-five imprisoned Blacks.[153] That was not an anomaly. During the early 1900s, Juneteenth paroles happened often.

Celebration Dates

Typically, Juneteenth celebrations are held during the weekend nearest June 19th. In 2017, a Juneteenth celebration was held somewhere in the nation on every weekend in June. In some locations, preliminary activities are held during the month of May. Preliminary activities include Juneteenth royalty pageants and fundraising events.

Watermelon, Barbecue and Red Lemonade

Nearly all remembrances of the earliest celebrations mention barbecue. Even now, consumption of barbecue and red drinks is a staple practice among veteran Juneteenth celebrants. Watermelon has become taboo. (See page 210)

In an essay on his Afroculinaria blog, culinary researcher Michael Twitty proposes potential rationale for the celebratory consumption of red food.

He offers, "The practice of eating red foods—red cake, barbecue, punch and fruit—may owe its existence to the enslaved Yoruba and Kongo brought to Texas in the 19th century. For both of these cultures, the color red is the embodiment of spiritual power and transformation."[154]

Emancipation Park

During the early post-emancipation years, freedmen in numerous Texas towns were not allowed to hold celebrations in public parks. Undaunted, celebrants raised funds to purchase their own parks. Some were named "Emancipation Park." The most noted of those properties—Houston's Emancipation Park—still exist and still hosts annual Juneteenth celebrations.[155] In 2017, Charlottesville, Virginia's Robert E. Lee Park, was renamed Emancipation Park.[156]

THE JUNETEENTH FLAG

As of this book's publication date, no "official" Juneteenth flag exist. A popular flag flown at celebrations nationwide is the property of the organization National Juneteenth Observance Foundation. Their copyrighted design was created in 1997 and later modified. Galveston's only ceremonial flag raising in June 1865 occurred on the 5th. The United States flag was raised.

A more historically appropriate flag to honor Juneteenth is the 25th Army Corps flag (pictured above.) An estimated 4,000+ members of the United States Colored Troops arrived in Galveston on June 19, 1865, under the command of Gen. G. Weitzel. They are depicted in Galveston's mammoth Juneteenth mural, "Absolute Equality" by artist Reginald C. Adams. The mural exist where General Order #3 was first issued.

The 25th Corps' swallowtail flag is blue, red and white. Some recreations of the flag use beige rather than white, replicating the now aged coloring of General Weitzel's personal silk flag.

The Underground Railroad - Texas

During the decades before the Civil War's end, an organization of bounty hunters guarded the Texas/Mexico border to prevent runaways from leaving the state.[157] Northbound routes of the famed Underground Railroad are well documented, preserved and celebrated. Less known are the southbound routes through Texas to Mexico. The National Park Service has not identified any still existing Texas facilities that were used as stations (rest stops) on the Underground Railroad.

> **ELI JACKSON CEMETERY**
>
> IN 1857, NATHANIEL JACKSON CAME FROM ALABAMA AND ESTABLISHED A RANCH IN THIS AREA. A FORMER SLAVE OWNER, JACKSON, WHO WAS WHITE, CAME WITH HIS WIFE MATILDA HICKS, WHO WAS BLACK, THEIR CHILDREN AND HIS FREED SLAVES. ON HIS 5,500-ACRE RANCH, JACKSON RAISED LIVESTOCK AND GREW VEGETABLES, COTTON AND SUGARCANE. HE ALSO ESTABLISHED A CHAPEL THAT SERVED FAMILY AND FRIENDS. HE WAS KNOWN FOR HIS GENEROSITY AND HOSPITALITY, AND MANY, INCLUDING RUNAWAY SLAVES, CAME TO THE RANCH IN NEED OF LODGING AND OTHER RESOURCES. UPON JACKSON'S DEATH IN 1865, HIS HEIRS DIVIDED THE PROPERTY. THE SHARE TO HIS SON ELI INCLUDED THIS SITE, THE FAMILY CEMETERY. ELI AND HIS WIFE, ELIZABETH KERR, AND THEIR CHILDREN CONTINUED THE FAMILY TRADITION OF HOSPITALITY. ELI SERVED AS A COUNTY OFFICIAL, AS DID HIS SON NATHANIEL "POLO" JACKSON. POLO'S DAUGHTER ADELA OPERATED THE RANCH AND CARED FOR THE CEMETERY UNTIL HER DEATH IN 1992.
>
> TODAY, THE ELI JACKSON CEMETERY REPRESENTS THE EARLY AREA RANCHING COMMUNITIES. THE BURIAL GROUND IS A TIE TO THE JACKSON FAMILY, AND TO THEIR FRIENDS AND NEIGHBORS FROM THE PAST WHO SHARE THIS AS A FINAL RESTING PLACE.
>
> HISTORIC TEXAS CEMETERY - 2005

Frederick Douglass Statue

After passage of the 13th Amendment, acclaimed abolitionist Frederick Douglass worked diligently, but unsuccessfully, to make January 1st a day to commemorate the proclamation.

In 2013, the 150th year of the Emancipation Proclamation, a statue of Douglass was placed in Emancipation Hall Capital Visitor Center (visitor center of the United States Capital). The statue was unveiled on Juneteenth.

R.I.P., HATER!

Rep. Claiborne Washington "Clay" Smothers of Dallas (pictured below) adamantly opposed recognizing Emancipation Day as a Texas State Holiday. In a letter to Texas Governor Bill Clements, he acknowledged the unpopularity of his opinion.

His letter started with barf-class schmoozing, "I have not relaxed my admiration, respect or confidence in you..." and "... how fortunate the state of Texas is having you at the head of its government..." Then he whined, "The only person who has been harmed by my outspoken objection is me.[158]

Such butt kissing happened because prior to the Juneteenth holiday bill's signing ceremony, Smothers called a press conference where he accused the bill's sponsor, Rep. Al Edwards, of "making an ass of himself." Smothers also described the governor-supported bill as "a meaningless piece of legislation for ceremonious grinning and bursting watermelons."[159]

Years earlier, this dude endorsed the presidential campaign of Alabama's segregationist ex-Governor George Wallace. In 1977, *Texas Monthly* magazine named him one of Texas' worse legislators. The magazine claims Clay said, "I am against Blacks, Mexicans, women, Indians, and queers talking to me about their rights" [160]

"UMPH, UMPH, UMPH!"

The Texas Almanac, is an annual directory of all things Texas. Publication began in 1857. The book's first acknowledgment of Juneteenth was published in 1961. Thereafter, each edition contained the following two sentences or a slight variation thereof:

"This date, June 19, has always been celebrated by Texas Negroes as Emancipation Day. It is popularly referred to by them as Juneteenth."

Likewise, in 1961, June 19 appeared in the publication's roster of state holidays along with this footnote:

"Not a legal holiday but generally observed by Negroes"[161]

After Emancipation Day became a state holiday, the footnote disappeared and the description changed.

TOO AFRAID TO CELEBRATE

Twice during Juneteenth's first 150 years, the celebration's popularity plummeted. The second slump and resurgence are both credited to the civil rights movement, albeit by different factions. Apparently, among some activists, rehashing slavery's end was not in step with Black empowerment. Such rejection was not a new idea. The placard below shows the aberrant measure folks in Richmond, Virginia took to avoid being associated with their state's annual commemoration of freedom. Fear of retribution from ex-confederates was the likely motivation.

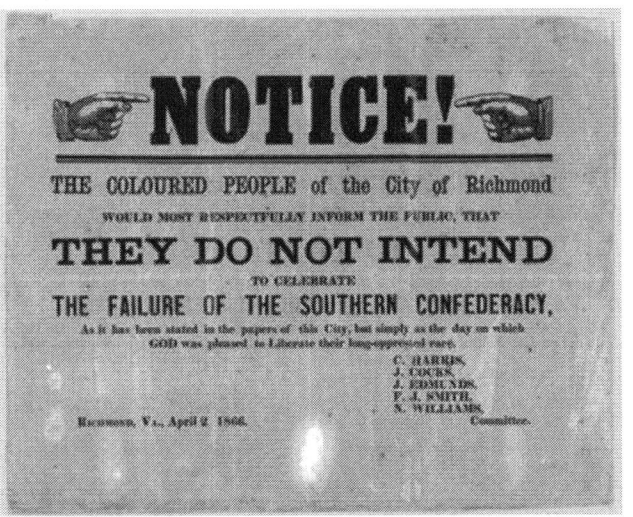

NOTICE!

THE COLOURED PEOPLE of the City of Richmond WOULD MOST RESPECTFULLY INFORM THE PUBLIC, THAT **THEY DO NOT INTEND** TO CELEBRATE THE FAILURE OF THE SOUTHERN CONFEDERACY, As it has been stated in the papers of this City, but simply as the day on which GOD was pleased to Liberate their long-oppressed race.

C. HARRIS,
J. COUSS,
J. EDMUNDS,
F. A. SMITH,
N. WILLIAMS,
Committee.

Richmond, Va., April 2, 1866.

1860 CENSUS

Recorded number of enslaved people in the United States:

Nationwide	3,950,528
Delaware	1,798
Kentucky	225,483
Texas	*182,566*

Some historians estimate 75% of Kentucky's slaves escaped or were freed[162] before the 13th Amendment was ratified. If that projection is correct, the 13th Amendment freed at least 56,000 Kentucky slaves in December 1865, making them the last freedmen.

Texas Freedom Timeline

1829	Mexico outlawed slavery in "Tejas."
1830	Mexico allowed slavery to continue in Texas.
1836	Texas became an independent nation and legalized slavery.
1845	After going broke, The Republic of Texas joined the U.S. to get out of debt.
1861	The State of Texas sided with confederates and succeeded from the union.
April 1865	Confederates began surrendering.
June 1865	The U.S. military assumed control of Texas and began enforcing the Emancipation Proclamation.

...but on June 20, 1865 ...

"NEW ORLEANS, June 20.—Gen. Herron has ordered runaway negroes back to the plantations of their former masters, for the common good of negroes and masters."

From The Tri-Weekly Tribune (Houston, Texas)

Transcription:
New Orleans, June 20. -- Gen Herron has ordered runaway negroes back to the plantations of their former masters, for the common good of negroes and masters.[163]

Texas' Final Slave Sale

On January 6, 1900, the last known payment for lawful purchase of an enslaved person in the United States occurred in the Dallas County Courthouse. An attorney representing heirs of Mr. D. H. Epperson (purchaser) paid $750 to an attorney representing Mr. W. J. McDonald, heir to the seller. The payment ended a series of court cases spanning more than three decades.

The original sale occurred in 1860, but the civil war created a financial hardship for the Epperson family, preventing complete payment. The enslaved person died shortly after emancipation in 1865, as did the seller and buyer. Payment remained incomplete. The feud over unresolved payment continued among heirs of the seller and buyer.[164]

The enslaved person was not identified in court records. The 1860 census recorded Mr. Epperson's slaves by description, not by name. Mr. W. J. McDonald is namesake of the acclaimed University of Texas McDonald Observatory.

How many? Not many!

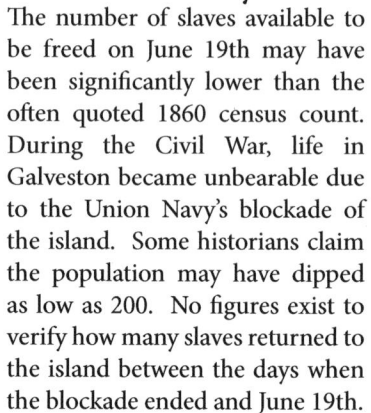

The number of slaves available to be freed on June 19th may have been significantly lower than the often quoted 1860 census count. During the Civil War, life in Galveston became unbearable due to the Union Navy's blockade of the island. Some historians claim the population may have dipped as low as 200. No figures exist to verify how many slaves returned to the island between the days when the blockade ended and June 19th.

A SLAVE PAID FOR.

After Forty Years a War Time Debt is Dischargd.

An incident occurred in Dallas yesterday that strongly smacks of the "old South" and of her practices in ante-bellum days. After forty years, a debt contracted for a Negro in Clarksville Tex., in 1860, was discharged and the entire matter ended forever. All the principals to the sale of the slave are gone. The black man went to his long resting place just as the first flowers of a new spring were blooming over the grave of the Southern Confederacy and while yet the

The Dallas Express
Vol. 7, No. 14, Jan. 13, 1900

A Note Given for a Negro in 1860, Paid in 1900.

Dallas Texas, January 6 —An echo of slavery times was heard in Dallas today. It was the settlement of a debt contracted in 1860 in which the sale of a negro slave was the basis of the transaction. In the days "before the war" the McDonald and Epperson families were among the leading planters of the Red river valley. The head of the Mc-

The Abilene Reporter,
Vol. 2, No. 12, Jan. 12, 1900

Juneteenth's Daddy

In 1979, The 66th Texas Legislature designated June 19th 'Emancipation Day in Texas'. The bill was authored by Texas State Rep. Al Edwards of Houston and signed by Governor William P. Clements. Whereas, this eventually ignited a wave of Juneteenth recognitions by numerous states, Edwards gained the title "The Father of Juneteenth."[165]

Juneteenth's Grandpa

In 1879, State Representative Robert J. Evans of Navasota, Texas filed legislation to secure official statewide recognition of Juneteenth.[166] That effort failed. This was the first recorded attempt in Texas to officially celebrate emancipation. Rep. Evans, a freedman, served two terms in political office—January 1879 through January 1883.

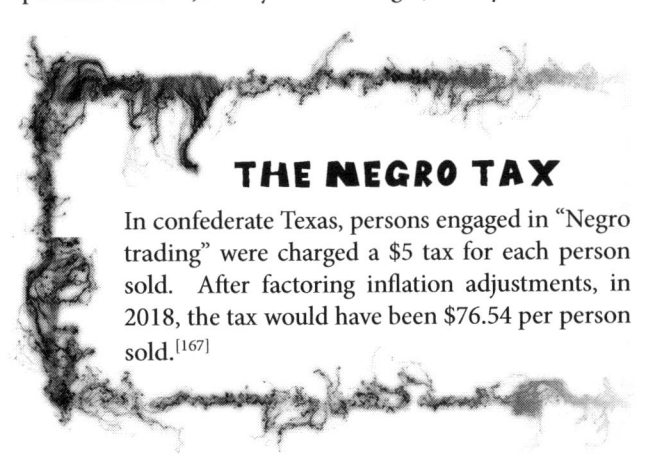

THE NEGRO TAX

In confederate Texas, persons engaged in "Negro trading" were charged a $5 tax for each person sold. After factoring inflation adjustments, in 2018, the tax would have been $76.54 per person sold.[167]

Up, Up and Whe-e-e!

June 19, 1925, was the first day Blacks in Texas were allowed to fly. Pilot Bessie Coleman treated a few brave Houstonians to free flights around the city. [168]

FREEDOM DAY STAMPS

Since 2009, the National Juneteenth Stamp Commission has campaigned for the issuance of a postage stamp commemorating Juneteenth. As of July 2021, that effort was unsuccessful. However, the United States Postal Service has issued two stamps commemorating the Emancipation Proclamation (pictured above). The designed below was submitted by the Commission for consideration.

Miss Juneteenth

Release date: Jan. 24, 2020. Received favorable reviews. Earned 34 award nominations. Won 9. Plot: A former beauty queen and single mom prepares her rebellious teenage daughter for the "Miss Juneteenth" pageant.

153

Commemorating Juneteenth

(Above) Memorial back.
(Right) Memorial front.

Texas African American History Memorial

The Juneteenth commemorative statue located in Galveston at Ashton Villa was funded by the Texas legislature and intended for display on the state capital grounds. After completion, lawmakers were concerned that it too closely favored Rep. Al Edwards, the lawmaker who spearheaded the project. Rather than discard the statue, it was relocated to Ashton Villa.

Location:	Grounds of the Texas State Capital Austin, Texas
Coordinated by:	Texas African American History Memorial Foundation
Unveiled:	Nov. 19, 2016
Sculptor:	Ed Dwight, Denver, Colorado
Size:	27' high, 32' wide

In 1991, Texas State Senators Rodney Ellis and Al Edwards ushered passage of a resolution that began a twenty year pursuit of a state Juneteenth memorial. The task ultimately required passage of a least six additional bills and resolutions.[169]

In 2012, the effort was aborted. In its place, a more comprehensive statue was commissioned. The new goal was to create a state memorial celebrating a much broader history of African Americans in Texas, rather than one event. The revised project cost $3 million. Half of that cost was raised by the Texas African American History Memorial Foundation. The remainder was provided by the Texas legislature.

The memorial, created by sculptor Ed Dwight, commemorates African* and African American involvement in Texas history from 1528 through the 20th century. In keeping with the original pursuit, and despite the changed design and purpose, the memorial remains dedicated to the emancipation of enslaved Africans in Texas.

* Prior to 1866, people of African descent could not have full American citizenship.

Juneteenth 101

TEXAS AFRICAN AMERICAN HISTORY MEMORIAL

155

Fibbery, Fables & Foolishness
A sample of incorrect Juneteenth news and statements

From: Politico

a) More than two years after President Abraham Lincoln signed the Emancipation Proclamation and two months after the South lost, Texas finally got the message that slavery was no more on June 19, 1865. That's the day Union Army Gen. Gordon Granger arrived in Galveston with the news.

b) The black power movement of the late 1960s also helped resurrect the day as something of a new Fourth of July, naming it Juneteenth and celebrating with parades, barbecues, fireworks, speeches and even readings of the Emancipation Proclamation.

c) On Jan. 1, 1980 (117 years after the Emancipation Proclamation), Juneteenth became an official state holiday in Texas, the first government-sponsored celebration of emancipation in the United States.[170]

Wrong

a) Texans knew about the proclamation, but chose to ignore it. b) The name Juneteenth was coined a century before the Black Power movement. c) The 1st federally-sponsored celebration of emancipation was National Freedom Day (1949).

From: Quotes123.com

JUNETEENTH

Juneteenth, also known as Emancipation Day, symbolizes the end of slavery and commemorates the reading of Republican President Abraham Lincoln's General Order #3 on June 19, 1865 in Texas, which announced the freeing of slaves.[171]

Wrong

President Abraham Lincoln did not issue General Order No. 3.

Juneteenth 101

Univ. of Texas at San Antonio

"the Emancipation Proclamation specifically excluded several border states, including Texas. It was almost two-and-a-half years after the Emancipation Proclamation that General Order No. 3 eradicated slavery within Texas."[172]

Nope

> Texas was one of the states *included* in the Proclamation.

From: Denison Daily Cresset

"Today is the anniversary of the Emancipation Proclamation"[173] (Published June 19, 1877)

False

> Is an explanation necessary?

From The Atlanta Journal-Constitution

"5 facts about Juneteenth, which marks the last day of slavery."[174]

Wrong

> This statement would be correct if it included two more words: "in Galveston."

From: TEXAS STATE LIBRARY AND ARCHIVES COMMISSION

"In the early days, Juneteenth celebrations included a prayer service, speakers with inspirational messages, reading of the Emancipation Proclamation, stories from former slaves, food, red soda water, games, rodeos and dances."[175]

Kinda False

> The accuracy of this statement depends on how "early" is defined. The earliest commemorations were political awareness events. Recreational activities were the second level of commemoration. Commercialism was third.

From Newsweek

"Every year on June 19, the anniversary of the end of slavery is recognized across the country."[176]

Wrong

> December 18 is the anniversary of the end of lawful slavery in the United States. Removing the words "the anniversary of" would correct this statement.

157

Juneteenth 101

From: U. S. Dept. of State & PBS LearningMedia

"On January 1, 1980, Juneteenth became an official state holiday in Texas, making it the first, and only, officially recognized emancipation celebration."[177]

Wrong

The first officially recognized emancipation celebration was National Freedom Day, Est. 1949.

University of Texas at Austin

"June 19, 1865: General Order No. 3, ended slavery in Texas two months after blacks were emancipated in the Union."[178]

Way Wrong

Assuming "in the Union" refers to northern states, emancipation began 84 years before the Civil War. Vermont was first. (See page 28 for the complete list of emancipation dates.)

All excerpts are examples of misinformation resulting from presumably well-intentioned efforts to inform. They are not intended to condemn the sources.

2019 JUNETEENTH in the Tré

Emancipation Park Historic District Celebrations!

Third Ward, Texas

Celebrating the abolition of slavery in the United States of America and the park where the world's Juneteenth Celebrations began!

Commemorating...

- **156 years** since the Emancipation Proclamation
- **154 years** since Texas slaves were granted freedom
- **147 years** of Emancipation Park area Freedom Celebrations &
- **46 years** of Third Ward Area Houston Freedom Parades

From Houston

"...the park where the world's Juneteenth Celebrations began."[179]

The first celebration of June 19th occurred in Galveston on June 19, 1866. Houston's enslaved Africans were freed on June 20, 1865. Their first celebration was held on June 20, 1866.

158

Juneteenth 101

From HuffPost

"The Emancipation Proclamation marked the end of the legalized institution of slavery in America, but in the small town of Galveston Island, Texas, black slaves had been carrying on their lives of bondage and subjugation, oblivious to the fact that they were actually free.

On June 19th, 1865, Major General Gordon Granger and his band of Union soldiers (who had been traveling throughout the South for two years spreading the word) arrived at Galveston Island to tell the last remaining slaves in the United States that they were finally free."[180]

Oo-wee Wrong!

A) The entire Union army was charged with "spreading the news", given that emancipation was a weapon of war.
B) Galveston was the second largest city in Texas, and its primary port. Some Civil War scholars suggest slaves there were aware of the Proclamation, but powerless to reap its benefits.
C) Galveston was not slavery's last stand.

For more great fibbery, search your favorite engine for "Juneteenth." Trust and believe, its there.

From Instagram (Originator unknown)

DID YOU KNOW?
Autochthons of America/FB
JUNETEENTH IS AN AMERICAN INDIAN HOLIDAY
On June 19, 1865–General Granger Announced the End of Slavery at Galveston, Texas (a date referred to as "Juneteenth").

• Galveston was not just a random or haphazard place picked to announce the Emancipation of Slaves in Texas. It was an Indian Empire where the enslaved Karankawa indians were reclassified as "Africans" and "Blacks".

Wrong

F.Y.I.: Galveston marked the eastern edge of the Karankawa tribe's territory. Per Anglo historians, the tribe was banished to Padre Island and Mexico, and eventually eradicated years before Juneteenth.[181] The tribe no longer exist to tell their own story.

Juneteenth 101

From Prof. Henry Louis Gates, Jr.

"Jan. 31: the date the 13th Amendment passed Congress in 1865, officially abolishing the institution of slavery."[182]

Partially False

On Jan 31, Congress proposed an amendment that would abolish slavery. They lacked authority to conclusively end slavery without approval from 2/3s of the states, which they did not have until Dec. 6, 1865.

From Texas Senator Ted Cruz[183]

> **Senator Ted Cruz**
> @SenTedCruz
>
> Today marks the 154th anniversary of #Juneteenth. On this day, U.S. Major General Gordon Granger delivered the long-overdue announcement to Texans in Galveston that the Emancipation Proclamation had been signed.
>
> 12:43 PM · Jun 19, 2019 · Twitter Web Client

Wrong

Whereas, Texans knew the Emancipation Proclamation was issued, it's a safe bet they also knew it was signed.

From Noire Histoir

JUNETEENTH
A Day of Remembrance

Juneteenth celebrates June 19, 1865, the date when Major General Gordon Granger and Union troops reached Galveston, TX with news of the Civil War's end. Taking place 2 1/2 years after the Emancipation Proclamation, it represented the end of slavery in the United States.

[184]

Wrong

Texans knew of the Civil War's end before the so-called "last battle" on May 12-13, 1865. They chose to continue fighting, fearing anticipated subjugation to Freedmen and the north, if they lost. (See page 61).

From TIME

Though President Abraham Lincoln delivered his Emancipation Proclamation on January 1, 1863, the news spread slowly to Texas. It wasn't until more than two years later that union soldiers reached the Lone Star state to make the announcement. [185]

Wrong

More accurately, "...more than two years later" Union soldiers enforced a proclamation that Texans had known about, but ignored since 1862.

From EBONY

"How did the government get the largest state in the Union to abide by the rules? They sent artillery and a general who wasn't one for losing battles. When Major General Gordon Granger arrived in Galveston, Texas, soldiers in tow, he made three announcements called General Orders."[186]

Yes! Yes! No!

Corrections: General Granger issued *four* General Orders on June 19th, not five. His first one was issued on the 17th. His troops arrived 1 to 3 days before Granger.

From FOX NEWS

"...Union Army Maj. Gen. Gordon Granger marched his soldiers to Galveston, Texas to spread the word that slavery had ended in America...

Gen. Granger's announcement that the immoral and brutal institution of slavery had at long last been abolished sparked widespread celebrations among newly freed black Americans, culminating with the establishment of a spontaneous holiday on June 19, 1865 that they called Juneteenth.

Although considered an official holiday in Texas since 1980, Juneteenth still goes largely unrecognized by our country as a whole. That's too bad."[187]

Wrong

a) Granger and company arrived aboard ships.
b) Only freedmen in or near Galveston celebrated.
c) The first "holiday" commemoration was in 1866. The name "Juneteenth" was coined years later.
d) At the time this report was published, 45 states and the District of Columbia had officially recognized Juneteenth.

Juneteenth 101

From CNN

On Jan. 1, 1863, President Abraham Lincoln issued the final Emancipation Proclamation, freeing those enslaved.

Wrong [188]

Lincoln's proclamation was not universal. Only *some* enslaved people were freed.

From The U. S. Army

In Shreveport, Louisiana on June 3, 1865, Captain WM. H. Clapp issued Special Order #20 by order of the Union Army's Major General Francis J. Herron. It stated: *"There are no longer any slaves in the United States. All persons heretofore held as such became free by virtue of the Executive proclamation of January 1, 1863, commonly known as the Emancipation Proclamation."* [189]

Wrong, even then.

From Nebraska Legislature

"For more than 130 years, Juneteenth National Freedom Day has been the oldest and only African-American holiday observance in the United States." [122]

No

1) As an "official observance," National Freedom Day predates Juneteenth National Freedom Day. 2) As a popular, but unofficial celebration of emancipation, Watch Night observances predate Juneteenth by three years. 3) There are numerous African American holiday observances in the United States. Many are designated by annual legislative and gubernatorial proclamations.

Juneteenth 101

From Donald J. Trump

THE WHITE HOUSE
Office of the Press Secretary

FOR IMMEDIATE RELEASE
June 19, 2017

Statement from President Donald J. Trump on Juneteenth

Melania and I send our warmest greetings to all those celebrating Juneteenth, a historic day recognizing the end of slavery.

Though President Lincoln issued the Emancipation Proclamation in 1863, news traveled slowly from Washington, D.C., to the southern states. More than two years later, on June 19, 1865, Major General Gordon Granger stood on the Ashton Villa balcony in Galveston, Texas, to deliver the belated message of the then-deceased President: all slaves were free.

Granger's astonishing words inspired soulful festivities and emotional rejoicing. Over the years, as freedmen and freedwomen left Texas, they took Juneteenth and its meaning with them. Today, we celebrate this historic moment in 1865, as we remember our Nation's fundamental premise that all men and women are created equal.

On Juneteenth 2017, we honor the countless contributions made by African Americans to our Nation and pledge to support America's promise as the land of the free.

###

[190]

Wrong, wrong, wrong, wrong!

This statement includes several of Juneteenth's most popular myths.
How many can you spot?

163

Juneteenth - Cedar Rapids, Iowa

164

Guess whose website offers this juicy fib:

"... Juneteenth Independence Day, June 19, 1865, the day on which slavery finally came to an end in the United States."

Answer on page 166

Answer:

The United States Congress!...'nem.

"Honey hush!"

"They ought'ta be ashame!"

"Seems like Congress would know when the 13th ratified."

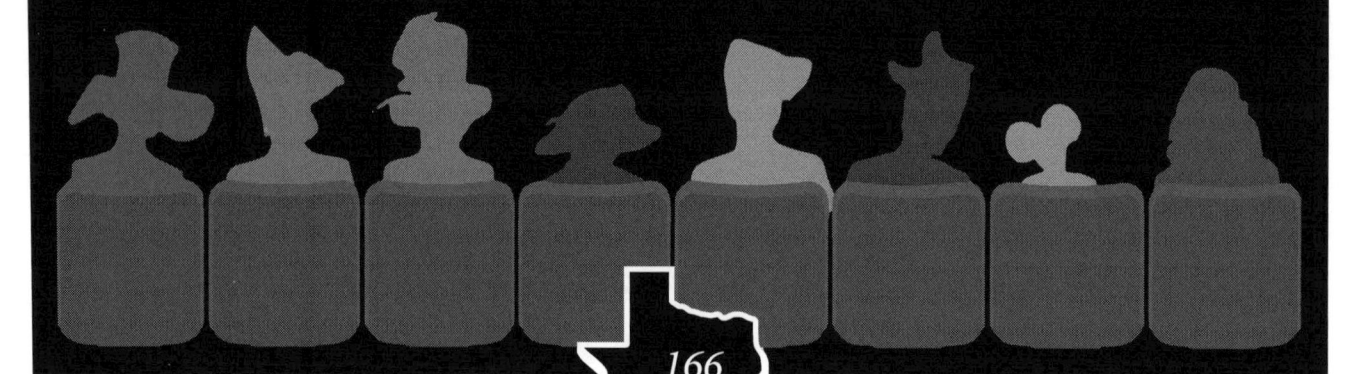

166

Senate Joint Resolution 11 (1997)[191]

Commemorating "Juneteenth Independence Day", June 19, 1865, the day on which slavery finally came to an end in the United States.

Whereas   news of the end of slavery came late to frontier areas of the country, especially in the American Southwest;

Whereas   the African-Americans who had been slaves in the Southwest thereafter celebrated June 19 as the anniversary of their emancipation;

Whereas   their descendants handed down that tradition from generation to generation as an inspiration and encouragement for future generations;

Whereas   Juneteenth celebrations have thus been held for 130 years to honor the memory of all those who endured slavery and especially those who moved from slavery to freedom; and

Whereas   their example of faith and strength of character remains a lesson for all Americans today, regardless of background or region or race: Now, therefore, be it

Resolved by the Senate and House of Representatives of the United States of America in Congress assembled, That the annual observance of June 19 as Juneteenth Independence Day is an important and enriching part of our country's history and heritage.

Sec. 2. That the celebration of Juneteenth provides an opportunity for all Americans to learn more about our common past and to better understand the experiences that have shaped our Nation.

Sec. 3. That a copy of this resolution be transmitted to the National Association of Juneteenth Lineage as an expression of appreciation for its role in promoting the observance of Juneteenth Independence Day.

Passed the Senate April 10, 1997.

105th CONGRESS
Sponsor: Trent Lott

As of *Juneteenth 101*'s original publication date, the United States Senate and House of Representatives had addressed 37 Juneteenth resolutions.[192]

Senate Res. 253 —
116th Congress (2019-2020)
A resolution designating June 19, 2019, as "Juneteenth Independence Day" in recognition of June 19, 1865, the date on which news of the end of slavery reached the slaves in the Southwestern States.

Sponsor: Sen. Cornyn, John [R-TX]
Introduced: 06/19/2019
Cosponsors: 57.

House Res. 448 —
116th Congress (2019-2020)
Expressing support for designation of June 19, 2019, as "Juneteenth Independence Day" in recognition of June 19, 1865, the date on which slavery legally came to an end in the United States.

Sponsor: Rep. Weber, Randy K., Sr. [R-TX-14]
Introduced: 06/19/2019
Cosponsors: 0.

House Res. 450 —
116th Congress (2019-2020)
Recognizing June 19, 2019, as this year's observance of the historical significance of Juneteenth Independence Day.

Sponsor: Rep. Jackson Lee, Sheila [D-TX-18]
Introduced: 06/19/2019
Cosponsors: 57.

Senate Res. 214 —
115th Congress (2017-2018)
A resolution designating June 19, 2017, as "Juneteenth Independence Day" in recognition of June 19, 1865, the date on which slavery legally came to an end in the United States.

Sponsor: Sen. Wicker, Roger F. [R-MS]
Introduced: 06/29/2017
Cosponsors: 44.

House Res. 948 —
115th Congress (2017-2018)
Recognizing June 19, 2018, as this year's observance of the historical significance of Juneteenth Independence Day.

Sponsor: Rep. Jackson Lee, Sheila [D-TX-18]
Introduced: 06/19/2018
Cosponsors: 53.

House Res. 386 —
115th Congress (2017-2018)
Recognizing June 19, 2017, as this year's observance of the historical significance of Juneteenth Independence Day.

Sponsor: Rep. Jackson Lee, Sheila [D-TX-18]
Introduced: 06/15/2017
Cosponsors: 57.

Senate Res. 547 —
115th Congress (2017-2018)
A resolution designating June 19, 2018, as "Juneteenth Independence Day" in recognition of June 19, 1865, the date on which slavery legally came to an end in the United States.

Sponsor: Sen. Wicker, Roger F. [R-MS]
Introduced: 06/14/2018
Cosponsors: 47
Latest Action: Senate - 06/14/2018 Submitted in the Senate, considered, and agreed to without amendment and with a preamble by Unanimous Consent.

House Res. 936 —
115th Congress (2017-2018)
Expressing support for designation of June 19, 2018, as "Juneteenth Independence Day" in recognition of June 19, 1865, the date on which slavery legally came to an end in the United States.

Sponsor: Rep. Weber, Randy K., Sr. [R-TX-14]
Introduced: 06/13/2018
Cosponsors: 1

House Res. 316 —
114th Congress (2015-2016)
Observing the historical significance of Juneteenth Independence Day.
Sponsor: Rep. Weber, Randy K., Sr. [R-TX-14]
Introduced: 06/15/2015
Cosponsors: 22.

Senate Res. 500 —
114th Congress (2015-2016)
A resolution designating June 19, 2016, as "Juneteenth Independence Day" in recognition of June 19, 1865, the date on which slavery legally came to an end in the United States.
Sponsor: Sen. Cornyn, John [R-TX]
Introduced: 06/16/2016
Cosponsors: 40.

Senate Res. 201 —
114th Congress (2015-2016)
A resolution designating June 19, 2015, as "Juneteenth Independence Day" in recognition of June 19, 1865, the date on which slavery legally came to an end in the United States.
Sponsor: Sen. Cornyn, John [R-TX]
Introduced: 06/15/2015
Cosponsors: 40.

House Res. 787 —
114th Congress (2015-2016)
Recognizing June 19, 2016, as this year's observance of the historical significance of Juneteenth Independence Day.
Sponsor: Rep. Jackson Lee, Sheila [D-TX-18]
Introduced: 06/15/2016
Cosponsors: 57.

House Res. 309 —
114th Congress (2015-2016)
Recognizing June 19, 2015, as this year's observance of the historical significance of Juneteenth Independence Day.
Sponsor: Rep. Jackson Lee, Sheila [D-TX-18]
Introduced: 06/11/2015
Cosponsors: 78.

House Res. 268 —
113th Congress (2013-2014)
Observing the historical significance of Juneteenth Independence Day.
Sponsor: Rep. Jackson Lee, Sheila [D-TX-18]
Introduced: 06/17/2013
Cosponsors: 40.

Senate Res. 474 —
113th Congress (2013-2014)
A resolution designating June 19, 2014, as "Juneteenth Independence Day" in recognition of June 19, 1865, the day on which slavery legally came to an end in the United States.
Sponsor: Sen. Levin, Carl [D-MI]
Introduced: 06/12/2014
Cosponsors: 44.

House Res. 632 —
113th Congress (2013-2014)
Recognizing June 19, 2014, as this year's observance of the historical significance of Juneteenth Independence Day.
Sponsor: Rep. Jackson Lee, Sheila [D-TX-18]
Introduced: 06/19/2014
Cosponsors: 45.

Senate Res. 175 —
113th Congress (2013-2014)
A resolution observing Juneteenth Independence Day, June 19, 1865, the day on which slavery finally came to an end in the United States.
Sponsor: Sen. Levin, Carl [D-MI]
Introduced: 06/19/2013
Cosponsors: 34.

Senate Res. 211 —
112th Congress (2011-2012)
A resolution observing the historical significance of Juneteenth Independence Day.
- *Sponsor:* Sen. Levin, Carl [D-MI]
- *Introduced:* 06/16/2011
- *Cosponsors:* 37.

Senate Res. 496 —
112th Congress (2011-2012)
A resolution observing the historical significance of Juneteenth Independence Day.
- *Sponsor:* Sen. Levin, Carl [D-MI]
- *Introduced:* 06/19/2012
- *Cosponsors:* 21.

House Res. 323 —
112th Congress (2011-2012)
Observing the historical significance of Juneteenth Independence Day.
- *Sponsor:* Rep. Davis, Danny K. [D-IL-7]
- *Introduced:* 06/22/2011
- *Cosponsors:* 0.

Senate Joint Res. 45 —
112th Congress (2011-2012)
A joint resolution amending title 36, United States Code, to designate June 19 as "Juneteenth Independence Day."
- *Sponsor:* Sen. Hutchison, Kay Bailey [R-TX]
- *Introduced:* 06/19/2012
- *Cosponsors:* 30.

Senate Res. 198 —
111th Congress (2009-2010)
A resolution observing the historical significance of Juneteenth Independence Day.
- *Sponsor:* Sen. Burris, Roland [D-IL]
- *Introduced:* 06/19/2009
- *Cosponsors:* 4.

Senate Res. 559 —
111th Congress (2009-2010)
A resolution observing the historical significance of Juneteenth Independence Day.
- *Sponsor:* Sen. Burris, Roland [D-IL]
- *Introduced:* 06/16/2010
- *Cosponsors:* 9.

House Res. 546 —
111th Congress (2009-2010)
Recognizing the historical significance of Juneteenth Independence Day, and expressing the sense of the House of Representatives that history should be regarded as a means for understanding the past and more effectively facing the challenges of the future.
Sponsor: Rep. Davis, Danny K. [D-IL-7]
Introduced: 06/15/2009
Cosponsors: 66.

Senate Res. 159 —
111th Congress (2009-2010)
A resolution recognizing the historical significance of Juneteenth Independence Day and expressing the sense of the Senate that history should be regarded as a means for understanding the past and solving the challenges of the future.
Sponsor: Sen. Burris, Roland [D-IL]
Introduced: 05/21/2009
Cosponsors: 4.

House Con. Res. 155 —
110th Congress (2007-2008)
Recognizing the historical significance of Juneteenth Independence Day, and expressing the sense of Congress that history should be regarded as a means for understanding the past and more effectively facing the challenges of the future.
Sponsor: Rep. Davis, Danny K. [D-IL-7]
Introduced: 05/23/2007
Cosponsors: 57.

Senate Res. 584 —
110th Congress (2007-2008)
A resolution recognizing the historical significance of Juneteenth Independence Day and expressing the sense of the Senate that history should be regarded as a means for understanding the past and solving the challenges of the future.
Sponsor: Sen. Durbin, Richard J. [D-IL]
Introduced: 06/05/2008
Cosponsors: 18.

Senate Res. 231 —
110th Congress (2007-2008)
A resolution recognizing the historical significance of Juneteenth Independence Day and expressing the sense of the Senate that history should be regarded as a means for understanding the past and solving the challenges of the future.
Sponsor: Sen. Durbin, Richard J. [D-IL]
Introduced: 06/12/2007
Cosponsors: 23.

House Res. 1237 —
110th Congress (2007-2008)
Recognizing the historical significance of Juneteenth Independence Day, and expressing the sense of the House of Representatives that history should be regarded as a means for understanding the past and more effectively facing the challenges of the future.
Sponsor: Rep. Davis, Danny K. [D-IL-7]
Introduced: 06/04/2008
Cosponsors: 70.

House Con. Res. 160 —
109th Congress (2005-2006)
Recognizing the historical significance of Juneteenth Independence Day, and expressing the sense of Congress that history should be regarded as a means for understanding the past and solving the challenges of the future.
Sponsor: Rep. Davis, Danny K. [D-IL-7]
Introduced: 05/19/2005
Cosponsors: 69.

Senate Res. 516 —
109th Congress (2005-2006)
A resolution recognizing the historical significance of Juneteenth Independence Day and expressing the sense of the Senate that history should be regarded as a means for understanding the past and solving the challenges of the future.

Sponsor: Sen. Obama, Barack [D-IL]
Introduced: 06/19/2006
Cosponsors: 4.

Senate Con. Res. 42 —
109th Congress (2005-2006)
A concurrent resolution recognizing the historical significance of the Juneteenth Independence Day, and expressing the sense of Congress that history should be regarded as a means for understanding the past and solving the challenges of the future.
Sponsor: Sen. Obama, Barack [D-IL]
Introduced: 06/15/2005
Cosponsors: 2.

House Con. Res. 163 —
107th Congress (2001-2002)
Recognizing the historical significance of Juneteenth Independence Day and expressing the sense of Congress that history be regarded as a means of understanding the past and solving the challenges of the future.
Sponsor: Rep. Watts, J. C., Jr. [R-OK-4]
Introduced: 06/14/2001
Cosponsors: 2.

Senate Con. Res. 51 —
107th Congress (2001-2002)
A concurrent resolution recognizing the historical significance of Juneteenth Independence Day and expressing the sense of Congress that history be regarded as a means of understanding the past and solving the challenges of the future.
Sponsor: Sen. Brownback, Sam [R-KS]
Introduced: 06/19/2001
Cosponsors: 1.

Senate Joint Res. 11 —
105th Congress (1997-1998)
A joint resolution commemorating "Juneteenth Independence Day," June 19, 1865, the day on which slavery finally came to an end in the United States.

Sponsor: Sen. Lott, Trent [R-MS]
Introduced: 01/23/1997
Cosponsors: 10.

House Joint Res. 56 —
105th Congress (1997-1998)
Celebrating the end of slavery in the United States.
Sponsor: Rep. Watts, J. C., Jr. [R-OK-4]
Introduced: 02/26/1997
Cosponsors: 25.

House Joint Res. 195 —
104th Congress (1995-1996)
Recognizing the end of slavery in the United States, and the true day of independence for African-Americans.
Sponsor: Rep. Collins, Barbara-Rose [D-MI-15]
Introduced: 09/17/1996
Cosponsors: 20.

~ ~ ~

This list was generated September 1, 2019. Bills and resolutions proposed after that date may be found on the websites of the United States Senate, the United States House of Representatives, and The Library of Congress.

Juneteenth - Maui, Hawaii

Who Devised All This Boo-Boo? pt. 1

Hear y'all! Hear y'all!

"Not us" cried the Never-wrongs.

Texas Newspapers in 1865—sole distributors of news and the primary recorders of local history—typically issued editorials written from the perspective of ex-confederates. There were no beat reporters assigned to chronicle emancipation from the freedman's viewpoint.

No evidence suggest such propaganda was coordinated. Rather, news reports were rife with missing details, creating opportunity for conjecture to germinate and fester.

Freedmen reports of emancipation recorded long after occurrence, verified popular assumptions and validated paramnesia, whether plausible or not. Public ignorance quickly adopted and nurtured the resulting legends, and still enables them. Examples:

- The "Juneteenth ended slavery" myth reveals limited understanding of how constitutional amendments are created.
- The "Buffalo Soldiers were present" myth exposes inadequate knowledge of Black military history.
- The Ashton Villa myth contends staunch ex-confederates offered hospitality and grace to victorious enemies formerly considered vitriolic evildoers.

Early southern newspapers portending civility freely paraded their disdain for freedmen's freedom. Yet, those rancorous writers did not create Juneteenth's distortions. In fact, the opposite is more accurate. Their bigotry-filled rhetoric exhibits the incessant hardships freedmen endured and preserves a glimpse of conditions under which Juneteenth grew into a worldwide celebration.

During the years shortly after 1865, few newspapers published news about Freedom Day celebrations—an omission insinuating freedmen affairs were irrelevant. With very few exceptions, celebrations were promoted verbally. The eventual merging of those celebrations reveals the statewide network Black Texans maintained without expendable resources or mass media.

Eventually, disregard yielded to annual one sentence celebration reports. Example: "Negroes throughout the state are making preparations for the celebration of emancipation on the 19th inst."[193]

As reports grew longer they became annual mockeries of the worse behaving celebrants, fueling racial prejudice and animosity. The Carbon News 1909 Juneteenth report was typical. They wrote: "One of the bucks also called "Mr. Coon" was arrested and fined for disturbing the peace by yelling while intoxicated."[194]

Newspapers in Houston and Galveston provided lengthier and less sarcastic overviews of celebrations there and elsewhere. Yet, in their

> This is the nineteenth of June, or the Juneteenth of nine or some other day, at any rate it is the Fourth of July for the colored people, and they are enjoying it at the Hancock park in proper style. The Leader is pleased to see them show their patriotism in remembering the day when their freedom was declared, and in teaching the younger ones the principles of government and economy. Very few of the older ones who were in slavery are now alive, and a few years more will see them all extinct. The younger generation, however, will keep up these celebrations and they will tend to keep the race in harmony and unity. No race of people under the sun has made such progress in forty years as the colored race, and they are entitled to full credit for their advancement.

(Above) Editorial from the Lampasas Daily Leader, June 19, 1905. Even now, more than a century later, non-Black-owned Texas-based media would be admonished for issuing the final sentence.

reports are signs of the celebration's changing purpose.

Prior to 1892, festivities focused on *when* freedom occurred. They were held only on June 19th. Modern celebrations commemorate *that* freedom occurred and are held on the weekend nearest June 19th. An 1892 report preserved public dismay with purpose-change in one protracted sentence. That same year, the first reports of commercialism appeared.

"There was not much of a crowd in from the country, and a good many of the town darkies declined to have anything to do with the celebration, for they say they can't see the use of celebrating the 17th and 18th, because Emancipation Day is the 19th, and in addition to this they charge the management is running the thing for the money there is in it and they don't think that the day of freedom should be utilized in that way."[195]

Eventually, profiteering won that battle. Businesses began crafting Juneteenth sales replete with paid advertisements posted primarily in newspapers boasting large African American readerships. That transformed Juneteenth into a commercial golden goose, albeit temporarily. When Juneteenth's popularity declined, special sales and advertisements also declined. Their remnants are vendor booths at present day celebrations.

In the twenty-first century, social media drives Juneteenth's popular myths. Seemingly, many advocates have found it easier to quote misinformed others than research nineteenth century sources. In turn, Juneteenth inaccuracies continue.

Juneteenth 101

In the early 1900's, Juneteenth was a cash cow for businesses catering to African Americans. Fashion outlets were first to benefit as Juneteenth was a dress-up affair. White women and men were the models. Other businesses followed, including grocery stores, dry goods stores, and entertainment venues.

QUALITY WITHOUT EXTRAVAGANCE

The Grand Leader Company
CONGRESS AT TRAVIS

"JUNETEENTH!"

THIS STORE is the proper place to purchase that Dress for the annual Emancipation celebration—because our stock is the most complete, our prices the most reasonable, our merchandise the best the market affords, combining to make this store your logical "Juneteenth" shopping Mecca.

See our Latest Creations in Dresses for Women and Misses, in all the wanted fabrics and colors; superb in quality, perfect in workmanship.

A. Harris & Company
Economy Basement
Every Buy A Bargain

Emancipation Day
SALE OF SUMMER'S
Pretty and Cool
DRESSES

Harris-Priced
$4.50
$5.95 TO $6.95 VALUE

Tissues   Linens   Voiles
Tub Silks   Crepe de Chines
Pongees

Every smart type for summer wear is included. Charming affairs for summer daytime activity. Tucked Frocks, Paneled Frocks, Pleated Frocks, Lace-Trimmed Frocks, Organdy-Trimmed Frocks — in fact, everything that's new in every shade.

Pretty Silk and New Wash Dresses
$8.75
All Regular and Some Extra Sizes

Pure Linens—Sheer Summery Voiles — Printed Crepes — Voiles and Linens Combined

Dainty Organdy Collars and Cuffs
Clever Vestees and Pockets
Drawnwork—Fancy Stitching
Dainty Laces—Ribbons—Embroidery
Straight-line Belted Styles
Lace Trimmed and Draped Effects
Graceful Pleated and Pieced Styles
Clever Tucked Skirts
Full Hip Models and Many, Many Others.

Harris'
Economy Basement

More Than 150 Charming Summer Frocks

Materials: Crepe de Chine, Flat Crepe, Foulards, Georgettes, Broades, Rashmaras, Sport Silks, Figured Crepes, Combinations

Colors: Brown, Black, Tan, Gray, Oyster, Nile, Jade, Copen, Yellow, White, Beige, Rust, Orange, Henna, Peach, Apricot.

Cool, refreshing frocks will delight both misses and women. Rich in simplicity they follow the ever straight, slim silhouette and depend for their loveliness on elaborate uses of lace artfully arranged to outline the frock or in some cases to form the vestee and trim collar, cuff and sleeves. Accordion pleated, gros-grain ribbons; colored embroidery; organdy or felt trims; glass button trims; ruffles scalloped effects; fobs and monograms make them very smart.

176

JUNETEENTH SPECIAL

Your feet take care of you, let "Weiss" take care of your feet

BETTER SHOES FOR LESS MONEY

WEISS SHOE COMPANY

GUNTER HOTEL BLDG.

328 N. ST. MARY'S ST.

(Page 176, left) The Houston Informer, June 16, 1923
(Page 164 right) Dallas Express, June 14, 1924

(Top) *San Antonio Express*, April 9, 1913.
(Botton) *Dallas Express*, May 26, 1923;

JUNETEENTH SPECIAL
FOR BEST VALUES HAVE YOUR SUIT MADE IN OUR OWN SHOP.
THE PERFECT FIT OF ALL TAILOR-MADE GARMENTS

For smart styles and careful hand-workmanship will appeal to your sense of economy.

Give us a trial. Very reasonable prices. Also cleaning and pressing called for and delivered.

PHONE Y-1648
RELIABLE TAILORS

308 South Ervay Street   Dallas, Texas

The Bankrupt Sales Store
FREE—MONEY FOR THE JUNETEENTH—FREE

118 W. HOUSTON—Opposite Strand Theater

Yes Sir! Yes Maam!

For Mother and Daughter
DRESSES
Dresses of Fine Organdie, Georgette, Lace and Satin, Sizes 14 to 52

$12.50 Dresses — **$4.95**
$10.00 Dresses — **$2.95**

Organdies are prettily ruffled and in floor lengths.

ADORABLE KNIT DRESSES
$1.95 $2.95 $3.95

HATS
Of finest Hair Braid and of Rough Straws.

$7.50 Values — **$2.95**
$3.00 Hats — **$1.85**

Cute Knit Hats
49c   79c

Slips and Panties
They Are Plenty Cut!
49c   98c

For Father and Son
Newest Hollywood Suits
Fifth Avenue Tailored

$33.00 Suits — **$18.95**
$15.00 Suits — **$8.95**

Blues, Tans, Greys and Navies
$12.50 Summer Suits — **$7.95**

Fine Tailored
SHOES
Ladies' Lovely Shoes. Plenty of Whites, Blacks, Blondes, etc. High and Low Heels. Sizes 3 to 10

$6.85 Values — **$3.85**
$5.00 Values — **$2.95**
$3.00 Values — **$1.85**

BATHING SUITS
You Will Adore Them!
$1.00 TO $2.95

JUNE BRIDES!
DRESSES—WREATHS—VEILS! Adorable Styles to delight you! Priced to please you!
Buy Your JUNETEENTH Outfit Here And Save Enough to Spend on the Celebration.

MAX POLUNSKY
BANKRUPT SALE STORE

Max Polunsky   118 W. Houston Street   Opposite Strand Theater

The Houston Informer, June 16, 1923

GIGOLO'S JuneTeenth Special

Tutti Fruitti Ice Cream

Place your order with the Gigolo for socials, parties and picnics

We make deliveries

Watch this space each Friday for Week-end Specials

The GIGOLO
907 So. Hackberry
L-20363

San Antonio Register, June 16, 1933

GOING OUT OF TOWN?
JUNETEENTH

To make your trip pleasant and safe for the family, sweetheart or yourself, start out with good rubber. Blowouts are dangerous and annoying.

Goodrich's Budget Plan Extends Easiest Credit in City. Come in Today and Buy. No Red Tape, No Delays, No Embarrassment, No Investigation! Small Payment Down--Balance to Suit You--As You Ride!

The new Goodrich *Safety* Silvertown

GOODRICH SILVERTOWN, Inc.
PAUL SAUER, Mgr.
LEXINGTON AT EUCLID   GARFIELD 7278

San Antonio Register, June 15, 1934

Eventually, businesses with minimal relation to Juneteenth celebrations began promoting Juneteenth specials, including auto dealers, dry good stores, and rental properties.

Juneteenth 101

JUNETEENTH SPECIALS

Don't throw your old shoes away. Bring them to Central Repair Company. We serve you with a "Smile." Old shoes made to look and wear like new.

CHILDREN'S FINE QUALITY HALF SOLES

Sewed on by Our New Lockstitch Method

50c The Pair

Half Soles WOMEN'S SHOES **65c**

Half Soles MEN'S SHOES **75c**

LADIES' LEATHER HEEL TAPS
Super X Leather, Pair 25c
2 Pair for 35c

MEN'S BEST QUALITY RUBBER HEELS
The Pair, Attached 35c

SHOES DYED 75c
ANY NEW SPRING COLOR

Shoes dyed with our new process penetrating dyes are applied by new factory methods. Will not fade, crack or rub off... makes your shoes look and wear like new. WHITE SHOES REDYED WHITE to look like new!

WE CALL FOR AND DELIVER—GARFIELD 5218

CENTRAL SHOE REPAIR CO.
THE BIG PLANT   323 ALAMO PLAZA

Yes! Here's Specials for Father and show it with FLOWERS very special Bargains Now

'81 PONTIAC TRANS AM
Beauty apple red, white letter tires rally wheels, stereo cassette, low miles, exceptional buy.......... **$7988**

'78 CHEVY MONTE CARLO
Beautiful copper tone has fine stereo cassette system, don't miss this.......... **$2988**

JUNETEENTH SPECIAL

'80 GRAND LEMANS
Bucket seats, console, stereo and tape. This is a little doll.......... **$4488**

'80 12 PASSENGER E250 CLUB WAGON
Dual a/c, roomy, runs like a top, take the family on a picnic July 4th, P/S, P/B, auto and more.......... **$6988** FULL PRICE

'75 FORD TORINO STA. WAG.
Plenty of room in this automatic, air conditioned good transportation wgn—You'll like this at only.......... **$1688⁰⁰**

And this is just the tip of the ice berg — Large inventory, two locations for your greater convience -- Don't forget to check on this available 12 mo/20,000 MIC Warranty Available here.

FLOWERS
PONTIAC-CADILLAC-HONDA
(FIRST IN SALES - FIRST IN SERVICE)
5915 BROADWAY — GALVESTON
744-5711 or Sat. 744-5714

---

page 180
(Left) *San Antonio Register,* June 15, 1934
(Right) *Galveston Daily News,* June 18, 1983

page 181
The Tribune (Hallettsville, TX) June *12, 1936*

180

Colored Folks' Juneteenth Celebration

The colored folks of Hallettsville are going to put on a real 19th Celebration. Brass band, public speaking and a big parade, rodeo and everything that goes to make this the outstanding of all other Juneteenth Celebrations in Hallettsville. Let nothing keep you away from Hallettsville on that day. And the best of all·

THE MEYERHOFF DRY GOODS CO.'s SPECIAL JUNETEENTH SALE.
STARTS TO-DAY, FRIDAY, JUNE 12th AND LASTS THRU FRIDAY, JUNE 19th.

Ladies' Rayon step-ins	10c
Ladies' rayon slips	35c
15c, 36-in. fancy print Batiste, yd.	12½c
36-in. fancy prints, yard	10c
59c, 40-in. rough and fancy novelty crepe, yard	49c
69-in. fancy and printed Acetate crepe, yard	59c
75c, 40-in. printed flat crepe, yard	65c
25c Ladies' rayon hose, all new spring and summer shades, pair	19c
45c Ladies' never mend pure silk hose, new shades, pair	39c
Ladies' Wash Frocks	50c
95c Ladies' Wash Frocks	79c
$1.69 Ladies' Wash Frocks	$1.39
$1.95 Ladies' Wash Frocks	$1.69
$3.95 & $3.45 ladies' rough and printed crepe dresses	$2.95
$6.45 ladies' printed crepe and triple sheer dresses	$4.95
$7.45 Ladies' printed crepe and triple sheer dresses	$5.95
$1.00 Ladies' hats, choice	75c
$1.50 Ladies' hats, choice	95c
$1.95 Ladies' hats, choice	$1.49
75c Ladies' sandals, white and fancy colored stripes, pair	59c
$1.25 Ladies' sandals, white and fancy, pair	89c
$1.95 Ladies' white and all styles sandals, Pair	$1.75
Men's fancy dress sox, pair	10c
Men's fancy dress shirts	39c
$1.25 Men's guaranteed fast color dress shirts	95c
REDUCTIONS ON ALL MEN'S DRESS SHIRTS FOR THE 19th SALE	
Men's dress Oxfords, solid white & black, Pair	$1.95
95c Men's dress pants, pair	85c
$1.25 Men's dress pants, pair	95c
$1.45 Men's dress pants, Pair	$1.25
$1.75 Men's dress pants, pair	$1.45
$2.45 Men's dress pants, pair	$1.95

DON'T FAIL TO GET IN ON MEYERHOFF'S JUNETEENTH SALE

MEYERHOFF DRY GOODS Co. (Inc.)
HALLETTSVILLE, TEXAS
"THE BIG STORE ON THE CORNER"

Juneteenth 101

JUNE-TEENTH

Just Ain't a Holiday without a good car to go some place!

LOOK AT THESE—

1946 Chevrolet Fleetmaster. Xtra Clean	$1295
1941 Chevrolet Master Deluxe 4-Dr. Sedan	$825
1941 Chevrolet Master Deluxe 2-Dr. Sedan	$795
1940 Ford Coupe. Radio, heater, fog lights, spot light	$545
1941 Ford Super Deluxe Tudor. A Bargain	$495
1938 Oldsmobile 6 Coupe —Lots of transportation	$225

J. M. BOLLS
Used Car Exchange
Phone 612   113 W. Tyler

EVERYTIME WE MAKE A DEAL WE MAKE A FRIEND

SPRING KIDS
For Sale
Nice for Juneteenth Bar-b-que
B. C. SLOVER
Tyler, Rt. 8   Ph. Bullard 2111

JUNETEENTH SPECIAL
100 LBS. BEEF
Cut & Wrapped
$99
CASH & CARRY

Left - Longview News-Journal, June 9, 1949

Center - Baytown Sun, June 19, 1983

Top Right - Tyler Morning Telegraph, June 19, 1914 (Note: "Kids" are goats)

Bottom Right - El Paso Times, June 19, 1950

87th Juneteenth
TEXAS EMANCIPATION DAY
Program By
Col. Louis A. Carter
Post No. 58A
American Legion Dept. of Texas

DOUBLE HEADER BASEBALL GAME
DUDLEY FIELD—2 P.M.
June 19, 1950

1ST GAME—
Col. Carter Post Girls' Teams
(Softball 7 Innings)

Emancipation Day Address
Mayor Dan Duke

2ND GAME—(Hardball)
El Paso Aces vs. Vado Giants
First Ball Pitched By
Judge Victor Gilbert

Prizes From Local Merchants Awarded Every Inning to Holders of Lucky Tickets

ADULTS 75c   CHILDREN 25c
SOLDIERS In Uniform 50c

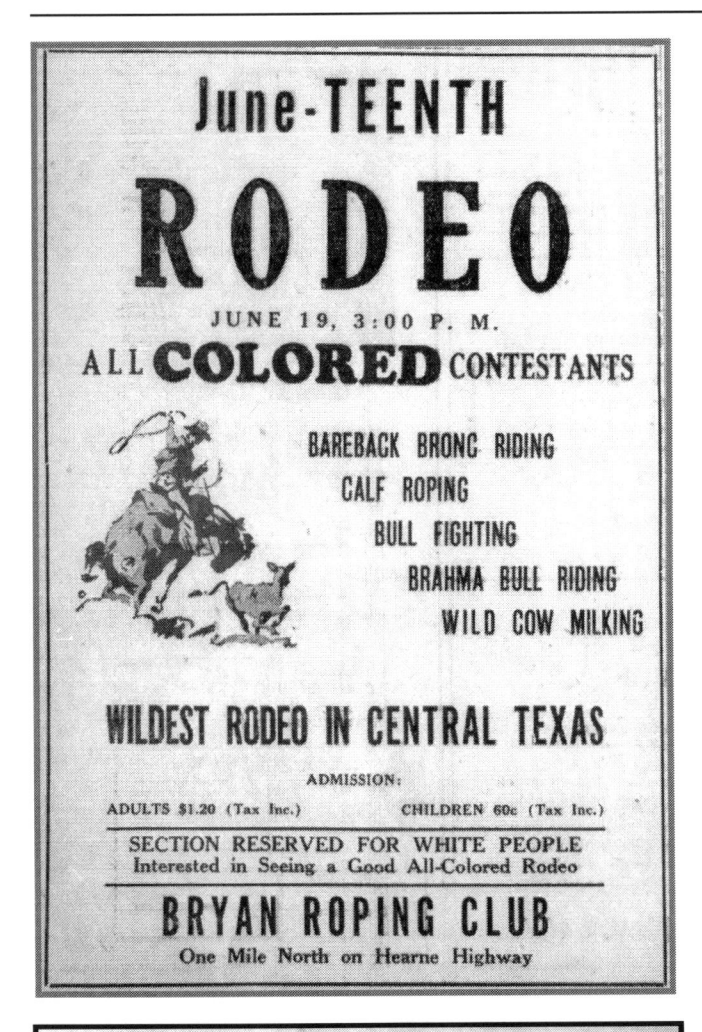

June-TEENTH RODEO

JUNE 19, 3:00 P. M.

ALL COLORED CONTESTANTS

- BAREBACK BRONC RIDING
- CALF ROPING
- BULL FIGHTING
- BRAHMA BULL RIDING
- WILD COW MILKING

WILDEST RODEO IN CENTRAL TEXAS

ADMISSION:
ADULTS $1.20 (Tax Inc.) CHILDREN 60c (Tax Inc.)

SECTION RESERVED FOR WHITE PEOPLE
Interested in Seeing a Good All-Colored Rodeo

BRYAN ROPING CLUB
One Mile North on Hearne Highway

NOTICE

As I wish to close Tuesday to give my driver the Juneteenth—will ask my customers to give me their orders Monday. Phone 15 and 18.

G. H. CONWAY
Corner Austin and Lafayette Sts.
6-17-19c

FLASH!
ROUND-BY-ROUND REPORTS OF THE
LOUIS-CONN FIGHT
Will Be Given on Loudspeaker at the
Juneteenth Rodeo at Bryan Roping Club

"Juneteenth"
TABLE D'HOTE DINNER

Rice Roof
Monday, June 19th

FINLEY'S ORCHESTRA
SINGING
DANCING

One Dollar and Fifty Cents Per Plate

Make Your Table Reservation Early

Phone Preston 8300

Homer D. Matthews, Manager

Top L - The Eagle (Bryan, Texas) June 14, 1946
Bottom L - he Eagle (Bryan, Texas) June 17, 1946
Top R - The Marshall Messenger June 17, 1923
Bottom R - The Houston Post, June 19, 1916

PLUS SIZES FOR WOMEN

The Only Plus Size Fashion Store on the Island

Sunday Only Juneteenth Sale

Come See the New Location & Save

We've Moved
1212 - 38th Street
Galveston

1212-38th Street   409-762-7777

Galveston Daily News, June 6, 1999

Hair Unlimited Juneteenth Special

Hair Unlimited is having a Juneteenth Special with 20 per cent off of curls, hair cuts relaxers, lustra curl, braids and relaxers. Hair Unlimited also specialize in braid extensions and cornrolls. Stop by Hair Unlimited, 1035 S. W. W. White Road or call 333-6344. Stop by and see Estella, Irene, Phillip, Dennis or Evelyn.

San Antonio Register, 1980

FOR RENT

Several houses abailable. Juneteenth special. Little deposit. call 532-7532 or 653-6032, weekly rates.

San Antonio Register, June 19, 1986

Much to-do occurred when Juneteenth was featured in an episode of Atlanta—a nationally televised comedy. Contrary to some reports, this was not Juneteenth's TV debut. During the 1970's and 80's, Texas television stations aired "Juneteenth Specials" created by local affiliates of the national networks. The schedule on page 185 is from the Baytown Sun (June 21, 1985), is an example.

Juneteenth 101

HARLEM THEATER

SHOWING SUNDAY and MONDAY

"Drums OF Fu Manchu"

"JUNETEENTH" SPECIAL!

(Above) *Marshall Messenger,* June 17, 1945
(Right) *The Caldwell News,* June 12, 1941
(Below) *Baytown Sun,* June 21, 1985

SATURDAY MORNING

6:00
- ③ PINWHEEL
- ⑪ AGRICULTURE U.S.A.
- ⑬ VIVA HOUSTON
- ⑰ (D) JIMMY SWAGGART
- ⑲ (F) CARTOONS
- ⑳ NEWS
- ㉓ (J) NEW JERSEY REPORT
- ㉕ (L) NEWS / WEATHER / SPORTS
- ㉗ CARRASCOLENDAS
- ㊱ OUTLOOK

6:05
- ⑥ BASEBALL BUNCH

6:15
- ⑲ (F) BUYERS FORUM

6:30
- ㊲ KIDD VIDEO
- ⑪ GUMBY AND PROFESSOR BILL
- ⑬ JUNETEENTH SPECIAL

Hey! Where Will You Be on the JUNETEENTH?

COME TO FAIR PARK, CALDWELL—FOR THREE FULL DAYS OF FUN AND FROLIC

Thursday, Friday, Saturday, June 19, 20 and 21. Meet all your old friends—make new friends. Street Parade, Carnival Attractions, Rodeo, Races for Fat Folks and Lean Folks, and Free Lunch for the Oldest, Youngest, Fattest and Leanest One in Attendance.

SIX BIG BASEBALL GAMES

THURSDAY, 2:00 P.M. — — TUNIS vs. MUMFORD
THURSDAY, 4:00 P.M. CALDWELL vs. SMITHVILLE
FRIDAY, 2:00 P.M.—SAND HILL vs. SMITH GRADED
FRIDAY, 4:00 P.M.—CALDWELL vs. HEMPSTEAD
SATURDAY, 2:00 P.M.—DIME BOX vs. ZION
SATURDAY, 4:00 P.M.—CALDWELL vs. BARTLETT

Admission ... 15c Single Game—25c Both Games

DANCE EVERY NIGHT

Music by Freeman High School Orchestra—Adm.: 25c !

Plenty of Eats and Refreshments of All Kinds !

DON'T MISS The RODEO Featuring "BUCK" TAYLOR

All Church May Have Stands ... Apply to A. F. Douglass, Secretary. THIS BIG CELEBRATION PERSONALLY SPONSORED BY BOBBIE GRIFFIN, COON BULLARD, T. B. GUNN, WESLEY TURNER, R. A. YOUNG, JOE SHARPE, JAMES I. LEE, H. L. MIDDLETON, IKE BULLARD, E. R. KERR, EMMETT THOMAS, ROBERT CONNOR, CHARLIE DOUGLASS, JNO. J. BOULDON and A. F. DOUGLASS, Secy.

185

More Boo-Boo Talk, pt. 2

No entity singlehandedly initiated the myths surrounding Juneteenth's birth, but every inaccuracy is a product of someone's ignorance. From each first speaking, many Juneteenth myths have spread statewide, nationwide, even worldwide.

As for potential harm, Maryland and Missouri are excellent examples. After being exempted from the Emancipation Proclamation, those great states voluntarily terminated slavery without military force. Yet, around 150 years later, rather than honoring their historic and noteworthy deed, the Maryland and Missouri legislatures chose to laud the day emancipation was militarily enforced in Texas. Likewise, Kentucky honors Texas' emancipation date, disregarding the continuance of slavery beyond that date in their own state. Proponents of these decisions claim national solidarity was the goal of such befuddlement. If that is correct, a more logical and appropriate commemoration date would have been when slavery was nationally outlawed and the last enslaved people were freed, which was not June 19, 1865.

Intelligence is benignant; ignorance is malignant.

Texas public schools are arguably the most pervasive distributors of erroneous Juneteenth lore. They do so openly and consistently with no apparent resistance. Here's how.

Texas History is required learning for all seventh graders in Texas public schools. During the 2016-17 academic year alone, the population of Texas seventh graders was a smidgen less than 400,000. For comparison, in 2016, Wyoming's entire population was 584,000.

That year, the Texas Education Agency (TEA) adopted three Texas History textbooks. All three publications contain inaccurate or misleading information about Juneteenth. They will not be replaced until 2023. By then, based on TEA's enrollment figures, approximately 2.8 million students will have skimmed the erroneous books. That's a heap of misinformed Texans.

It is unlikely that textbooks preceding the current editions were more accurate. Assuming Juneteenth first appeared in school books when it became a state holiday (1980), it's a safe bet that all seventh grade Texans since 1980 may have been infected with bogus Juneteenth information.

Understanding juneteenth properly is not a matter of singing the correct songs. The justifications for understanding emancipation and American independence are identical. To the degree that one is important, so is the other. Whereas, awareness is the adviser and fortification of freedom, lack of awareness breeds oafish, uninformed and untenable decisions. Of this law, the only exceptions are coincidental.

See pg. 174 for Boo-Boo. pt. 1

Juneteenth 101

[196]

[197]

[198]

"The state's 200,000 enslaved African Americans who gained freedom at war's end, were the few Texans who benefited significantly from the war." (pp 313)

"The African American community celebrates Juneteenth each year. This celebration is held on June 19 to commemorate the time in 1865 when slaves in Texas learned that they were free." (pp 568)

This textbook contains numerous facts about African Texans. These are the only two statements expressly addressing emancipation in Texas.

> Neither of these three publications include the words emancipation, manumission, or chattel in the glossary.

"On June 19, a large Union force commanded by General Gordon Granger arrived in Galveston to take control of the state." (pp 434) **Correction: The "force" arrived June 16th through 18th.**

"News of the proclamation spread slowly, but in most cases, Texas slave holders voluntarily complied." (pp 434) **Correction: News of the proclamation began spreading across Texas in 1862. Emancipations began in 1865 after the Union army arrived to force compliance.**

"It marks Juneteenth, June 19, 1865, which began as a celebration of the date the news of the end of slavery arrived in Galveston, Texas." (pp 715) **Correction: In Galveston, news of universal emancipation began circulating in 1862.**

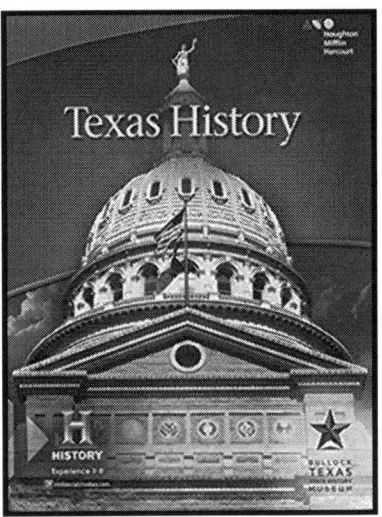

187

"During the summer and fall of 1865, Texas roads were crowded with former slaves loaded down with their possessions." (pp 397) **Correction: The Texas Constitution outlawed ownership of property by enslaved people. Freedmen had nothing to carry. On June 22, 1865, Gordon Granger outlawed travel on public thoroughfares by freedmen.**

"Even after the Civil War, freed people who fell into debt could be auctioned as servants to pay off the debt. (pp 399) **This statement is presented without clarification. The Black Codes adopted in 1866 do not include this information.**

"Juneteenth - June 19, day celebrated as the day on which Union General Gordon Granger landed at Galveston and issued the Emancipation Proclamation freeing Texas slaves." (pp R31) **Correction: Maj. Gen. Granger decreed General Order No. 3 which referenced the Emancipation Proclamation.**

Juneteenth 101

HELP WANTED
Bunk Busters
No experience needed.

Duties:
  Help abolish inaccurate Juneteenth reports.

Qualifications:
  Possession of accurate information, good listening skills, patience

Perks:
  Work from home.
  Flexible hours
  Overtime available
  No supervision, no meetings,
  No performance quotas.

Pay:
  Satisfaction and personal gratification

Job begins immediately

This is not an equal employment opportunity. Applicants addicted to legend and delusions need not apply.

Orientation

5 Tips for Successful Bunk Busting

Welcome!
Thanks for joining the Juneteenth Bunk Busters Guild. There are no required strategies, but the following tips may be helpful.

1. Do not assume myths will self-correct.
Address fiction immediately. Fear no fibber. Respond appropriately to fact-free friends and family, erroneous news reports, and misinformed officials.

2. Fact check frequently.
Discussions of Juneteenth's origin not verifiable by 19th century sources are not creditable.

3. Avoid negotiations.
Discussions with die-hard myth tellers can morph into bartering transactions. Avoid that. Truth has worth and is non-negotiable. Fallacy is valueless trash.

4. Question everything / Assume nothing
History becomes clearer as information surfaces. Before the Internet existed, access to mid-nineteenth century publications was limited. The net expanded access significantly, but also provided a platform for opinions posing as fact.

5. Know truth; value the importance of truth; and recognize truth vandals.
Without knowing how or why Juneteenth occurred, it is possible to celebrate wrong ideas. Educate liberally, but know ignorance has a huge, unshakable fan club.

"Only an educated and informed people will be a free people."
President John F. Kennedy

Suggested Responses

What is Juneteenth?
Nationally, Juneteenth commemorates the general emancipation of Africans enslaved in America regardless of when they were actually freed. The holiday's date (June 19th) acknowledges the first day the Emancipation Proclamation was militarily enforced in Texas.

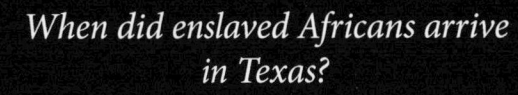

When did enslaved Africans arrive in Texas?
The first recorded enslaved African in Texas was documented in 1528. His name was Mustafa Azemmouri, (slave name: *Estevanico*). Virginia's "twenty and odd" who arrived in 1619, are considered the first enslaved Africans in America's thirteen original colonies.

Note: The name "Mustafa Azemmouri" was given to this person by the people of Morocco, the place where he was sold. His actual birthplace is believed to be much farther south on the African continent

Newspapers don't prove that slaves knew about emancipation before Juneteenth.
What the slaves did or did not know is insignificant. Emancipating themselves made them runaways. Emancipation made them freedmen.

Isn't Juneteenth a celebration of being tricked and deceived?
Juneteenth is a celebration of what the freedmen lauded—their freedom.

When did slavery end in Texas?
An 1868 decision by the Texas Supreme Court recognized the surrender of the confederate states as the point where slavery legally ended in Texas. June 19, 1865 was the date of formal declaration.

How should the enslaved be identified?
Enslaved people referenced in this book are identified as "enslaved Africans." The term "African American" is not used because they did not have American citizenship. The term "slave" is used in regard to their social status while enslaved. After emancipation, that status changed to "freedmen."

Why did slave owners ignore the Emancipation Proclamation?
There are many reasons. The strongest are:
(1) Confederates believed they would win the war. Had they won, the Proclamation would be obsolete.
(2) The proclamation was a mandate from their enemy.

Juneteenth celebrations are embarrassing.
Walk away quickly.

Fa-la-la...

Other things to know

a.k.a.

It ain't over 'til ...

190

EXTRA! JUNETEENTH NEWS EXTRA!

Untitled

The colored people are to have an excursion on Tuesday, June 19th 1877, in commemoration of the order of Gen. Granger, which declared emancipation to the slaves in Texas on that day, twelve years ago. We understand that Indianola will be the objective point of this excursion, and that extra trains on the railroad have been obtained for the occasion.

Victoria Advocate (Victoria Texas) May 26, 1877

Liberty (Co.)
The Colored People Celebrate

(Special Telegram to the News)
Liberty, June 19 –

The colored people of this county celebrated the thirteenth anniversary of their freedom. The order of the day was a grand barbecue, after which they were addressed by L. C. Chambers, S. C. Perryman and W. C. Harris.

Galveston Daily News June 20, 1878

Corsicana, June 18

The streets were thronged this morning at an early hour with darkies from the surrounding country, coming to town to assist our colored citizens in celebrating Emancipation Day. They formed in line, and, headed by the colored brass band, marched to a grove in the northeast part of town. Mr. A. Zadek addressed the assemblage, giving them good, wholesome advice. He was followed by Mayor Miller and others.

Galveston Daily News, June 19, 1881

Letters From the People

Editor Constitution – Why do negroes in Texas celebrate their emancipation on the 19th of June? What is the value of property owned by negroes in the southern states and in the other states of the union?

Edward North
Starrville, Ga. May 11, 1898.

The negroes in Texas celebrate their emancipation on the 19th of June because of the promulgation of General Granger's emancipation order on that date, 1865. General Granger was in charge of the federal troops in that state.

The total value of property owned by negroes in the southern states and in the other states of the union is estimated at $300,000,000.

Atlanta Constitution (Atlanta, Georgia)
May 15, 1898

Closed For The Day

There's nothing doing at either the oil mill or the compress today. It's "Juneteenth" and the negro laborers refused to work for either love or money. It is reported that the oil mill gang turned down a proposition of $100 above their salary to work today.

Daily Bulletin (Brownwood, Texas), June 19, 1907

Untitled

Yesterday was the day when the average colored damsel and the average colored dude hied[sic] themselves forth to celebrate the 19th of June and the busy housewife had to wend her way to the kitchen and do menial work.

Austin American Statesman, June 20, 1899

Washington (Co.)

The colored people of this county will hold a grand emancipation celebration in this city on the 19th of June. Preparations are already being made for the occasion...colored emissaries are said to be working quietly and secretly among the colored people of this city, with a hope of inducing emigration to the panhandle.

Galveston Daily News, May 21, 1879
Reprinted from Brenham Banner.

Fort Worth, May 13, 1880

The emancipation celebration by the colored people occurred to-day. There was a procession of several hundred, principally Sunday-schools, with their banners, among which the old stars and stripes were conspicuous.

Dallas Daily Herald, May 14, 1880

Wound Up In A Row

The second day's festivities of the Emancipation celebration were carried out as per scheduled programme with some sensational features thrown in for good measure.

Before the turmoil came, C. N. Love, in a neat speech, awarded the "loving" cup donated by Messrs. Sweeney and Fredericks to the Sheridan Guards. The various prizes were awarded to the crack bicyclists, societies and winners in the pony races. The fireworks display was brilliant and an appropriate finale to what has been the most successful celebration held in many years.

The first trouble came about noon yesterday, when, despite the fact that it had been publicly announced that a meeting would be held at 4 p.m. to elect trustees of the park of the coming year, the old board of trustees got together and reelected themselves. .

Houston Daily Post, June 21, 1899

Untitled

Today is Emancipation Day with our colored population and the most of them will celebrate some way or other.

The Cass County Sun, June 19, 1900

Emancipation Tame Show

(By Associated Press)

Dallas, Texas, June 19 –

Emancipation day more commonly known as "Juneteenth" has been shorn of its chief attraction to the Negroes of the south this year. In view of the war, the much-looked-for barbecue and basket picnic features will be eliminated as a food conservation measure. Even "red lemonade" has been "tabooed" to conserve sugar. Elaborate demonstrations have always accompanied this date in the history of the Negro, but this year about the only thing left for the Negro is the ball game.

Palestine Daily Herald, June 19, 1918.

Dallas Will See Interracial Track Meet 'Juneteenth'

Dallas, June 18 – (ANP) –

In conjunction with the annual "Juneteenth" celebration of Emancipation Day, to be staged June 19 at the Negro exhibits building of the Texas Centennial Exposition, what is said to be the first interracial track meet in the history of the South will be run off in Dallas.

Pittsburgh Courier, June 20, 1936

Untitled

To-day was the fourteenth anniversary of emancipation, and it was duly celebrated by the negroes. Davis and others orated, chiefly against the exodus to Kansas, which, until lately, had not struck this section.

Fort Worth Daily Democrat, June 20, 1879

Emancipation Day [Train rates]

All stations, June 19. Rate: One and one-third fare between all stations. Dates of sale: Evening trains of 18 and all trains of 19. Final limit, June 20.

The Van Zandler, (Van Zandt, TX), June 8, 1900.

Brenham

Judy Daly (colored) of this city paid up her taxes to-day and says she was born in 1767. She is in good health, and bids fair to see several more emancipation days.

Galveston Daily News, June 19, 1881

Emancipation
(Abridged)

The colored people of the county observed Emancipation day yesterday, part of them going to Mineral Wells, the larger portion however, assembled at the Park and appeared to enjoy the occasion very much.

The white speakers were Mayor Putman and Hon. D. M. Alexander. Mayor Putman's speech was in part as follows:

Speaking for the white people of Weatherford, and I believe I know their sentiments, I will say that the white people of Weatherford; the dominant element at least, are your friends.

…You need fewer lawyers and preachers and more mechanics and farmers…Prove to the white people that it is fixed purpose to respect law, order and virtue, and prove to them further that you will respect prosperity rights and that you will cultivate habits of thrift and industry.

Do this and we will stand by you and protect you even unto death."

The Weekly Herald (Weatherford, TX) June 21, 1900

Texas Items

A child fainted and died at the emancipation celebration at Brenham.

Christian Messenger (Bonham, TX), June 10, 1878

Walked from Gonzales
Four Small Children Wanted to See Juneteenth Celebration in San Antonio

The celebration of the freedom of the Texas slaves is still being held at San Pedro Springs. Crowds are going to the park all the time and the Negroes are making a three days celebration of it. Dancing is indulged in in the evening. In the afternoon the celebration is in the nature of a picnic.

One incident attracted attention among the picnickers yesterday. Two small boys and two small girls walked from Gonzales, a distance of seventy-five miles, to attend the celebration here. The police were notified the children had run away from home and found them at the celebration. They missed part of the celebration, for they were detained by the police.

The girls are aged 13 and 12 and the boys are 11 and 9 respectively. When the Officers Krushall and Thompson found the children they were unwilling to believe that children of their ages could have walked twenty-five miles a day. The children said that they all work on a from near Gonzales chopping cotton. After deciding to spend June 19 in San Antonio they walked into the town one evening, drew their pay and started out along the railroad track leading to San Antonio.

Jessie James Ross, the older boy, said he intended to start back to Gonzales this evening had they not been arrested. It is now very likely they will make the return trip on a train. He said they had lived with a Miss Stewart while in San Antonio, but could not give her address.

The Daily Express, San Antonio, June 21, 1906

Juneteenth 101

I don't celebrate Juneteenth.

And you shouldn't. Only people with good sense appreciate freedom.

EXTRA! JUNETEENTH NEWS EXTRA!

Titles Timeline

Mammoth Celebration: Negroes of Austin to Fittingly Observe Emancipation Day
Austin Daily Statesman, June 12, 1911

Program Ready for Emancipation Day Grande Street Procession in Morning will End at Park Followed by Exercises
Houston Post, June 9, 1912

Negro in his Glory Tomorrow - It is Juneteenth and Wherever the Sons of Ham are Found They Celebrate the Day Properly
Laredo Weekly Times, June 21 1914

Local Colored People Observed Juneteenth Parade, Baseball Game, Prayer Meeting and Other Features on the Days Program
The Corpus Christi Caller, June 20, 1915

Watermelons Are More Plentiful on Market Big Demand from Negroes on the "Juneteenth"
Houston Post, June 20, 1916

Celebrate Emancipation Picnic at Brooker Park and Many Go Elsewhere
Corsicana Daily Sun, June 19, 1916

Negroes to Finance Juneteenth Program Former Plan to ask their White Friends for Donations Abandoned
Corpus Christi Caller, June 7, 1917

Three Bartlett Blacks Die of Juneteenth Overeating
Austin Statesman, June 24, 1923

Quietest Juneteenth of Austin History Celebrated Yesterday
Austin Statesman, June 20, 1924

"Juneteenth" Quiet in City of Corsicana
Corsicana Daily Sun, June 20, 1924

City had Quiet Day Juneteenth
The Marshall News Messenger, June 20, 1925

You'll Have to Eat Out of the Ice Box For It's Juneteenth: Waco Dusky Swains and Damsels to Celebrate Freedom with Watermelons and Barbecue
The Waco News-Tribune, June 19, 1926

3-Day Juneteenth Celebration Planned
Austin Statesman, June 17, 1927

Colored Folk Turn Out En Masse Tues For Juneteenth Jubilee
The Waxahachie Daily Light, June 19, 1928

Austin Housewives Face Cooking for Day as Juneteenth Draws Near
Austin American June 19 1929

June'Teenth Ball Game to be Held Here: Dusky Nines from Amarillo and Childress will Clash.
The Amarillo Globe-Times, June 18, 1929

Valley Negroes Trek Towards Melon Country for Juneteenth
Valley Morning Star (Harlingen, TX), June 21, 1931

Dusky Bathing Beauty Contest on Juneteenth
Tyler Morning Telegraph, June 19, 1931

Outbreak of Measles Causes Postponement of Juneteenth Barbecue and Frolic
Waco Tribune-Herald, June 18, 1933

May Pass Case of Negro Here, Witnesses for Robbery Trial Ask Off for Juneteenth
Abilene Reporter-News June 18, 1933

Navasota Plans Negro Marathon for Juneteenth
The Eagle (Bryan, TX), June 12, 1935

Negroes Celebrate Juneteenth Today You'll have to cook your own meals.
The Austin American, June 19, 1936

Darkies Spruce Up for Big Juneteenth Affair Galveston Center of Texas Celebration Valley Negroes Meet in San Benito
Valley Morning Star (Harlingen, Texas), June 18, 1936

City Sees 'Juneteenth' Pass with Quiet Demeanor as Few Leave Jobs
The Monitor (McAllen, TX), June 20, 1937

Today's Juneteenth and Negroes of Texas Converge in Dallas Saturday
Valley Morning Star (Harlingen, TX) June 19, 1937

Valley Air Base Colored Soldiers to be Honored on Juneteenth
The Monitor (McAllen, TX), June 18, 1942

Beaumont Expects Quiet June-Teenth After Rioting
The Taylor Daily Press (Taylor, TX) June 17, 1943

Negroes Forego Big Doings on Wartime Emancipation Day
Abilene Reporter-News, June 19, 1944

All-Negro Rodeo Is Now Planned for Juneteenth
The Eagle (Bryan, TX), June 12, 1946

Negro City Employees To Get 'Juneteenth'
The Austin American, June 19, 1946

No Work, Traditional Tips, Ball Game by Gals, Barbecue Party, And Last But Not Least, Atomic Dancing—That's Juneteenth
Corsicana Daily Sun, June 19, 1947

It's Juneteenth: 10,000 Negroes Swarm to Park for Celebration
The Austin Statesman, June 19, 1947

Once Known for Watermelons and Brawls Big Juneteenth Celebrations Are Planned All Over Texas
Lubbock Evening Journal, June 18, 1947

Today's "Juneteenth" But Dusky Corsicanans Started Celebration Last Night, Jail Records Indicate
Corsicana Daily Sun June 19, 1948

Abilene Negroes Swap Yarns, Feast at 'Juneteenth' Gathering
Abilene Reporter-News June 20, 1950

Monday's the Day: Local Colored Folks to Mark Juneteenth
The Weimar Mercury (Weimar, Texas) June 16, 1950

Little Whoopee, Juneteenth Is Dead
Austin American June 18, 1960

Juneteenth 101

BEFORE JUNETEENTH

The first enslaved African in the territory that became Texas was recorded in 1528.
At the time, Texas was governed by multiple Native American nations.

1528 1529 1530 1531 1532 1533 1534 1535 1536 1537 1538 1539 1540 1541 1542 1543 1544 1545 1546
1547 1548 1549 1550 1551 1552 1553 1554 1555 1556 1557 1558 1559 1560 1561 1562 1563 1564 1565
1566 1567 1568 1569 1570 1571 1572 1573 1574 1575 1576 1577 1578 1579 1580 1581 1582 1583 1584
1585 1586 1587 1588 1589 1590 1591 1592 1593 1594 1595 1596 1597 1598 1599 1600 1601 1602 1603
1604 1605 1606 1607 1608 1609 1610 1611 1612 1613 1614 1615 1616 1617 1618 1619 1620 1621 1622
1623 1624 1625 1626 1627 1628 1629 1630 1631 1632 1633 1634 1635 1636 1637 1638 1639 1640 1641
1642 1643 1644 1645 1646 1647 1648 1649 1650 1651 1652 1653 1654 1655 1656 1657 1658 1659 1660
1661 1662 1663 1664 1665 1666 1667 1668 *196* 1669 1670 1671 1672 1673 1674 1675 1676

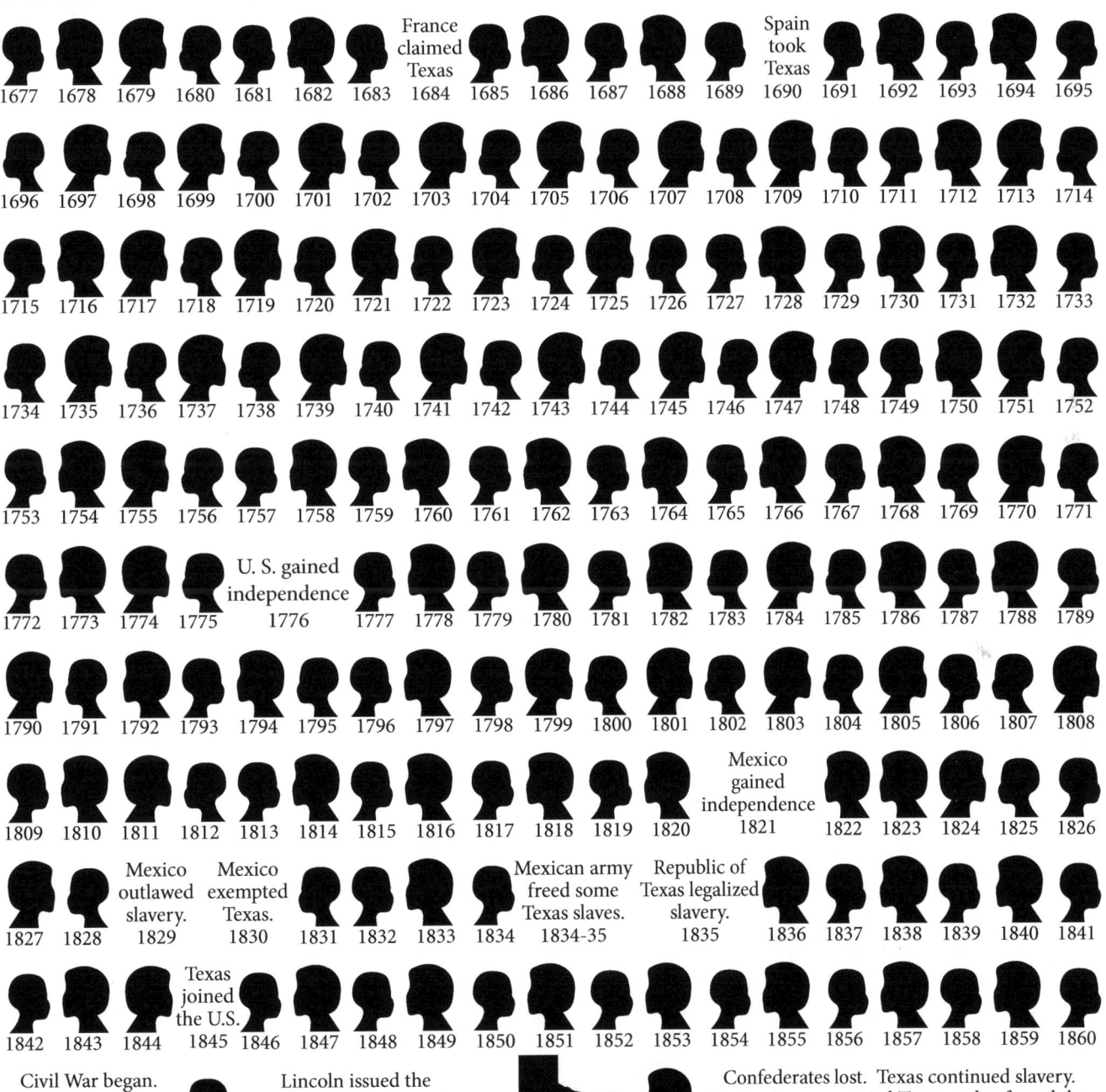

Juneteenth 101

Year	Event
1677–1683	
1684	France claimed Texas
1685–1689	
1690	Spain took Texas
1691–1775	
1776	U. S. gained independence
1777–1820	
1821	Mexico gained independence
1822–1828	
1829	Mexico outlawed slavery.
1830	Mexico exempted Texas.
1831–1833	
1834-35	Mexican army freed some Texas slaves.
1835	Republic of Texas legalized slavery.
1836–1844	
1845	Texas joined the U.S.
1846–1860	
1861	Civil War began. Texas joined the confederates.
1862	
1863	Lincoln issued the Emancipation Proclamation. Texans ignored it.
1864	
1865	Confederates lost. Texas continued slavery. Union Army occupied Texas and enforced the Emancipation Proclamation, birthing Juneteenth.

WITH FRIENDS LIKE THESE …

After June 19, 1865, southern journalists frequently referred to former masters being "the best friends" of the formerly enslaved. The following article clarifies the boundary of that relationship. It appeared on the front page of the Galveston Daily News one day before Juneteenth.

The problem most difficult to solve just now, s how to dispose of the Negro. His northern brethren have proclaimed him in some places to be free. "Here is a distressed negro" – proclaim they – "who much prefers idleness to work – should not he be free to choose which? Is he not a man and a brother? Clearly here are two legs and no feathers: let us vote him millions of money, and thousands of lives, and oceans of blood, and myriads of cripples and deformed bodies, and miseries for whole generations of his white brothers for enfranchisement, and so secure him the blessings of the gods. They proclaim, in the gross, as if it had become credible lately, all two legged animals without feathers to be free," Sambo was tolerably happy until the philanthropists got hold on him. He had good pork and beef and bread to eat, had plenty to wear, was housed from the inclemencies of the seasons, unused when he was sick, had his children well taken care of (for Sambo would not do this himself) and was made to do his share of honest labor. The philanthropists thought Sambo would be better off without labor and so undertake to proclaim him free. Well, what then? He won't work and must be supported in idleness. It is not fair that his pseudo friends, the philanthropists, should bid him work or starve. They have taken him out of a happy condition and should exchange him into one that is happier. The English did the same thing once. That is they took Sambo out of his happy condition – took him away from the nurturing care of his natural guardians and friends and bid him "root hog or die." Fortunately for Sambo the Island of Jamaica abounded in spontaneous pumpkin and plantain, and so he was enabled to live without work. Up to his knees in vegetables that grow without culture, and the in costume even more primitive than fig leaves of our anti-diluvian parents, Sambo has so rapidly progressed towards that happier condition in which his friends the British philanthropists, would raise him, that his race is becoming extinct, and those that remain are the most idle, worthless, pilfering, lying, impure vagabonds on the face of the earth. Sambo of the Jamaica isle is rapidly nearing his destiny, and what, with his laziness and his pumpkin, will soon reach the goal towards which the philanthropists would have him go.

But fortunately for Sambo of the Southern States, the soil is not to genial to his vagabondising qualities as to produce for him the spontaneous pumpkin and plantain; it requires to be tilled, "not tickled with a hoe and laughing with a harvest" – tilled plough-deep and oxen strong, and we know that Sambo is not up to this kind of voluntary servitude. Then, with "his strong paternal and maternal instincts," which his northern friends laud so highly, he must, in addition to shelter and feed and clothing for himself and dusky partner, take care of, provide for and raise his sooty offspring. He has to do the nursing in sickness and pay the doctor's bill and all other sorts of bills, or else he must starve and die. Sambo is, of course well qualified for all this, and is prepared to take his stand, without work, in the community as a free and equal member of society. He will not abandon his family to destitution and starvation. "Oh no!" say the philanthropists, "Sambo is a creature of refined and chivalrous sensibilities, and never abandons his family." But the philanthropists would have him to live without work, and, of course, the philanthropists will support him in this idleness, "But we are not able to do this," again they say; "and if Sambo does not go to work for an honest livelihood we will ship him to the country of this progenitors." Good! They would place the Negro in a happier condition than from whence they have taken him. They would refine enlighten and Christianize him and for these great ends they will send him to that land of Christianity and civilization, the congenial Africa – there, of course, to become high-toned gentlemen and pure moralits of the Fetish school, like their forefathers were before them. The philanthropists are making out a brilliant destiny for Sambo. They tell him to go into crowded communities and work for big wages and little work – New Orleans, for instance. Well Sambo mayhap thinks he can make a living by draying, which was profitable under the old regime. He runs counter to a while laborer and is hit over the head with a dray-stick, accompanied with the euphourious "git out! of this, you d—d nigger," or with something more guttural Tentonic untransferable to paper. He has no natural guardian to protect his rights and redress his wrongs. He is driven forth by the superior energy of his white brother, and is denied even the privilege of working as he would wish. Sambo, in his benightenment, cannot see the poetical justice of this – there is in it something his dilatory reason cannot grasp at; but, for all this, it is justice and retributive justice at that. His friends, the philanthropists, have proclaimed him, free, and he must in all time to come stand on his own bottom.

But then, Sambo does not like to work – will not work if he can help it. He would rather steal, lie and loaf for a living; vile the police reports of the New Orleans courts, from whence Mr. and Mrs. Sambo daily are sent up in crowds to the penitentiary, work-house and house of corrections, for all sorts of vicious vagabondage. He is proclaimed free, and of course freemen are able to take care of themselves. Consequently, Sambo unlike others of puerile natures, needs no guardianship wherewith to take care of his thriftless and ignorant self, and in return for all such good care, is compelled to do his part for the general good. "Six days shalt thou labor" was thundered form Mount Sinai ever so many hundred years ago. But then, the philanthropists say that Sambo is an exception to all this – that he is a peculiar specimen of the genus homo, and is excepted from all moral and divine obligations. Sometimes, in the excess of their humanity, the philanthropists appoint camps of instruction for this new, full of equal rights revelation, to teach him how to enjoy his new blessings in this happier condition to which they have elevated him. That is, they give him spare rations and worse quarters, and try to make him work. Sambo does not exactly appreciate this kind of teaching and his happier condition, and seeks to return to that from which they had taken him. The former was good enough for him. He was taken care of and had no distracting thought to disturb his mental equilibrium. Now all this is rank ingratitude on the part of Sambo – this want of appreciation for the efforts of his philanthropic brethren; but then they console themselves that republics always were ungrateful. The Negro of Jamaica, with his pumpkin and his plantain, is nearing his destiny rapidly enough. The Negro of the South without the necessary and spontaneous pumpkin, will travel the same road more rapidly. The Indian has fulfilled his destiny on his continent, and Sambo, thanks to the efforts of the philanthropists, will complete his in a much shorter space of time. The extinction of slavery is simply the extinction of the Negro race.

Galveston Daily News, July 18, 1865

Juneteenth 101

AFTER JUNETEENTH

"Yet with a steady beat have not our weary feet, come to the place for which our father's signed."

From *Lift Every Voice and Sing*

- **1865**: 13th Amendment ratified
- **1866**: Reconstruction begins. Texas adopts Black codes. Texas State Central Committee of Colored Men holds first convention.
- **1868**: *Freedman's Press*, a newspaper for Black Texans, begins.
- **1869**: New state constitution, grants voting rights to Black men. Sixteen Black state legislators elected.
- **1870**: 15th Amendment grants suffrage to Black men.
- **1872**: Paul Quinn College becomes Texas' 1st college for Blacks. Blacks in Houston create Emancipation Park.
- **1876**: Alta Vista A&M College of Texas for Negroes opens
- **1877**: Reconstruction ends.
- **1880**: First state bill to commemorate emancipation fails.
- **1882**: Texas legislature approves a classical university for Blacks similar to U. of Texas.
- **1889**: Texas State Fair creates Colored People Day.
- **1893**: A black teenager in Paris, Texas was tortured, hanged, and burned without trial. His body parts were sold as souvenirs.
- **1898**: A Texas Supreme Court decision prevents creation of a classical university for Blacks.
- **1901**: Prairie View Normal School begins teaching college courses in classical and scientific studies.
- **1902**: Poll tax limits voting.
- **1907**: 5 Black-owned banks open. (Dallas, Ft. Worth, Palestine, Tyler, Waco)
- **1908**: Jack Johnson becomes Boxing Heavyweight Champion.
- **1910**: Dallas designates race-based neighborhood boundaries.
- **1915**: Penalty for interracial relationships increases to 2 - 5 years imprisonment. El Paso citizens organize Texas' 1st chapter of the NAACP.
- **1917**: Harassment by Houston Police sparked a race riot by 156 Black soldiers.
- **1918**: Blacks required to use separate libraries. Texas Colored Baseball League begins.
- **1919**: Rumors of a mixed race couple in Longview sparks a 3-day race riot.
- **1920**: 19th Amendment grants suffrage to women.

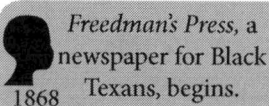

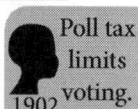

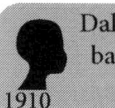

200

Juneteenth 101

- **1920**: PV Interscholastic League begins Black school competitions.
- **1921**: Texan Bessie Coleman becomes 1st Black woman pilot.
- **1923**: Democratic party bars Blacks from primary elections.
- **1925**: Law requires racial segregation in schools.
- **1926**: Dallas Black businessmen establish the first Negro Chamber of Commerce in Texas. Texas Negro Peace Officers Association founded.
- **1931**: Texas legislature declares Confederate General Lee's birthday a state holiday.
- **1942**: Navy Cross awarded to Dorie Miller (1st Black).
- **1943**: Segregated seating required in all buses. A rumor of rape sparked anti-Black rioting in Beaumont.
- **1944**: U.S. Supreme Court ends White's Only Democratic primary.
- **1947**: Texas State University for Negroes created to avoid desegregating U. of Texas.
- **1948**: Pres. Truman desegregates U.S. Military.
- **1949**: Texas ignores creation of Nat'l Freedom Day
- **1950**: Separate facilities required for state park visitors. U.S. Supreme Court opens UT Law School to Blacks.
- **1954**: Texas school districts create rules rejecting Supreme court ordered school desegregation.
- **1957**: Gov. sends Rangers to prevent integration of Mansville High School.
- **1958**: The New Year's Cotton Bowl game featured an integrated football team.
- **1960**: Students at Texas Southern U. begin sit-ins that helped desegregate Houston businesses.
- **1964**: Civil Rights Act of 1964 passed.
- **1965**: Voting Rights Act outlawed discriminatory voting practices
- **1966**: Texas' 1st Black female state senator elected.
- **1968**: Civil Rights Act of 1968 passed.
- **1971**: Houston's 1st Black City Councilman elected.
- **1972**: 1st Black female state representative elected
- **1974**: Oscar DuCongé elected 1st Black mayor of a major Texas City (Waco).
- **1975**: Morris Overstreet becomes 1st Black elected to a Texas statewide office.
- **1977**: Texan Azie Morton becomes 1st Black U.S. Treasurer.
- **1980**: Emancipation Day becomes a Texas state holiday
- **1991**: Martin Luther King, Jr. Day becomes a Texas state holiday.
- **1995**: Chelsi Smith becomes 1st Black Miss Texas USA; and 1st Black Miss. Universe.
- **2001**: James Byrd Jr. Hate Crimes Act signed into state law
- **2008**: Barack Obama elected President of the United States

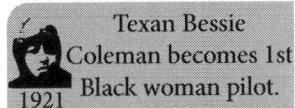

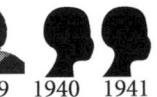

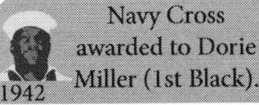

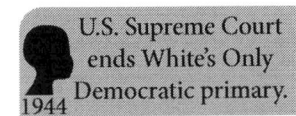

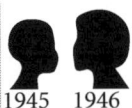

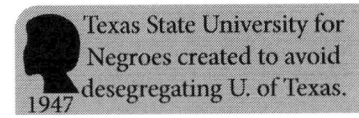

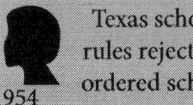

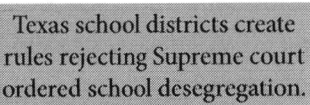

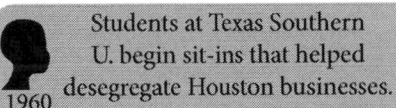

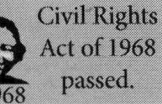

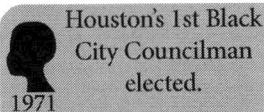

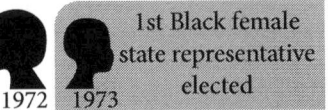

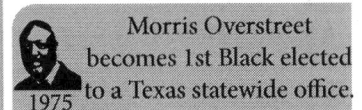

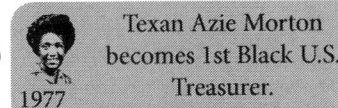

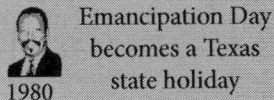

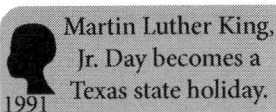

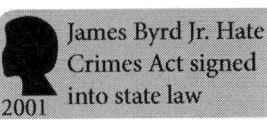

AFTER JUNETEENTH

BUREAU Refugees, Freedmen and Abandoned Lands,

Enforcement of the Emancipation Proclamation in Texas ended slavery for a majority of the state's enslaved Africans, but not all. Throughout its brief existence, the Freedmen's Bureau received reports of men, women and children who remained enslaved years after June 1865. One of the more bizarre discoveries occurred in 1868 when a Texan named Alex Simpson was hanged for stealing horses. After his death, a search of his property revealed numerous enslaved Africans he had not released. [199]

A report by B. V. Gen. Abner Doubleday provides an intriguing description of conditions for freedmen in post-Juneteenth Galveston County. (See page 204.)

A bird's eye view of
The Freedmen's Bureau - Texas

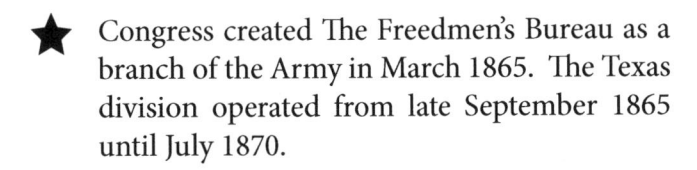

★ Congress created The Freedmen's Bureau as a branch of the Army in March 1865. The Texas division operated from late September 1865 until July 1870.

★ The agency's mission:
- provide relief to people left homeless by the Civil War (Blacks and Whites);
- supervise freedmen affairs; and
- administer land abandoned by or confiscated from confederates.

★ National Commissioner:
    Gen. Oliver Otis Howard
Texas Assistant Commissioners:
    Edgar M. Gregory, (9 months)
    Joseph Kiddoo, (8 months)
    Charles Griffin, (8 months)
    Joseph J. Reynolds, (4 months)
    Edward R. S. Canby
Other Texas Bureau positions:
    Superintendent of Education
    Surgeon-in-chief
    Traveling Inspector
Subassistant Commissioners managed the local offices. Some Subassistants had Assistant Subassistants.

★ Texas was considered the bureau's most difficult state to manage. At its largest, the state had fifty-nine districts. Texans hostile to the Bureau's mission wounded or threatened managers. Some managers were killed. District size was based on the army's ability to provide protection.

★ Best achievement: The bureau established 150 freedmen schools serving 9,086 students while battling intense opposition from Texans opposed to educating Blacks.

★ Before 1867, only the staff members who were army officers received payment. Civilian staff members were not paid because Congress did not appropriate funding for the first two years of operation.

★ Freedmen used the bureau primarily for legal redress and for help locating relatives.

★ Political equity acquired by African Texans via the Freedmen's Bureau was lost when reconstruction ended.

★ To view records of daily reports created by Freedmen Bureau—Texas administrators, visit: https://www.archives.gov/research/african-americans/freedmens-bureau

If ya can't figure it out how to find records, call the National Archives.

Source: "The Freedmen's Bureau and Black Texans" by Barry Crouch[200]

Report from the B.R.F.A.L. - Galveston County

Written March 1, 1867
by Brevet Major General Abner Doubleday

In obedience to circular letters dated Headquarters, Bureau of Refugees, Freedmen and Abandoned Lands, Galveston, Texas December 31, 1866, I have the honor to submit the following report:

Comparatively few criminal and civil cases have occurred during the month, in which freedmen have been parties, and none of a serious character. A list of those arbitrated by this office and those brought before the civil courts under the recent order of the [Asst.] Commissioner is subjoined. Many complaints made by freedmen are of a trivial character. Even when the complainant is undoubtedly in the right it frequently results that cases cannot be brought before the civil courts on account of a lack of evidence, thus throwing the cost upon the freedmen. In all such cases I have endeavored to collect the debts by getting the parties together and advising them, if necessary, to compromise in preference to going to law. A large number of claims have been thus adjusted by Alain Reid, Justice of the Peace, who appears to be a just and efficient officer – one that advises the freedmen, untaught in law. The best and most economical manner of settling their difficulties. I am informed by him that he has succeed in every case where it was possible to collect the claim of freedmen. When the parties could not be reconciled and the defendants did not possess property which could be attached for debt, he has advised the claimants to take no action whatever as it would involve them in expense and be of no avail.

Nearly all claims presented by freedmen are for small amounts. To collect them in due process of law frequently involves an expense double the amount for which suits are brought. The cost of employing an attorney alone is usually greater than the claim. This I find to be the greatest obstacle the freedman has to contend against in obtaining his just dues. Hence in most instances it is expedient to lose a debt rather than take the chance and suffer the cost of a civil prosecution. Heretofore these collections have been made by the Bureau without expense to the freedmen.

The mayor of this city, Chas. H. Leonard, shows a disposition to make no distinction with regard to color in dispensing justice. He claims that white and black receive the same privileges and attention. And I am pleased to say that but few cases have yet come under my observation where partiality has been shown. (These are referred to in the last-paragraph of this report.)

There have been three schools for freedmen in operation during the month of February, having an attendance of 468 pupils. Five teachers have been employed. All efforts for the education of freed people have come from the government of the United States and benevolent societies of the North. No assistance has been rendered by White residents here although public sentiment it is said, favors the education of the colored people. Little aid can be expected since the educational system for the whites is so deficient and imperfect. If they will not perfect the school system for their own race, they certainly will not for another. The freed people are very desirous of receiving an education and have assisted to the utmost in furthering the object by giving the use of their churches and rendering such other assistance as lay in their power. The schools have been very full – in many instances pupils having been turned away for want of room. That all may receive the benefits of an education, the Bureau is cooperating in completing a building erected by the M. E. Church which has been leased, at a nominal price, for the term of five years, with the privilege of five more, for the use of schools. This house will soon be completed and sufficient accommodation will then be offered for those who choose to avail themselves of the opportunity of receiving a primary education.

Every kind of business, wherein freedmen are concerned is transacted by this office when consistent with the laws and regulations of this Bureau. Many letters have been written to agents in other sections and states to obtain information concerning the relatives of freedmen who have been separated for years and in nearly all instances the desired information has been received.

In exercising an advisory care over the freed people scarcely a day has passed in which many difficulties have not been settled which civil law could not reach.

My office hours are from 9 o'clock A. M. until 4 P.M. of each day (Sundays excepted, and I have been absent from my office no day during the month.

Five companies of Infantry are stationed at this post; and I have had no occasion to call upon them for assistance in the performance of the duties of this office during the past month. With regard to how far the civil authorities would meet out justice to the freed people in case the troops were withdrawn, I can only say that in my opinion some judges would do justice; while others would disregard all the rights and privileges of the colored population.

The active provisions of the "Labor Laws" passed at the regular session of the eleventh Legislature of this state, have in no instance been enforced.

The majority of freed people work for monthly wages, but a large number engage in a successful business of their own.

Owing to the frequent efforts made by planters in other portions of the state to swindle the freed people and deprive them of the fruits of their labor by selling their share of the proceeds to the plantations, I would recommend sever punishment for fraudulent attempts of this kind. Hitherto the custom has been simply to seize the cotton and other products and thus enforce a settlement. In my opinion there should be some additional penalty awarded.

Some laws though just in themselves, seem to be enforced here only as regards the freed people. I notice that several colored men have been fined for carrying concealed weapons. I doubt very much if this law has been enforced against White people

I am sir,
Very respectfully, Your [Obedient] Servant,
A. Doubleday
Bvt. Maj. Gen. U.S.A.
Sub-Asst. Commissioner B.R.F.A.L.
For Galveston County[201]

Brevit Major General Abner Doubleday

A Sample of Post-Juneteenth Shenanigans in the Lone Star State As Reported by The Freedmen's Bureau - Texas

September 7, 1867
Jim Ward (*Freedman*) Vs. **D. Autry** (*White*)

"Ward accused Autry of threatening to kill him. Accusation was based on hearsay and dismissed as frivolous."

Later, same day
D. Autry Vs. **Jim Ward**

"Autry accused Ward of threatening to kill him. Accusation was based on hearsay and dismissed as frivolous."

Later, same day
Timpe Ward (*Freedwoman*) Vs. **D. Autry**

"Tempe Complained that D. Autry pulled her hair, shook, and otherwise abused her. *(later)* Complaint was "dismissed as frivolous on account of non-appearance." [202]

Centerville Bureau

August 29, 1867
Ben (*colored*) and **Edmunsin**

"Ben freedman charges that Edmunsin called for drinks and cigars in his saloon and when requested to pay for them, refused, broke a glass and etc., and Ben was obliged to close his place. Charges proven. Ordered to pay costs $5.85 and fined $10."[203]

Waco Bureau

Oct. 5, 1868
Henrietta Grobuk (*Colored*) **vs. Dr. Philips** (*White*)

"Dr. Philips has a girl, my daughter. Has had her all her life. She is 15 years old. C. C. Preatin[sic] went after her. I sent by him $20.00 to pay her way home. He Preaton[sic] asked her if she wanted to come home. She said she did but was afraid of Dr. Philips as he said to her that she should not go home. He could not get her; consequently brought the money back. I have written to her often but cannot get an answer and believe they will not allow her to write."[204]

Houston Bureau

March 24, 1867
Edmond Whiting (*freedman*) **vs. Matthew Williams** (*freedman*)

"Edward Whiting (freedman) states that a boy by the name of Matthew Williams went blind a year ago this month, working and living on the (???) Plantation with him (CM Summers)

Since which time he has been compeld [sic] to surport [sic] and pay Dr. bill to amount of fifty dollars. And asks if The Freedman's Bureau cannot relieve him of the charge or pay something towards his surport [sic] He is now on the place of CM Summers,

Edward Whiting also states that one of Mr. Summers hands that he brought from South Carolina is about to run away, by the name of John Inglim. He has made arrangements with some teamsters to take him to Milicas [sic]."[205]

Marlin Bureau

Oct. 12, 1868

Ann Hanhieser *(white)* and State vs. John Thompson *(Freedman)*

"Rape.

Evidence adduced was positive that John Thompson on – 10th of May 1868, came to the house of Mrs. H. about an hour before day. She was on the bed, he ??? her, beat bruised and raped her person. John was working for Bernard Miller a neighbor, who with Joe Ferlin ??? – and John Phillip Clark were standing guard that night, watching a corn field to prevent cattle braking in. Ferlin took first watch. Phillip 2nd & Thomas 3rd. Mrs. Miller hearing noise, got up we??? to ???? & found Thompson about—??? about the hour Mrs. H was assaulted. Mrs. T swore positively he was the man.

Motion for new trial & subsequent arrest of judgment by counselor ???? on ground that an error had been made. Affidavit of Jas Good and J H Caller offered to show Thomas was in Columbus on night 10 May. Sentenced to be hung on 18th day of December, 1868."[206]

Columbus Bureau

Dec. 7, 1868

Frances Fitzgerald *(Colored)* vs. Owens McGowen *(Colored)*

"Refusing to support her child. Ordered to appear on Tuesday, December 8, 1868 at 10 AM.

(Later) Ordered to support mother and child until he could marry her."[207]

Houston Bureau

After Juneteenth

Feb. 15, 1867

Nelson Lee *(colored)* vs. Oscar F. Nash, planter

"[Lea] states that he was working on the place of Nash under contract about 4 miles from Bastrop. This morning Nash beat him with his fist because he would not make his wife go out to work. That his wife was not on the contract and was not rationed by Nash. Nelson offered no resistance as Nash had a pistol belted on him. Lee further states that Nash took out a knife and told him that he would cut his neck clean off if he opened his mouth.

A man named Barnes, a friend of Nash came in and wanted the Negro forced back; acknowledged that Nash had beat him.

Referred this case to Mr. Allen, Justice of the Peace who had Nash arrested and bound up and set his trial for the 18th.

Nash appeared but the complainant and witnesses not appearing he was discharged."[208]

July 1, 1867

"Nelson complains that he cannot get a settlement with Nash for last year's services. Thinks Nash has charged him too much.

After examining the accounts of Nash striking out lost time and found that there was a balance due Nash who offered to give a receipt in full.

Settled.

Nash gave Lea a receipt in full of all demands to date."[209]

Bastrop Bureau

After Juneteenth

Text of standard work agreement for freedmen in Grimes County, Texas[210]

County of Grimes
State of Texas

    Know all men by these presents, that we _____ of Grimes County and State of Texas of the first part and the undersigned colored men and women of the second part, Witnesseth:
    That the said ___*(name of employer)*___ of the first part hereby promises and agrees to pay to the said parties of the second part ___*(name of freedman/woman)*___ to furnish provisions, and provender, and all things necessary for farming purposes, to give the usual attention to the sick and furnish medicine. Should a doctor be required the laborer is to pay for the attention.

In consideration of which the parties of the second part hereby promise and agree to do all labor needed on the plantation to wit: Making fences, building cabins &c.. to work diligently and faithfully and to obey and comply with all reasonable rules and regulations for the proper management of the plantation.
    It is further agreed that the laborers will not willfully absent themselves from the field or shirt the performance of duty; that all time lost by idling, sickness, or any other cause will be charged to each individual laborer thus losing time and be deducted from his or her _____.
    It is also agreed that should any laborer leave the plantation before the expiration of the time specified, he or she forfeit all _____.
    Ten hours is a day's work and six days a week's work; the women are to have Saturday afternoon of each week to wash for themselves and all the men.
    The hours of labor to be regulated by the manager of the plantation. All children and persons not laboring chargeable with board.

And it is further agreed, that in case either of the parties to this contract fail to comply with the requirements thereof the aggrieved party is hereby required to refer the question at issue to the Agent of the Bureau of Freedmen for final settlement.
    This agreement to be and remain in full force until the 25th day of December 1867
IN witness whereof the contracting parties hereunto annex their names, this _____ day of _____, 1867.

Signed and sealed in the presence of
_____
_____

Wharton Bureau

Juneteenth's Siblings

Multiple times before June 19th, freedom teased Texas slaves. Mexico's "Decree No. 56", (signed May 5, 1828) stated: "All contracts, ... that have been entered into in foreign countries, between emigrants who come to settle in this State, or between the inhabitants thereof, and the servants and day laborers or working men whom they introduce, are hereby guaranteed to be valid in said State." [217]

That translates to: All contracts made in other nations (i.e., United States) between emigrants (to Texas, a Mexican state) and their laborers are valid in Texas.

Slave owners heading to Texas responded by freeing their slaves, but required them to sign contracts indenturing them and their children for life. Owners declared a slave's worth - an amount requiring a lifetime or longer to repay at $20 per year. Existing children worked for free until age 18, and future children until age 25, whereupon they too, would begin bartered payments. [218]

Slave owners already in Texas took their chattel to Louisiana and signed contracts, some reportedly requiring the "laborers" to work either until age 100 or 100 years.

The following year (1829), Mexico passed a law completely outlawing slavery. The law was never implemented in Texas. Instead, after intense lobbying, Texas was exempted from the law in 1830.

Mexico's General Santa Anna disliked the exemption.[211] During the Texas Revolutionary War, his troops were allowed to free all slaves encountered along their path.

For protection, emancipated freedmen trailed the Mexican Army, similar to how freedmen later trailed the Union Army during the Civil War.

In 1836, a significant number of enslaved Africans gained freedom during the Texas Revolution thanks to a six-week fortuitous incident called "The Runaway Scrape." Slave owners afraid of Santa Anna ran en masse to Louisiana, often leaving their possessions and slaves behind.

The war was a blessing, but ultimately, the 18-minute Battle of San Jacinto which Texans revere, was a tragic loss for enslaved Africans. Shortly after the war, Texas President Sam Houston ordered the Republic's army to round up all 'runaways' and return them to their former owners.[212]

Mexican Generals were required to release everyone they emancipated. Only one general cooperated. Others hid the freedmen and ushered them to freedom in Mexico.

Historically, Texas school books have ignored this happenstance, preferring to claim enslaved Africans were captured, stolen, seized or abducted when describing their emancipation by the Mexicans.

The most famous saga associated with this effort is often told in terms that vilify the Mexicans. It is the story of Emily West (Morgan), the fabled Yellow Rose of Texas - an indentured servant. A popular travel website exemplifies how some prefer to recount Ms. West's saga.

> "Emily Morgan was captured along with other members of her household by the Mexican army and was forced to travel with the forces of General Antonio López de Santa Ana."[213]

It is commonly reported that Ms. West was entertaining Santa Ana when the Texans' historic attack began. One legend claims she conspired with the Texans to keep Anna occupied while they attacked. For that to be correct, Ms. West needed access to Sam Houston to plot the ploy. No records verify such interaction occurred.

The WATERMELON Mess

Once upon a time, sharing a watermelon on Juneteenth was as conventional—if not compulsory—as carving turkeys on Thanksgiving. No normal person ate a whole watermelon alone, and freedmen had no refrigerators. Therefore, every burst fruit became a communal delicacy shared by families and friends.

Watermelons were delicious treats which celebrants grew for themselves or bought cheaply from White planters who openly mocked Black customers while profiting immensely from their annual Juneteenth gorging. Juneteenth provided newspapers an opportunity to entertain readers with harsh sarcasm about the watermelon penchant of emancipation celebrants. Meanwhile, consumption by Whites was encouraged (see pg. 211.)

Many years, that inequity was ignore, possibly, because Black appreciation of independence and the thrill of community unity were valued above insults from people not known for kind words. Eventually, that changed.

Somewhere during the early 1900's, insults from Whites were granted credibility. Publicly enjoying watermelon became an embarrassment in the Black community. No exception was made for Juneteenth.

Now — a century later — many African Americans still consider watermelons a potent symbol of racism. Other racist irritants have lost their sting (e.g., spade, picaninny, Sambo, Golliwogg, Topsy, Sapphire, Jemima, etc.), but mentioning watermelon in mixed company remains socially hazardous.

Conceivably, avoiding the fruit for image purposes reveals self-hate. African Americans embrace soul food as a treasured cultural heritage. Though Watermelon is part of that heritage, it isn't considered soul food. Therefore, it lacks the reverence given to neckbones, collard greens and sweet potato pie. Racists attacks were made on other soul foods, but none prevailed like the watermelon siege. Blacks succumbed to White criticism and continue to placate it today. Such obedience arms bigots and xenophobes whose artillery is otherwise exhausted.

Watermelon hate is not unique. Other groups have embraced the sting of culinary insults, but ignored them. East Asians are not ashamed of eating sushi. Italians consider pizza consumption a cherished legacy. Mexicans embrace their affinity for tacos. Wealthy people worldwide devour slugs and call it an extravagance.

A survey of African American youth suggest change is slowly happening. Of 100 teenagers surveyed, six had learned watermelon was a social scourge. None were unfamiliar with the vintage insults mentioned above. If that changes, it will likely be because African American adults taught them to value insults from other races.

Like it or not, historically correct Juneteenth celebrations include plump watermelons - the freedmen's confection of choice.

210

Coloreds

The watermelon season has been formally inaugurated along with the initial ceremonies incident to the pulling off of the twenty-third annual manumission celebration. *(This article referenced Juneteenth as a joke.)*
Brenham Daily Banner, June 18, 1898, page 4.

The melon harvest is at hand, the Juneteenth is approaching and our brother in black is in his glory.
Halletsville Herald, June 22, 1905, page 6.

Bad For Melons

If you had a Melon patch; Yesterday you've lost the batch; While last night was drifting by; Juneteenth makes the melons fly.
The Houston Post, June 19, 1913, page 6

Milt Rutherford, four miles southeast of town, broke all watermelon records by bringing in a load of fine ripe ones Monday. He brought in the second load this morning, just in time to help the darkies celebrate the "Juneteenth."
Rockdale Reporter and Messenger, June 19, 1913, page 3

...The only thing that had a tendency to curtail their enjoyment and contribute to the sadness of the occasion was the lack of the luscious watermelon in sufficient quantities to appease the normal appetite of the Negro, which at this season of the year is "something fierce."
El Campo Citizen, June 27, 1913, Page 1

The negroes of Waco are organizing a movement to have January 1st observed as emancipation day, that being the date in 1862 when president Lincoln issued his proclamation. The date was later changed to June 19th in order that the early watermelon crop might be ready for the celebrations. Just what use a negro has for emancipation without watermelons the Waco reformers do not state.
Daily Bulletin (Brownwood, TX), Jan. 6, 1910, pg. 2

Whites Only

...The immense crowd was invited to the sumptuous barbecue with the privilege of plenty of watermelons, ice cream, and a full soda fount.
Evening Telegraph (Houston) July 2, 1870, page 2

A watermelon party was a part of the enjoyment and the entire occasion was one that will long be remembered by those who were fortunate enough to be there.
The Temple Daily Telegram, June 20, 1908, Page 7

...After the program, a contest and various games were enjoyed. Delicious refreshments of ice cream, cake and watermelon were served.
The Schulenburg Sticker, June 23, 1910, Page 2

In order to give the watermelon raisers of Lavaca county a chance to get the Herald for one year free, we are going to make the following offer: To the one bringing in the largest melon will be given a year's subscription...
LaGrange Journal, June 17, 1909, Page 1

The favorite way of eating a melon is to tote [one] to the corner of the field, burst its head with a stump and dig out the heart and just eat without frills or form. Another way, almost as good, is to assemble the neighborhood on the back gallery and carve the melon through and through and then slice in long slices, and grasping the slice in both hands, bury the face in the heart of the meat....There are other approved ways of eating melons, but the two above ways are the most approved.
Palestine Daily Herald, June 6, 1910, page 4

Watermelons are occupying the center of the stage, the receipts growing heavier daily. Good melons can be brought now at 10 cents and 15 cents. The 5-cent kind may show up by Monday in celebration of the "Juneteenth." *San Antonio Express, June 18, 1911*

Juneteenth 101

What the Scholars Say

Lest a discussion of watermelon warfare be considered trite and insignificant, a scholarly study on the topic by historian William R. Black, Ph.D, argues otherwise.

"How Watermelons Became Black: Emancipation and the Origins of a Racist Trope."

Abstract

This article explicates the origins of the racist watermelon trope and its relationship to white Americans' attitudes toward emancipation. The trope had antecedents in Orientalist depictions of the growing, selling, and eating of watermelons, but the fruit was not associated with African Americans until after emancipation. Freedpeople used watermelons to enact and celebrate their freedom, especially their newfound property rights. This provoked a backlash among white Americans, who then made the fruit a symbol of African Americans' supposed uncleanliness, childishness, idleness, and unfitness for the public square. The trope spread in U.S. print culture throughout the late 1860s and supported the post-emancipation argument that African Americans were unsuited for citizenship.

BLACK, WILLIAM R. "How Watermelons Became Black: Emancipation and the Origins of a Racist Trope." Journal of the Civil War Era, vol. 8, no. 1, 2018, pp. 64–86.

The Morning Announcements

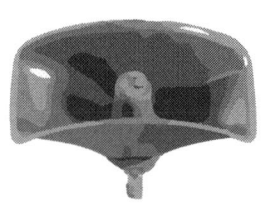

"A great way to end this watermelon foolishness is to stop being offended. Why y'all letting other people control your feelings? Quit needing approval! Asking others to stop offending you leaves them in control of your feelings, Sugar. Yes, they might stop temporarily, but if they later resume their bad behavior, where will you be? I'm saying, if you stop buying other people's objections, they'll stop selling 'em. I'll tell you what. I gonna bust me a watermelon, sit on my porch with friends, and eat it. Anyone who don't like it can kiss lick my spoon. Happy Juneteenth, Everybody!"

Assignment

Find someone who believes watermelon is a racist symbol. Ask her/him to explain why that is so, without saying, "because 'they...'"

The Coon's Trade-Mark
A Watermelon, a Razor, a Chicken and a Coon
Words & Music by Tom Logan ~ Pub. 1898 by Jos. W. Stern & Co.

Now listen and a fact I'll show
A pointer that all do not know,
As certain and sure as Holy writ,
And not a coon's exempt from it.
Now, you've heard about birds of a feather:
Four things you'll always find together,
Regardless of condition of sun or moon
A watermelon, razor, a chicken and a coon!
    CHORUS
  All coons need their razors
    when they go to fight,
  A chicken and a coon are fast friends
    on a cloudy night!
  Ev'rybody shout this trademark,
    everybody sing this tune
  A watermelon, razor, a chicken and a coon!

Three gem-men of color one day did steal
A melon for their noonday meal;
A lesson in fractions, with razors gave,
For an equal share each coon did crave;
Til a runaway team dashed past the door,
'Twas a load of chickens, they waited no more.
But rushed pell-mell the fowls to assail,
Not a pullet was left to tell the tale.
    (Chorus)

The Blue Vein Club chose Darktown Hall,
The proper place for their full dress ball.
Had watermelons and chickens galore,
So the hall was crowded to the door.
A peddler stood near the entrance, quite
three tubes of razors he sold that night;
Each coon bought one, with a grateful smile.
They'd rather be dead than out of style.
    (Chorus)

Rather than ignoring White disapproval, Blacks embraced it, causing decades of shame and acceptance-seeking.

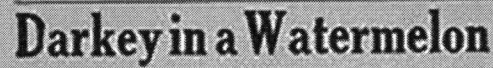

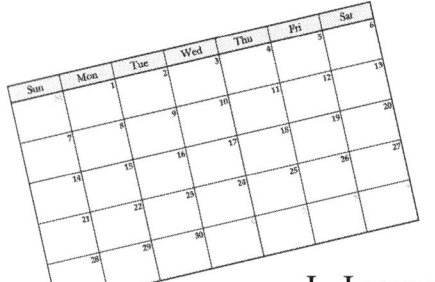

2020 too, was a Juneteenth Milestone

I. Larger Gallery

Circa 2020: Pandemic-related mandates restricting large public gatherings caused the downsizing or cancellation of an incalculable number of Juneteenth celebrations. Despite the contraction, public awareness of Juneteenth increased significantly due to a herculean clash of incompatible ideologies -- intrinsic tactlessness and insensitivity vs. tradition and deep seated pride. The latter contingent won.

Long before 2020, local Juneteenth celebrations were held in all fifty states, D.C., and several other nations. Even so, an enormous surge of public enlightenment began nine days before Juneteenth 2020, after the Trump presidential re-election campaign ignited a Juneteenth public relations firestorm.

Trump's opponents considered his "Make America Great Again" (MAGA) rallies to be political ova bearing racism and bigotry when fertilized with his rhetoric. In turn, scheduling a MAGA rally on Juneteenth was viewed by some as an intentionally blatant offense, intensified by its location - Tulsa, Oklahoma.

Shortly before the rally was announced, Tulsa had commemorated the 99th anniversary of its infamous Tulsa Race Massacre where highly prosperous African American community was destroyed.

News of Trump's Juneteenth rally quickly garnered massive negative attention. Normally, his campaign profited from controversy - invigorating his core supporters. Not so this time.

A multi-day barrage of news reports across all media platforms included explanations of Juneteenth's origin and its historic significance. The history-filled reports fueled public outrage and opposition to the campaign rally, especially among political fence sitters.

Instead of acknowledging a misstep, the White House falsely claimed to be unfamiliar with Juneteenth, despite having previously issued glowing press releases about the annual commemoration.

Public fury forced Trump's campaign to reschedule their rally. But by then, Juneteenth had garnered a national wave of attention no press release or standard news report could hope to match.

The increased notoriety was unquestionably expansive and noteworthy. But given the broad popularity Juneteenth enjoyed prior to 2020, an compelling argument can be made that the awareness groundswell was buoyed primarily by people indifferent to African American history and unlikely to commemorate emancipation.

214

II. Wider Slate

2020's second, less contentious, and more beneficial Juneteenth offering was an expanded cache of commemoration activities. Imaginations were challenged, but perseverance prevailed.

Since the celebration's origin in 1866, organizers have successfully surmounted numerous elimination-level conditions, including the Spanish Flu epidemic, Red Summer, World War I, the depression, and ironically, disdain from factions of the African American Civil Rights Movement. Contemporary organizers refusing to bow to Covid-19, successfully revived the fortitude of their predecessors, generating innovative activities that would not have been considered if not for the national lock down.

When cancellation became foreseeable, there were no examples of "socially distanced" holiday celebrations. For many celebrants, virtual commemorations were inconceivable as community assembly was considered one of Juneteenth's paramount and rudimentary assets.

Yet, for a majority of locations, especially upstart celebrations, virtual events were the only options, and so they happened.

Tenacious creativity birthed a wealth of virtual activities, which in turn, welcomed new participants. Best of all, the virtual activities were much less costly to produce, a significant bonus since organizers were unable to conduct their traditional fundraisers. Though many virtual activities were merely placeholders, some were designed to continue after Covid-related restrictions end.

III. Deeper Pockets

2020's third major contribution to Juneteenth was the unsolicited arrival of major corporate endorsements. Lured by the groundswell of public support, corporations were thirsty for photo opps. Unfortunately, most in-person celebrations had already been canceled. The few remaining ones were complete.

Without existing avenues to parade their support, corporations launched a haphazard oneupmanship spree - jumping on a crowded bandwagon with no driver. Universities that previously held minor Juneteenth celebrations - if any at all - closed in observance of the holiday.

Numerous companies did likewise, giving employees an unexpected holiday - a questionable benefit, since many were already working from home. Other corporations issued hastily assembled email campaigns and conducted special sales. At least one major bank (Chase Bank) placed a Juneteenth recognition statement on its automated teller machines.

The return of in-person celebrations in 2021 was expected to test the sincerity of the 2020 observances. Expectations were not high, given that the holiday was on a Saturday and the 2020 limelight had faded.

Such speculation proved to be wrong. Creation of the new national holiday delivered a bounty of credibility and attention that dwarfed the 2020 levels.

* * *

In hindsight, these three unplanned perks were excellent harbingers for Juneteenth 2021's legacy - the first official national celebration of emancipation.

P.S. Accuracy Matters

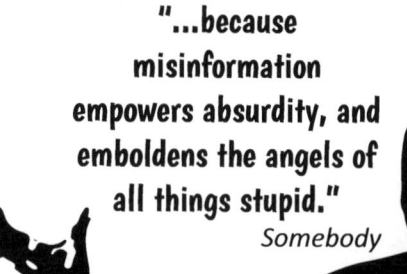

"...because misinformation empowers absurdity, and emboldens the angels of all things stupid."
Somebody

"Well!"

Think back to the three seemingly benign questions that prompted this study (page 9.) The pursuit of answers revealed many more questions of which one quandary remains: How are inaccuracies about events occurring over 150 years ago effectual today?

Contemporary civic turmoil suggest inaccuracy spawns poor judgment, causing strenuous confusion.

Consider this. Hiding an injury makes the injury unseen, not healed. Furthermore, corollaries resulting from the injury can be misidentified if their true origin is unknown. Then misdiagnoses induce false remedies.

Applying that theory to Juneteenth exposes distressing dilemmas. Here are two examples:

First, the idea that enslaved people in Texas would have been freed earlier had they known about the Emancipation Proclamation rejects the reality that they were someone else's property, governed like domesticated animals unable to make decisions regarding their own fate. More so, the fallacy ignores a concept often but incorrectly attributed to Sojourner Truth: some slaves didn't know they were slaves.

Second, failure to accept the dismal status of enslaved people grants undeserved gentility to slave owners. Example: Texas schoolbooks that claim slave owners voluntarily released slaves imply said owners possessed untapped compassion, civility, and humanity which General Order #3 released. Did they, really?

While harboring misinformation is awful, justifying it is worse.

An email exchange between the author of this

study and a Texas university librarian exemplifies how easy it is to discount African American history and values.

The university was contacted regarding their promotion of Juneteenth as the oldest continuous celebration of emancipation in the United States - an often repeated myth. The source was informed about Watch Night's beginning.

Below is the school's reply and the interpretation of that reply by a panel of African Americans assembled to review it. *(LR = Librarian's reply.)*

LR:	***Other people were already conducting vigils on that day.***
Panel:	'Europeans' were already conducting vigils on that day.
LR:	***While both dates likely hold significance for many that choose to commemorate the anniversary of the end of slavery...***
Panel:	while both dates are valued by Black people...
LR:	***Watch Night does have alternative meaning for several religious sects outside of this historical abolitionist context.***
Panel:	Other people don't associate Watch Night with emancipation.
LR:	***Meanwhile Juneteenth, though not yet recognized as a national holiday, holds the status as a state holiday in over 40 states."[214]***
Panel:	Forty groups of primarily White legislators have deemed Juneteenth to be worthy of recognition, thereby lifting its significance above the Black definition of Watch Night.

The reply is silent on how Europe's Watch Night is applicable to a comparison of Juneteenth and Watch Night, the freedom vigil. Also, the reply does not refute the belief that abolitionists and pockets of enslaved people held emancipation vigils on New Year's Eve, 1862. In fact, the source used to inject Europeans into the discussion reveals how enslaved people successfully held secret vigils in multiple states simultaneously. They co-opted an existing event.[219]

The authority to appraise the worth of either observance was forged by - and will forever rest in - the hands of freedmen and their descendants, unless said heirs give it away by passively accepting falsehoods and inaccuracies.

The "which came first" debate may appear petty, but as Juneteenth has become the day to celebrate slavery's end nationwide, failure to do so, correctly creates unintended hazards. Examples:

1) Claiming slavery ended on June 19, concurrently ignores Kentucky's refusal to outlaw slavery, and discounts the worth of all enslaved people there who were forced to wait until the 13th amendment passed.

2) Failure to acknowledge the presence of Black troops in Galveston disparages the thousands of Black veterans who witnessed history. By the way, Black troops who mutinied to avoid journeying to Texas were hanged by the Union Army for not trusting their White officers. They were villains in the 1800's, but heroes by today's standards.

Commemorating emancipation is an undertaking much too meaningful to denigrate. It should not cost truth. It should not be a fad. It must not be negotiated to placate anyone's discomfort. Most of all, laundering Juneteenth with erroneous or incomplete details is intolerable.

~ ~ ~

NOTE: The university web page that prompted this post script was removed soon after this discussion. Other organizations and schools promoting the same misstatement assert they do so solely because they found the claim on sites they deemed reputable. Some sources ambiguously describe Juneteenth as the oldest celebration "of its kind."

A Proclamation

Whereas, these words are a fundamental element
of Gordon Granger's General Order #3:
*"In accordance with a Proclamation
from the Executive of the United States,
all slaves are free."*

And whereas,
The Emancipation Proclamation does not
include those words, nor anything similar.

And whereas
President Abraham Lincoln never said
those words, nor anything similar.

Therefore,
the often repeated myth that Texas was last
to free slaves may plausibly be attributed
to the inaccuracy of
Major General Gordon Granger's
General Order #3.

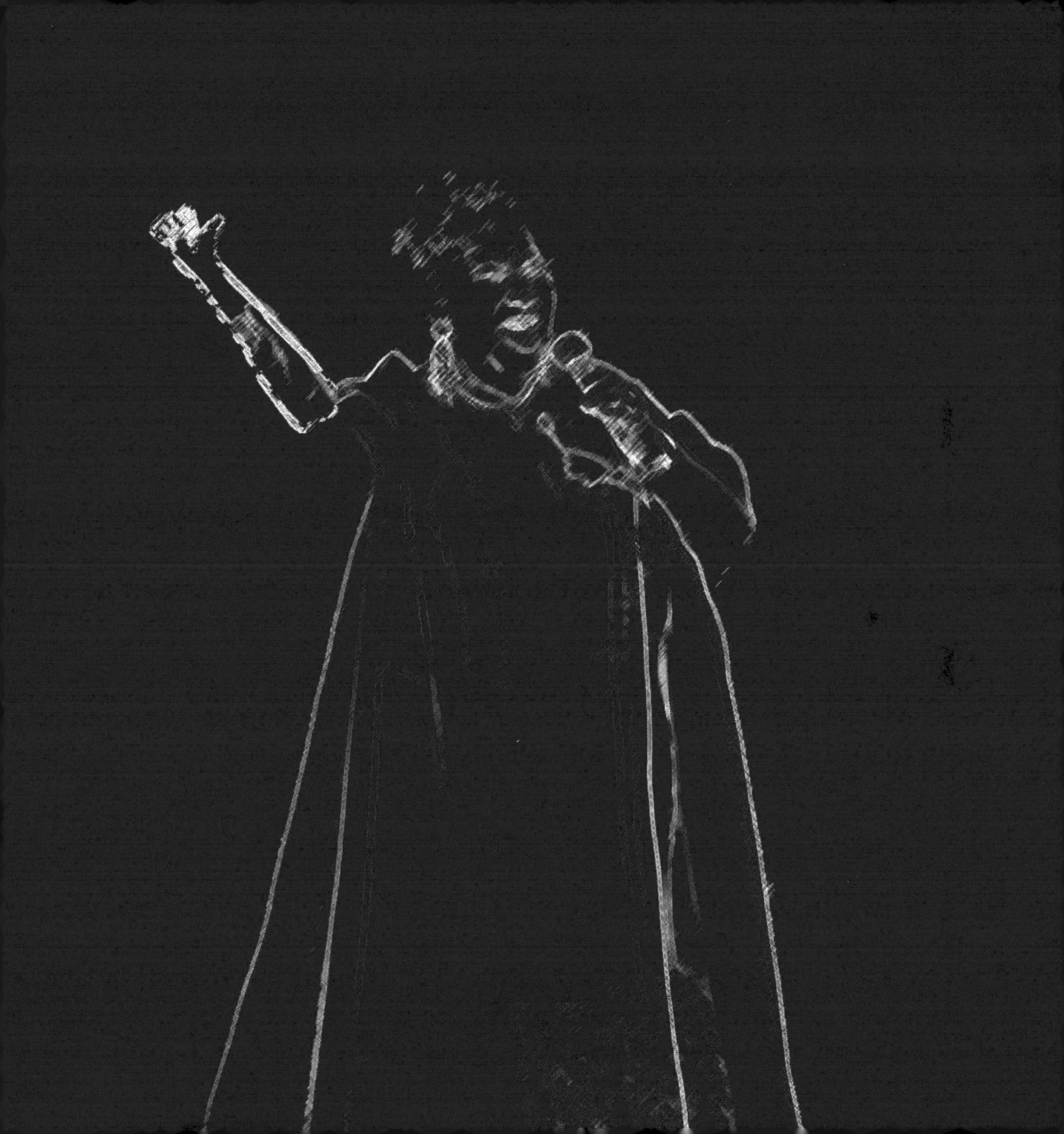

Bibliography

Web Abbreviations:

Chronicling = Chronicling America Historic American Newspapers. Library of Congress. https://chroniclingamerica.loc.gov/

Portal = Portal to Texas History. University of North Texas. https://texashistory.unt.edu/

Newspapers = Newspapers.com

The War [A]= United States. War Records Office, et al.. The War of the Rebellion: A Compilation of the Official Records of the Union and Confederate Armies. Washington: Govt. Print. Off., 18801901. Special Orders, No. 2. Series 1, Volume 48, Part 2 Correspondence. Chapter LX. Cornell University. https://hdl.handle.net/2027/coo.31924077723025

The War [B]= United States. War Records Office, et al.. The War of the Rebellion: A Compilation of the Official Records of the Union and Confederate Armies. Washington: Government Printing Office, - Series 1 Volume 46, Part 1, Reports: Section 1. Cornell University. https://hdl.handle.net/2027/coo.31924079575332

The War [C]= United States. War Records Office, et al.. The War of the Rebellion: A Compilation of the Official Records of the Union and Confederate Armies. Washington: Govt. Print. Off., Series 2: Volume 8: Cornell University. https://hdl.handle.net/2027/coo.31924079575233

NARA = National Archives and Records Administration microfilm publication M1912 (Washington, D.C.)

Access Dates:

On December 29, 2019, the web addresses listed in this bibliography were re-verified for accuracy and accessibility. All web sources without access dates were found to be still available and unchanged. One source was no longer accessible (#88). Another changed its content (#190). Both were available on the stated dates.

Access weblinks electronically at www.http//juneteenth.university. Under the "Learn Stuff" tab, click "Library".

1. "Major General Gordon Granger Arrived." *Flake's Tri-Weekly Bulletin* (Galveston, TX) 20 June 1865: pp 2, col 1. Web: Portal. https://texashistory.unt.edu/ark:/67531/metapth178695/m1/2/

2. "Galveston Formally Taken Possession of by the U.S. Naval Forces." *Flake's Tri-Weekly Bulletin*. (Galveston, TX) 8 June 1865, pp 1. Web: Portal. https://texashistory.unt.edu/ark:/67531/metapth178690/

3. "Juneteenth–The Day Slavery was Abolished in Texas." *Texas General Land Office Save Texas History Program*. 16 June 2016. Web: https://medium.com/save-texas-history/juneteenth-the-day-slavery-was-abolished-in-texas-7ec6d50868fc

4. Lee, George. "Special Orders, No. 2." *The War* [A], pp 1093. Web: https://babel.hathitrust.org/cgi/pt?id=coo.31924077723025&view=1up&seq=1095

5. "Human Trafficking What We Investigate. FBI. U.S. Department of Justice," Web: https://www.fbi.gov/investigate/civil-rights/human-trafficking

6. "DeMorse, Charles. The Amnesty and the Emancipation Proclamation." *The Standard* (Clarksville, TX) pp 1. 24 June 1865. Web: Portal. https://texashistory.unt.edu/ark:/67531/metapth234396/m1/2/

7. DC Compensated Emancipation Act, 16 April 1862; Record Group 11; General Records of the United States Government; National Archives. Web. United States Senate. Art and History. The Civil War: The Senate's Story. https://www.senate.gov/artandhistory/history/common/civil_war/DCEmancipationAct_FeaturedDoc.htm

8. "Compensated Emancipation." *Tri-weekly Telegraph* (Houston, TX) pp 3. Dec. 29, 1862. Web. Portal. https://texashistory.unt.edu/ark:/67531/metapth236466/m1/3/

9. Dueholm, James A. "A Bill of Lading Delivers the Goods: The Constitutionality and Effect of the Emancipation Proclamation." *Journal of the Abraham Lincoln Association*, Vol. 31, No. 1, 2010: pp 22–38. Web:

www.jstor.org/stable/25701807

10. "Washington County, July 12, '65." *Flake's Weekly Bulletin* (Galveston, TX) pp 2. 19 July 1865. Web: Portal. https://texashistory.unt.edu/ark:/67531/metapth178696/m1/2

11. Hamilton, A.J. "Proclamation." *Flake's Daily Bulletin* (Galveston, TX) pp 2. 26 July 1865. Web: Portal. https://texashistory.unt.edu/ark:/67531/metapth178527/m1/2/

12. "Govenor Hamilton's Houston Speech." *Flake's Weekly Bulletin* (Galveston, TX) pp 4. 9 Aug 1865. Web: Portal. https://texashistory.unt.edu/ark:/67531/metapth178699/m1/4/

13. "The Austin Intelligencia." *Houston Tri-Weekly Telegraph*, pp 2. 6 Sept 1865. Web: Portal. https://texashistory.unt.edu/ark:/67531/metapth235167/

14. "Courtney, Grimes County. June 28th, 1865." *Houston Tri-Weekly Bulletin*, pp 4. 10 July 1865. Web: Portal. https://texashistory.unt.edu/ark:/67531/metapth232754/m1/4/

15. Nieman, Donald G. "African Americans and the Meaning of Freedom: Washington County, Texas as a Case Study, 1865-1886 - Freedom: Politics." Illinois Institute of Technology Chicago-Kent College of Law. 541 (1994): pp 547. Web: https://scholarship.kentlaw.iit.edu/cgi/viewcontent.cgi?article=2970&context=cklawreview

16. Spivack, Miranda S. "The Not-Quite-Free State: Maryland Dragged its Feet on Emancipation During Civil War." *The Washington Post*. 13 Sept. 2013. Web: https://www.washingtonpost.com/local/md-politics/the-not-quite-free-state-maryland-dragged-its-feet-on-emancipation-during-civil-war/2013/09/13/a34d35de-fec7-11e2-bd97-676ec24f1f3f_story.html

17. "Missouri State Archives Guide to African American History." Office of the Secretary of State. Web: Missouri Digital Heritage. https://www.sos.mo.gov/archives/resources/africanamerican/guide/image005c

18. "The House Joint Resolution proposing the 13th Amendment to the Constitution." 31 Jan 1865; Enrolled Acts and Resolutions of Congress, 1789-1999; General Records of the United States Government; Record Group 11; National Archives. Web: https://www.ourdocuments.gov/doc.php?flash=false&doc=40

19. "Proclamation of the Secretary of State Announcing the Ratification of the Thirteenth Amendment to the Constitution", 18 Dec. 1865; General Records of the United States Government; Record Group 11; National Archives. Web: https://www.archives.gov/historical-docs/todays-doc/index.html?dod-date=1218

20. "Records of the Alabama constitutional convention of 1865." Alabama Department of Archives and History. pp 11-12. Web: http://digital.archives.alabama.gov/cdm/ref/collection/legislature/id/213539

21. "Juneteenth and Emancipation Day in Florida." 19 June 2015. Florida Memory State Library and Archives of Florida. Web: The Florida Memory Blog. http://www.floridamemory.com/blog/2015/06/19/juneteenth-and-emancipation-day-in-florida/

22. Johnson, Alfred S. "Guam." *The Cyclopedic Review of Current History*. Vol 10. 1900. pp 54. Current History Company (Boston, MA). Web: Wayback Machine. https://archive.org/details/cyclopedicreview10bostuoft/Pg/54

23. "Polly Strong's Slavery Case." Indiana Historical Bureau. Web: https://www.in.gov/history/markers/4267.htm

24. "When Did Slavery End in New York State?." New York Historical Society Museum and Library. http://www.nyhistory.org/community/slavery-end-new-york-state

25. "Minnesota Constitution 1858." Office of the Minnesota Secretary of State Steve Simon. https://www.sos.state.mn.us/about-minnesota/minnesota-government/minnesota-constitution-1858/

26. "Covenant Commonwealth of the Northern Mariana Islands Law Revision Commission," https://cnmilaw.org/cnmicovenant.html

27. Meyerhoff, Al. "The Law, Slaves and Jack Abramoff." 5/25/2011. *Huffpost*. https://www.huffingtonpost.com/al-meyerhoff/the-law-slaves-and-jack-a_b_41185.html

28. Lincoln, Abraham. "Abraham Lincoln papers." Series 2. General Correspondence. 1858 to 1864: Abraham Lincoln to Horace Greeley, Friday, Clipping from 23 Aug. 1862 Daily National Intelligencer, Washington, D.C. 1862. Manuscript/Mixed Material. Web: Library of Congress, www.loc.gov/item/mal4233400/

29. "The Immediate Effects of the Emancipation

Proclamation." Historical Society of Pennsylvania. https://hsp.org/education/unit-plans/the-immediate-effects-of-the-emancipation-proclamation

30. Greely, A. W. "The Military-Telegraph Service." *Signal Corps Association.* Web: http://www.civilwarsignals.org/pages/tele/telegreely/telegreely.html

31. Franklin, John H. "The Emancipation Proclamation An Act of Justice." *Prologue Magazine.* Summer 1993. National Archives. Web: 7 Dec. 2017. https://www.archives.gov/publications/prologue/1993/summer/emancipation-proclamation.html

32. Krystyniak, F., "Houston, The Emancipator." Sam Houston State University. Web: http://www.shsu.edu/today@sam/samhouston/HouEman.html

33. Downs, G. "The Hidden History of Juneteenth." *Talking Points Memo.* 18 June 2015. https://talkingpointsmemo.com/cafe/hidden-history-of-juneteenth

34. Gardiner, Richard. "The Last Battlefield of the Civil War and Its Preservation." *The Journal of America's Military Past*, Vol. 38, No 2. (2013): pp 9. Council of America's Military Past. Manassas, VA.

35. Hunt, Jeffery W., "The Last Battle of the Civil War: Palmetto Ranch". *Shirley Caldwell Texas Heritage Series.* July 2002. University of Texas Press. Austin, TX.

36. "Slaves." *The Constitution of the State of Texas as Amended in 1861.* pp 35. Article VIII. Sec. 2. Web: https://babel.hathitrust.org/cgi/pt?id=dul1.ark:/13960/t6j10vv9n&view=1up&seq=36

37. P. H. Sheridan to Gordon Granger, 13 June 1865, in *The War* [A], pp 866. Web: https://babel.hathitrust.org/cgi/pt?id=coo.31924077723025&view=1up&seq=868

38. "General Orders No. 3." *The War* [A]. pp 929. Web: https://babel.hathitrust.org/cgi/pt?id=coo.31924077723025&view=1up&seq=931

39. National Park Service, "Ashton Villa." *South and West Texas, A National Register of Historic Places Travel Itinerary* Web: https://www.nps.gov/nr/travel/tx/tx49.htm

40. Durham, J., Galveston Historical Foundation, 30 April 2018, email to author.

41. Cotham, Ed. "Juneteenth: Four Myths and One Great Truth." *The Daily News* (Galveston Co.) 18 June 2014. https://www.galvnews.com/opinion/guest_columns/article_73af8892-f75d-11e3-8626-001a4bcf6878.html

42. "General Orders, No 1." *The War* [A], pp 910. https://babel.hathitrust.org/cgi/pt?id=coo.31924077723025&view=1up&seq=912

43. "By Telegraph: Galveston, June 18, 3 PM." *Tri-Weekly Telegraph* (Houston, TX) pp 4. 19 June 1865. Web: Portal. https://texashistory.unt.edu/ark:/67531/metapth235157/m1/4/

44. "By Telegraph, Galveston June 16th." *Houston Tri-Weekly Telegraph*, pp 3. 19 June 1865. Web: Portal. https://texashistory.unt.edu/ark:/67531/metapth235157/m1/3/

45. "Arrival of the Army Transport Corinthian from Mobile." *Flake's Tri-Weekly Bulletin* (Galveston, TX). 17 June 1865, pp 2. Web: Portal. https://texashistory.unt.edu/ark:/67531/metapth178694/m1/2/

46. "Letter from Galveston." *Houston Tri-Weekly Telegraph.* 21 June 1965, pp 2. Web: https://texashistory.unt.edu/ark:/67531/metapth235158/m1/2/

47. "Telegraphic News - General Granger Assumes Command in Texas." *Evening Star* (Washington, DC) 23 June 1865, pp 1. Web: Chronicling. https://chroniclingamerica.loc.gov/lccn/sn83045462/1865-06-23/ed-1/seq-1/

48. "New Orleans, June 17." *Daily Davenport Democrat* (Davenport, IA). 20 June 1865, pp 4. Web: Chronicling. https://chroniclingamerica.loc.gov/lccn/sn83045646/1865-06-20/ed-1/seq-4/

49. "Troops Going to Texas." *The Highland Weekly News.* (Highland County, OH) 22 June 1865, pp 2. Web: Chronicling. https://chroniclingamerica.loc.gov/lccn/sn85038158/1865-06-22/ed-1/seq-2/

50. "Later from N. Orleans and Mobile." *Flakes' Tri-Weekly Bulletin.* (Galveston, TX) 20 June 1865, pp 1. Web: Portal. https://texashistory.unt.edu/ark:/67531metapth178695/m1/1/

51. "By Telegraph: Galveston, June 18, 1865." *Houston Tri-Weekly Telegraph.* 19 June 1865, pp 4. Portal. https://texashistory.unt.edu/ark:/67531/metapth235157/m1/4/

52. Stanton, Edwin, "The Blockade Ended." *The Norfolk Post* (Norfolk, VA), 26 June 1865, pp 2, col 5.

53. G. Granger to P. H. Sheridan, 19 June 1865 in *The War* [A], pp 927. Web: https://babel.hathitrust.org/cgi/pt?id=coo.31924077723025&view=1up&seq=929
54. W. W. Woodard to R. C. Shannon, 27 July 1865 in *The War* [A], pp 1142. Web: https://babel.hathitrust.org/cgi/pt?id=coo.31924077723025&view=1up&seq=1144
55. "By Telegraph - Galveston June 19." *Houston Tri-Weekly Telegraph*. 21 July 1865. pp 2. Web: Portal. https://texashistory.unt.edu/ark:/67531/metapth235158/m1/2/
56. F. W. Emery to F. W. Moore, 19, June 1865, in *The War* [A], pp 931. https://babel.hathitrust.org/cgi/pt?id=coo.31924077723025&view=1up&seq=933
57. "Yesterday morning...," *Houston Tri-Weekly Telegraph*. June 21, 1865." pp 4, Col 3. Web: Portal. https://texashistory.unt.edu/ark:/67531/metapth235158/m1/4/
58. "Sheridan Moving into Texas." *Daily Ohio Statesman*. June 20, 1865, pp 3. Web: Chronicling America. https://chroniclingamerica.loc.gov/lccn/sn84028645/1865-06-20/ed-1/seq-3/
59. "Late News." *Spirit of Democracy* (Woodsville, OH) June 28, 1865. pp 2. Col 5. Web: Chronicling America. https://chroniclingamerica.loc.gov/lccn/sn85038115/1865-06-28/ed-1/seq-2/
60. "By Telegraph from New Orleans." *Wheeling Daily Intelligencer*. Wheeling, WV. pp 5, col 6. 20 June 1865. Web: Newspaper Archive www.newspaperarchive.com/us/west-virginia/wheeling/wheeling-daily-intelligencer/1865/06-20/page-5
61. "Planters and Freedmen." *Houston Tri-Weekly Telegraph*. 16 June 1865. pp 4, Col 3. Web: Portal. https://texashistory.unt.edu/ark:/67531/metapth235156/m1/4/
62. "It seems to be settled policy." *Houston Tri-Weekly Telegraph*. June 7 pp 4. Col. 1. Web: Portal. https://texashistory.unt.edu/ark:/67531/metapth235152/m1/4/
63. Johnston, Theodore. "Near Courtney, Grimes County." *The Houston Tri-Weekly Telegraph*, June 30, 1865. pp 2, Col 5. Web: Portal. https://texashistory.unt.edu/ark:/67531/metapth232750/m1/2/
64. "The Lawlessness and Absolute Robbery." *Houston Tri-Weekly Telegraph*. 15 June 1865. pp 2, Col 1. Web. Portal. https://texashistory.unt.edu/ark:/67531/metapth235156/m1/2/
67. Conner, Robert. "General Gordon Granger: the savior of Chickamauga and the man behind Juneteenth." Havertown : Casemate, 2013.
66. Cullum, George. "Gordon Granger." *Biographical Register of the Officers and Graduates of the U.S. Military Academy at West Point*, N.Y. pp 237. Boston : Houghton, Mifflin, 1891 https://babel.hathitrust.org/cgi/pt?id=coo.31924092703937&view=1up&seq=245
67. Hunt, W. "Battle of Palmito Ranch." Texas State Historical Association. 15 June 2010. Web: https://tshaonline.org/handbook/online/articles/qfp01
68. National Park Service, *62nd Regiment, United States Colored Infantry* Web: The Civil War, Battle Unit Details https://www.nps.gov/civilwar/search-battle-units-detail.htm?battleUnitCode=UUS0062RI00C
69. Redkey, Edwin S. (1992) *"A Grand Army of Black Men – Letters from African-American Soldiers in the Union Army, 1861-1865."* Cambridge University Press. New York. pp 278.
70. "Weitzel Arrives with Troops in Galveston." *Flake's Tri-Weekly Bulletin* (Galveston, TX). 20 June 1865. pp 2 col. 1. Web: Portal. https://texashistory.unt.edu/ark:/67531/metapth178695/m1/2/
71. B. W. Gray to Herron, 22, June 1865, in *The War* [A], pp 968. https://babel.hathitrust.org/cgi/pt?id=coo.31924077723025&view=1up&seq=970
72. Grant to Sheridan, 17 May 1865, in *The War* [A] pp 476. https://babel.hathitrust.org/cgi/pt?id=coo.31924077723025&view=1up&seq=478
73. Gordon Granger to R. H. Jackson, 8 June 1865, in *The War* [A], pp 821. https://babel.hathitrust.org/cgi/pt?id=coo.31924077723025&view=1up&seq=821
74. "From Washington." *Burlington Free Press*, June 30, 1865. Burlington, Vt., pp 4, Col 1. Web: Chronicling. https://chroniclingamerica.loc.gov/lccn/sn84023127/1865-06-30/ed-1/seq-4/
75. "Highly Important – Mutiny Among the Colored Troops – They do not Want to go to Texas." *The Spirit of Democracy*, Woodsville, Ohio. 28 June 1865 pp 2. Col 3. Web: Chronicling. https://chroniclingamerica.

76. Miller, Edward A. Jr. *The Black Civil War Soldiers of Illinois: The Story of the Twenty-Ninth U. S. Colored Infantry* University of South Carolina Press. Columbia, South Carolina. 1927. pp 153 - 157
77. "Third Brigade, Second Division *The War* [B]. pp 143. Web: Chapter LVIII. The Richmond Campaign. https://babel.hathitrust.org/cgi/pt?id=coo.31924079575332&view=1up&seq=165
78. "Marshall, T.B. *History of the Eighty-Third Ohio Volunteer Infantry*. (1912) Cincinnati: Eighty-Third Ohio Volunteer Infantry Association, pp 170 Internet Archive. Web. https://ia802606.us.archive.org/11/items/historyofeightyt00marsh/historyofeightyt00marsh.pdf
79. 28th Regiment, United States Colored Infantry The Civil War, Battle Unit Details, United States Colored Troops, National Parks Service. https://www.nps.gov/civilwar/search-battle-units-detail.htm?battleUnitCode=UUS0028RI00C
80. Miller, Edward A. Jr. *The Black Civil War Soldiers of Illinois: The Story of the Twenty-Ninth U.S Colored Infantry* University of South Carolina Press. Columbia, South Carolina. 1927. pp 154
81. "Civil War Colored Troops Units with New York Soldiers or Officers." New York State Military Museum and Veterans Research Center. New York State Division of Military and Naval Affairs: Military History Web: March 19, 2008. https://dmna.ny.gov/historic/reghist/civil/other/coloredTroops/coloredTroopsMain.htm#31stInf
82. "By Friday's Mail," The Weekly State Gazette. (Austin, TX) 28 June 1865. pp 1, Col 1. Web: Portal. https://texashistory.unt.edu/ark:/67531/metapth181604/m1/1/
83. *General Laws of the Tenth Legislature (called session) with the Provisional and Permanent Constitutions of the Confederate States* Chapter V. pp 4. 1864. Houston, Texas: Galveston News Book and Job Office. Web: Wayback Machine. https://archive.org/details/generallawsoften1864texa/Pg/4
84. "City Matters," *Flake's Daily Bulletin* (Galveston, TX). 22 June 1865. pp 2, Col 1. Web: Portal. https://texashistory.unt.edu/ark:/67531/metapth178499/m1/2/
85. Granger, Gordon. Circular. Office of Provost Marshall General 28 June 1865. Galveston Daily News, pp 1, col 5. 7 July 1865 Web: Newspaper Archive. www.newspaperarchive.com/us/texas/galveston-daily-news/1865/07-07
86. Chism, Jonathan Langston. *Watch Night Cultural Resources* The African American Lectionary. 31 Dec. 2010. Web: http://www.theafricanamericanlectionary.org/PopupCulturalAid.asp?LRID=184
87. "Emancipation Celebration," The Flakes Daily Bulletin. 2 January 1866. p. 5, col 1. Web: Newspaper Archive. www.newspaperarchive.com/us/texas/galveston/galveston-flakes-daily-bulletin/1866/01-02/page-5
88. "History of the Mother Church of Texas," Reedy Chapel African Methodist Episcopal Church. Web: http://reedychapel.com/about-us/history/ Accessed July 1, 2018. NOTE: This web page was accessed prior to the second edition of Juneteenth 101. It was not accessible on publication date of the 3rd edition.
89. "Nelson, R. Speech of the Hon. Richard Nelson," *The Representative* (Galveston, TX). 26 June 1871. pp 3. Web: Portal. https://texashistory.unt.edu/ark:/67531/metapth203066/m1/3/
90. "Freedom Day," *The Representative* (Galveston, TX). 26 June 1871. pg. 2, col 1. Web: https://texashistory.unt.edu/ark:/67531/metapth203066/m1/2/
91. Haber, E. *The History of Juneteenth* Historic Oakland Foundation. June 11, 2018. Web: https://www.oaklandcemetery.com/the-history-of-juneteenth/
92. "Voting Rights, the Poll Tax," *Dallas Public Library*. (2010). https://dallaslibrary2.org/mbutts/assets/lessons/L9-voting+rights/Marion%20Butts%20-%20Voting%20Rights(PPT).pdf Accessed 20 July 2018.
93. Weeks, O. Douglas. "Election Laws," *Handbook of Texas Online*, July 25, 2016. Texas State Historical Foundation. http://www.tshaonline.org/handbook/online/articles/wde01
94. Acosta, Teresa P. "Juneteenth," *Handbook of Texas Online*. Texas State Historical Association. Web: https://tshaonline.org/handbook/online/articles/lkj01
95. Edwards, Al "Address by Representative Al Edwards,"

House Journal: 66th Legislature. Regular Session. 28 May 1979. pp 4951. Legislative Reference Library of Texas. https://lrl.texas.gov/scanned/Housejournals/66/05281979_83_4843.pdf

96. Alabama Secretary of State, *SJR157 Recognizing the Celebration of Juneteenth Day.* Web: http://arc-sos.state.al.us/PAC/SOSACPDF.001/A0008917.PDF

97. Alaska State Legislature, *SCS HB 100(STA): An Act establishing the third Saturday of each June as Juneteenth Day.* Web: http://www.legis.state.ak.us/basis/Bill/Text/22?Hsid=HB0100B

98. Arizona State Legislature, *1-315. Juneteenth Day* Web: https://www.azleg.gov/ars/1/00315.htm

99. Arkansas State Legislature, *SB263 - An Act to Establish the Third Saturday in June as Juneteenth Independence Day* Web: http://www.arkleg.state.ar.us/assembly/2005/R/Acts/Act2101.pdf

100. California Legislative Information, *Chapter 7. Holidays. Code 6719* Web: http://leginfo.legislature.ca.gov/faces/codes_displaySection.xhtml?lawCode=GOV&sectionNum=6719

101. Colorado General Assembly, *House Joint Resolution 04-1027* Web: http://www.leg.state.co.us/Clics2004a/csl.nsf/fsbillcont3/893DFCA6C29C630487256DB9006DE5CB?Open&file=HJR1027_enr.pdf

102. Connecticut General Assembly. "*Chapter 164 Educational Opportunities.* Web: https://www.cga.ct.gov/current/pub/chap_164.htm#TOC

103. State of Delaware, "*Chapter 269 formerly Senate Bill No. 282.*" Web: https://delcode.delaware.gov/sessionlaws/ga140/chp269.shtml

104. Council of the District of Columbia, *A Resolution 15-109* Web: http://lims.dccouncil.us/Download/5262/PR15-0160-ENROLLMENT.pdf

105. Florida Department of State, *General Acts Resolutions and Memorials.* pp 2434. Web: http://edocs.dlis.state.fl.us/fldocs/leg/actsflorida/1991/1991V1Pt3.pdf

106. Georgia General Assembly, *2011-2012 Regular Session - SR 164 Juneteenth Celebration Day.* Web: http://www.legis.ga.gov/Legislation/en-US/display/20112012/SR/164

107. Idaho Legislature, *2001 Legislature Senate Concurrent Resolution no. 101.* Web: https://legislature.idaho.gov/sessioninfo/2001/legislation/SCR101/

108. Illinois General Assembly, *Illinois Compiled Statutes.* Web: http://www.ilga.gov/legislation/ilcs/ilcs3.asp?ActID=134&ChapterID=2

109. Indiana General Assembly, *House Concurrent Resolution 0038* Web: http://archive.iga.in.gov/2010/bills/PDF/HRESP/HC0038.pdf

110. Iowa Legislature, *Chapter 1105 Juneteenth National Freedom Day S.F. 2273.* Web: https://www.legis.iowa.gov/docs/publications/iactc/79.2/CH1105.pdf

111. Kansas Senate, *Senate Resolution No. 1860* Journal of the Senate. pp 262. Web: http://www.kansas.gov/government/legislative/journals/2007/sj0402.pdf

112. Kentucky General Legislature, *2.147 Juneteenth National Freedom Day* Web: https://apps.legislature.ky.gov/law/statutes/statute.aspx?id=54

113. Louisiana State Legislature, *House bill 1672* Web: http://www.legis.la.gov/legis/ViewDocumoteent.aspx?d=818716

114. Maine State Legislature, *An Act To Establish Juneteenth Independence Day.* Web: http://legislature.maine.gov/legis/bills/bills_125th/chapters/PUBLIC53.asp

115. Maryland General Assembly. *HB0549 CH0602.* Web: http://mgaleg.maryland.gov/mgawebsite/Legislation/Details/hb0549?ys=2014RS&search=True

116. Commonwealth of Massachusetts, *An Act Relative to the Annual Observance of Juneteenth Independence Day.* Web: https://malegislature.gov/Laws/SessionLaws/Acts/2007/Chapter51

117. Michigan Legislature, *Juneteenth National Freedom Day; Sojourner Truth Day (Excerpt).* Web: http://www.legislature.mi.gov/(S(qdaons3lpesj5gwf3sbw2ucb))/mileg.aspx?page=getObject&objectName=mcl-435-361&highlight=Juneteenth

118. Minnesota Legislature, *Minnesota Session Laws - 1996.* Regular Session Sec. 10. [10.55] Web: https://www.revisor.mn.gov/laws/1996/0/390/

119. Mississippi Legislature, *Senate Concurrent Resolution 605.* Web: http://billstatus.ls.state.ms.us/2010/pdf/history/SC/SC0605.xml

120. State of Missouri, "*9.161. Emancipation Day Established,*" Web: http://revisor.mo.gov/main/OneSection.aspx?section=9.161
121. Montana Legislature, *Provide for Montana Calendar Observance of Juneteenth.* Web: http://laws.leg.mt.gov/legprd/LAW0203W$BSRV.ActionQuery?P_SESS=20171&P_BLTP_BILL_TYP_CD=&P_BILL_NO=&P_BILL_DFT_NO=&P_CHPT_NO=291&Z_ACTION=Find&P_ENTY_ID_SEQ2=&P_SBJT_SBJ_CD=&P_ENTY_ID_SEQ=
122. Nebraska Legislature, *One Hundred First Legislature First Session Legislative Resolution 75.* Web: https://nebraskalegislature.gov/FloorDocs/101/PDF/Intro/LR75.pdf
123. Nevada Legislature, *Chapter 29 2011 Statutes of Nevada.* pp 128. Web: https://www.leg.state.nv.us/Statutes/76th2011/Stats201102.html#Stats201102Pg128
124. General Court of New Hampshire, *Chapter 95 SB 174 - Final Version* Web: http://gencourt.state.nh.us/bill_Status/billText.aspx?sy=2019&id=1019&txtFormat=html
125. New Jersey Legislature, *36:2-80 Juneteenth Independence Day Designated.* Web: https://lis.njleg.state.nj.us/nxt/gateway.dll?f=templates&fn=default.htm&vid=Publish:10.1048/Enu
126. New Mexico Compilation Commission, *Laws 2006 Chapter 68.* Web: https://laws.nmonesource.com/w/nmos/Laws-2006#!fragment/zoupio-_Toc970034/BQCwhgziBcwMYgK4DsDWszIQewE4BUBTADwBdoAvbRABwEtsBaAfX2zgE4B2ABh4GYALAEoANMmylCEAIqJCuAJ7QA5CtERCYXAjkLlajVp0gAynlIAhZQCUAogBk7ANQCCAOQDCd0aTAAjaFJ2YWEgA
127. New York State Assembly, *Bill No. S01519* Web: https://nyassembly.gov/leg/?default_fld=&leg_video=&bn=S01519&term=2003&Summary=Y&Actions=Y&Text=Y
128. North Carolina General Assembly, *An Act Recognizing Juneteenth National Freedom Day in North Carolina.* Web: https://www.ncleg.net/Sessions/2007/Bills/House/PDF/H1607v4.pdf
129. "5.2247 Juneteenth National Freedom Day," *Lawriter Ohio Laws and Rules.* Web: http://codes.ohio.gov/orc/gp5.2247
130. "25-82.4," University of Oklahoma College of Law. Web: http://oklegal.onenet.net/oklegal-cgi/get_statute?99/Title.25/25-82.4.html
131. Oregon State Legislature, *71st Oregon Legislative Assembly--2001 Regular Session* Web: https://www.oregonlegislature.gov/bills_laws/archivebills/2001_ESJR31.pdf
132. Pennsylvania General Assembly, *June 19 as Juneteenth National Freedom Day - Designation and Holiday Observance.* Web: https://www.legis.state.pa.us/cfdocs/legis/li/uconsCheck.cfm?yr=2019&sessInd=0&act=9
133. State of Rhode Island General Assembly, *2013 -- S 0169.* Web: http://webserver.rilin.state.ri.us/billtext13/senatetext13/s0169.htm
134. South Carolina Legislature. *Session 117 - (2007-2008).* Web: https://www.scstatehouse.gov/billsearch.php?billnumbers=4731&session=117&summary=B
135. Tennessee General Assembly, *House Joint Resolution 170.* Web: http://www.capitol.tn.gov/Bills/105/Bill/HJR0170.pdf
136. "Edwards, Al. *A Bill to Be Enacted.* pp 30. Legislative Reference Library of Texas. Web: https://lrl.texas.gov/LASDOCS/66R/HB1016/HB1016_66R.pdf#Pg=30
137. Utah State Legislature, *H.B. 338 Juneteenth Holiday Observance* Web: https://le.utah.gov/~2016/bills/static/HB0338.html
138. Vermont General Assembly, *Establishing Juneteenth National Freedom Day.* Web: http://www.leg.state.vt.us/database/status/summary.cfm?Bill=H%2E0432&Session=2008
139. Virginia's Legislative Information System. "*House Resolution No. 56.* Web: http://lis.virginia.gov/cgi-bin/legp604.exe?071+ful+HR56ER
140. Washington State Legislature. *RCW 1.16.050* Web: https://app.leg.wa.gov/rcw/default.aspx?cite=1.16.050
141. West Virginia Legislature. *House Resolution No. 19* Web: http://www.wvlegislature.gov/Bill_Text_HTML/2008_SESSIONS/RS/Bills/hr19%20intr.htm

142. Wisconsin State Legislature, *2009 Wisconsin Act 91*. http://docs.legis.wisconsin.gov/2009/related/acts/ 91

143. State of Wyoming, *SF0098 - Juneteenth Holiday*. Web: https://www.wyoleg.gov/Legislation/2003/SF0098

144. A joint resolution amending title 36, United States Code, to designate June 19 as "Juneteenth Independence Day". S.J.Res.45, 112th Congress, 19 June 2012. Web: Library of Congress. https://www.congress.gov/bill/112th-congress/senate-joint-resolution/45/text

145. NARA, The House Joint Resolution proposing the 13th amendment to the Constitution, 31 Jan 1865; Enrolled Acts and Resolutions of Congress, 1789-1999; General Records of the United States Government; Record Group 11. Web: *Our Documents*. Web: https://www.ourdocuments.gov/doc.php?flash=false&doc=40

146. Harry Truman. "Proclamation 2824 — National Freedom Day," Truman Library Institute. Jan 25, 1949. Presidential Proclamations: National Freedom Day. Web: 1 Feb 2017. Web: https://www.trumanlibraryinstitute.org/presidential-proclamations-national-freedom-day/

147. "Origin of the Song," *Yale University Library*. Web: http://exhibits.library.yale.edu/exhibits/show/lift-every-voice/songs

148. Hall, R. "The story of the John Brown song 2017," *American Music*. Web: http://www.americanmusicpreservation.com/JohnBrownSong.htm

149. "Civil War Music: the Battle hymn of the Republic," *American Battlefield Trust*. Web: https://www.battlefields.org/learn/primary-sources/civil-war-music-battle-hymn-republic

150. "Manumission Anniversary," *Brenham Daily Banner*. (Brenham, TX). pp 4, col 2. Web: Portal. https://texashistory.unt.edu/ark:/67531/metapth484021/m1/4/

151. "House of Representatives," *Galveston Daily News*. pp 1, col 5. 20 June 1876. Web: Portal. https://texashistory.unt.edu/ark:/67531/metapth464501/m1/1

152. F. W. Emery to Thomas Carothers, June 19, 1865, in *The War*. [C] pp 659. https://babel.hathitrust.org/cgi/pt?id=coo.31924079575233&view=1up&seq=671

153. "Condensed News Items of Interest from Everywhere," *Mt. Pleasant Daily Times*, (Mt. Pleasant, TX). June 17, 1925, pp 4, col 3. Web: Portal. https://texashistory.unt.edu/ark:/67531/metapth785167/m1/4/

154. Twitty, M. "Terroir Noire: African American Foodways in Slavery, Texas," *Afroculinaria*. Feb. 4, 2011. Web: afroculinaria.com/2011/02/04/terror-noire-african-american-foodways-in-slavery-texas/

155. "Third Ward's Emancipation Park designated historic landmark," (2007, November 14). *Houston Chronicle*. Web: https://www.chron.com/news/article/Third-Ward-s-Emancipation-Park-designated-1531082.php

156. Fortin, Jacey; Alan Feuer (August 13, 2017). "The Statue at the Center of Charlottesville's Storm," *The New York Times*. Web: https://www.nytimes.com/2017/08/13/us/charlottesville-rally-protest-statue.html

157. Leanos, Raynaldo, Jr. "This underground railroad took slaves to freedom in Mexico," *Public Radio International: The World*. April 8, 2017. Web: https://theweek.com/articles/690709

158. "Letter exchange between William P. Clements and State Representative Clay Smothers regarding the declaration of Juneteenth as a state holiday," June 1979 University of Texas at Austin. Web: http://tx.clementspapers.org/clementstx/37880

159. Woolley, Brian. "Juneteenth, Texas, and Clay Smothers," *Dallas Times Herald*. 17 July 1979

160. Paul Burka and Richard West. "1977: The Ten Best and Ten Worst Legislators," *Texas Monthly*. July 1977. Web: https://www.texasmonthly.com/articles/the-ten-best-and-ten-worst-legislators-1977/

161. "Holidays, Anniversaries and Festivals, 1966 and 1967," *The Texas Almanac*. 1967. pp 29. Dallas, TX: A. H. Belo Corporation. Web: https://texashistory.unt.edu/ark:/67531/metapth113808/m1/31/

162. Hornsby, A. (2011, August 31) *Black America: a state-by-state historical encyclopedia*, vol. 1., p.307. Santa Barbara, CA: ABC-CLIO/Greenwood

163. "New Orleans, June 20," *The Houston Tri-Weekly Telegraph*. June 26, 1865. pp 2, col 5. Web: Portal. https://texashistory.unt.edu/ark:/67531/metapth235160/m1/2/

164. "An Echo of Slavery Times," *The Abilene Reporter.* Vol. 19, No. 2, Ed. 1. 12 Jan. 1900. Pg: 3, col 5. Web: Portal. https://texashistory.unt.edu/ark:/67531/metapth331142/m1/3
165. Representative Jackson-Lee of Texas speaking for Juneteenth on 20 June 2006. Congressional Record – House," Volume 152, Number 80. H4320. Web: Library of Congress. https://www.congress.gov/crec/2006/06/20/CREC-2006-06-20-pt1-PgH4320.pdf
166. Douglas Hales, "Evans, R. J.," *Handbook of Texas Online,* Web: http://www.tshaonline.org/handbook/online/articles/fev16
167. "Chap. 33," *The Texas Almanac* 1864. pp 15. Portal. Web https://texashistory.unt.edu/ark:/67531/metapth123770/m1/17/
168. "First Texas Flight." *Houston Informer,* 27 June 1925. pg. 1.
169. "New Texas African American Monument," Legislative Reference Library of Texas. (14 Feb. 2017). Web: http://www.lrl.state.tx.us/whatsNew/client/index.cfm/2017/2/14/New-Texas-African-American-Monument
170. Andrews, Helena. "Juneteenth Still Struggling for Legitimacy," *Politico.* 19 June 2008. Web: https://www.politico.com/story/2008/06/juneteenth-still-struggling-for-legitimacy-011208
171. Sam H. Pintrest re-post. Creator unknown. Acquired from Events. Web: https://www.pinterest.com/pin/407505466256111178/
172. Rockstroh, Liz. "UTSA celebrates freedom on Juneteenth," 14 June 2017. https://www.utsa.edu/today/2017/06/story/Juneteenth.html
173. *Denison Daily Cresset.* 19 June 1877. pp 1, col 1. Web: Portal. https://texashistory.unt.edu/ark:/67531/metapth524354/m1/4/
174. "5 facts about Juneteenth, which marks the last day of slavery," *Atlanta Journal-Constitution.* Web: https://www.ajc.com/lifestyles/facts-about-juneteenth-which-marks-the-last-day-slavery/7c6hmnKk2IRO7grn5bmsJI/#
175. "Juneteenth," Texas State Library and Archives Commission. 19 June 2019. Web: https://www.tsl.texas.gov/ref/abouttx/juneteenth.html
176. Godlewski, Nina. "Juneteenth 2018 Facts, Significance: History of the Holiday," *Newsweek.* 19 June 2018. Web: https://www.newsweek.com/juneteenth-holiday-history-984506
177. U.S. Dept. of State, 2014. "Juneteenth," PBS Learning Media. pp 94. Web: https://d43fweuh3sg51.cloudfront.net/media/media_files/juneteenth.pdf
178. Walker, Juliet. "The United States Flag," (1866-present) *Black History under the Six Flags of Texas: A Chronology.* 18 April 2003. University of Texas at Austin. Web: https://www.laits.utexas.edu/texasblackhistory/Chronology.html
179. "EmancipationUSA," Houston. Web: http://www.juneteenthfest.com (NOTE: click EmancipationUSA)
180. Blay, Zeba. "These Photos Show Why You Should Celebrate Juneteenth Black Voices," *Huff Post* 18 June 2016. Web: https://www.huffpost.com/entry/juneteenth-photos_n_57640f77e4b0853f8bf08d36
181. Gatschet, Albert S. "The Karankawa Nation after 1835; Its Decline and Extinction." *The Karankawa Indians, the Coast People of Texas.* Pp. 45-51. Archaeological and Ethnological Papers of the Peabody Museum. Vol. I. No. 2. 1891 Cambridge, Mass. Peabody Museum of American Archeology and Ethnology.
182. Gates, Henry Louis. "What is Juneteenth?." PBS. *The African Americans: Many Rivers to Cross with Henry Louis Gates, Jr.,* PBS. 2013. Web: https://www.pbs.org/wnet/african-americans-many-rivers-to-cross/history/what-is-juneteenth/
183. Ted Cruz, Twitter post, 19 June 2019 [12:43 PM] Web: https://twitter.com/SenTedCruz/status/1141401036839706625
184. Noire Histoir. Pinterest. Web: https://www.pinterest.com/pin/701998660637805886/
185. Dockterman, Eliana. "Here's How America Observes Juneteenth". *Time.* 20 June 2014. Web. https://time.com/2903414/how-america-observes-juneteenth/
186. Dingle, Joicelyn. "Explaining an Unsung Holiday." *Ebony* https://www.ebony.com/exclusive/juneteenth-

explaining-an-unsung-holiday/
187. Hunt, Jeremy. "Tuesday is Juneteenth – a holiday most Americans have never heard of, but need to know about." *Fox News*. Published 18 June 2018. https://www.foxnews.com/opinion/tuesday-is-juneteenth-a-holiday-most-americans-have-never-heard-of-but-need-to-know-about
188. "What You Should Know About Juneteenth." *CNN*. June 10, 2019. https://www.cnn.com/ampstories/us/what-you-should-know-about-juneteenth
189. Clapp, WM. H., "General Orders No. 20." 3 June 1865. *The War* [A]. Pg. 749. https://babel.hathitrust.org/cgi/pt?id=coo.31924077723025&view=1up&seq=751
190. Donald Trump, "Presidential Message on Juneteenth." The Whitehouse. (June 19, 2017). Web: https://www.govinfo.gov/content/pkg/DCPD-201700414/pdf/DCPD-201700414.pdf
191. A joint resolution commemorating "Juneteenth Independence Day,," - June 19, 1865, the day on which slavery finally came to an end in the United States, S. J. Res.11, 105th Congress, 23 Jan 1997. Web: Congress.Gov. https://www.congress.gov/bill/105th-congress/senate-joint-resolution/11
192. Library of Congress. Web. https://www.congress.gov/search?q=%7B%22source%22%3A%22legislation%22%2C%22search%22%3A%22juneteenth%22%7D&searchResultViewType=expanded
193. "State News." *Jasper News-Boy*, 4 June 1880. pp 2, col. 4. Web: Portal. https://texashistory.unt.edu/ark:/67531/metapth235469/m1/2/
194. "The colored population," *The Carbon News*, (Carbon, TX) July 1, 1909, pp 3, col. 1. Portal. https://texashistory.unt.edu/ark:/67531/metapth521959/m1/3/
195. "A Free Summer Normal." *Galveston Daily News*. 18 June 1892. pp 1, col 7. Web: Portal. https://texashistory.unt.edu/ark:/67531/metapth468049/m1/1/
196. Buenger, Walter L., Emilio Zamora. *Texas History*. Pearson Education, Inc. 2016. Boston, Massachusetts. Pg. 397, 399.
197. Anderson, Adrian N., Ralph Wooster. *Texas History*. McGraw-Hill Education 2016 Columbus, Ohio pp 434 and 715.
198. de la Teja, Jesus, V. Garnier, K/ Green, K. Harman, A. Shaw-Kelly. *Texas History*. 2016. Houghton Mifflin Harcourt. Orlando, Florida.
199. Glasrud, Bruce and Pitre, Merline. *Black Women in Texas History*. pp 42. Texas A&M University Press, College Station, Texas, 2008
200. Crouch, Barry. *The Freedman's Bureau and Black Texans*. University of Texas Press. Austin Texas. 1992
201. NARA, "Letter to Kirkman from A. Doubleday". 12 March 1867. Texas, *Freedmen's Bureau Field Office Records*, 1865-1870; Galveston. Roll 19, Letters sent, vol 1 (93), Jan 1867-June 1868. Images 28-30.
202. NARA, "Complaint from Jim Ward". Sept. 7, 1867. Centerville. Roll 14, *Register of complaints*, vol (89), July-Oct 1867. Image 8.
203. NARA, "Complaint from Ben Davis and Wife". 1867. Waco. Roll 27, *Registers of complaints*, vol 1 (169), July 1866-May 1868. Image 21.
204. NARA, "Complaint from Henrietta Gropbuk". 5 Oct. 1868. Houston. Roll 22, *Registers of complaints*, vol 1 (107), Dec 1865-Dec 1868. Image 21.
205. NARA, "Complaint from Edmond Whiting". n.d. Marlin. Roll 24, *Register of complaints*, vol (131), Jan-Oct 1867. Image 47.
206. NARA, "Complaint from Ann Hanhieser". 12 Oct 1868. Columbus. Roll 18, *Register of complaints*, vol (75), Apr 1867-Nov 1868. Image 63.
207. NARA, "Complaint from Frances Fitzgerald. Houston. Dec. 7, 1868. Roll 22, *Registers of Complaints*, vol. 1. Dec 1865-Dec 1868. Image 44.
208. NARA, "Complaint from Nelson Lee". Bastrop. Feb. 15, 1867. Roll 13, *Register of complaints*, vol (62), Feb 1867-Dec 1868. Image 4.
209. NARA, Complaint from Nelson Lee". July 1. 1867. Bastrop. Roll 13. *Register of complaints*, vol (62), Feb 1867-Dec 1868. Image 14.
210. NARA, Standard Work Agreement. County of Grimes, State of Texas. Wharton. Roll 28. *Records relating to complaints*, Mar 1867-Oct, 1868. Image 46.
211. Anna, Santa. "Mexico's Leaders Condemn Slavery in Texas." Feb. 16, 1836. Web: University of

Houston. http://www.digitalhistory.uh.edu/disp_textbook.cfm?smtid=3&psid=3657

212. Lack, Paul D., "The Texas revolutionary experience: a political and social history, 1835-1836". College Station, Texas A&M University Press, c1992.

213. "The Emily Morgan San Antonio - a DoubleTree by Hilton Hotel." *Historic Hotels Worldwide.* Web: https://www.historichotelsworldwide.com/hotels-resorts/the-emily-morgan-san-antonio-a-doubletree-by-hilton-hotel/?from=rezconsole

214. Stayton, Jenn. University of North Texas Library, 27 January 2020, email to author.

215. Paschal, George W. *Reports of Cases Argued and Decided in the Supreme Court of the State of Texas during part of Galveston session 1868, All of Tyler and Austin session 1868, and Galveston Session 1869.* Vol. XXXI. W.H. & O.H Morrison, Washington D.C. 1870. pp 732.

216. Collins, Samuel. Juneteenth Legacy Project. July 12, 2021. Email to author.

217. Gammel, Hans Peter Mareus Neilsen. "Decree No. 56." *The Laws of Texas, 1822-1897,* Volume 1, 1898; Austin, Texas. pp 213. Web: *Portal to Texas History.* https://texashistory.unt.edu/ark:/67531/metapth5872/m1/221/ Accessed 7/1/2021.

218. Bugbee, Lester G. "Slavery in Early Texas. I", *Political Science Quarterly,* Vol. 13, No. 3, Sept., 1898, (pp. 411-412.) Web: *The Academy of Political Science.* https://www.jstor.org/stable/2140047

219. "The Origin of Watch Night." Dec. 13, 2006. Web: *Snoops Media Group.* https://www.snopes.com/fact-check/watch-night/

220. Hawaii State Legislature. *31st Legislature 2021. SB939 HD2 CD1.* https:// www.capitol.hawaii.gov/measure_indiv.aspx?billtype=SB&billnumber=939&year=2021

221. North Dakota Legislative Branch. *Senate Bill No. 2232.* https://www.legis.nd.gov/assembly/67-2021/documents/21-0131-04000.pdf

Notes

70. Dates in this article do not agree with dates in other articles.
79. Approximate number of troops (896) was calculated by manually counting soldiers that mustered out after October 1, 1865 or died in Texas. Actual number may have been higher. Number does not include their White officers.
81. Estimated number of troops (823) was calculated by subtracting total losses (177) from a full regiment of 1,000 troops. Actual number may have been higher as some loses may have occured after troops reached Texas.

Website Access:

For easy access to websites visit juneteenth.university. Click "Library", then "Juneteenth 101 bibliography".

Photo Credits

Pgs. 11, 22, 24, 27, 28, 45, 48, 66, 70, 73, 82, 84, 86, 133, 137, 193	Depository: Library of Congress
Pg. 10	Juneteenth Music Festival Corporation Denver, Colorado Photographer: Kathryn Scott, Denver Post
Pg. 19	Caraway Photography Denton, Texas
Pg. 30	Journal Sentinel Milwaukee, Wisconsin
Pg. 35	Sarah Miller, photographer 2016 Juneteenth Gospel Explosion Tyler, Texas
Pg. 36	Atlanta Parade and Music Festival Atlanta, Georgia
Pg. 44	Philadelphia Juneteenth and Music Festival Philadelphia, Pennsylvania
Pg. 51	City of Grambling, Louisiana
Pg. 69	Juneteenth of Buffalo, Inc. Buffalo, New York
Pgs. 72, 74	Galveston Convention and Visitors Bureau.
Pg. 79	Galveston Historical Foundation.
Pg. 83	Valley of the Sun Juneteenth Celebration Phoenix, Arizona
Pg. 102	San Francisco Juneteenth Festival Committee San Francisco, California
Pg. 107	B. Hager / E Brumley, Las Vegas Review, 67Journal. Las Vegas, Nevada
Pg. 120	The Cooper Family Juneteenth Celebration San Diego, California
Pg. 131	Inland Northwest Juneteenth Coalition Spokane, Washington
Pg. 134	Memphis Juneteenth Festival http://www.memphisjuneteenth.com Leslie Thompson Photography Studio
Pg. 152	James Caldwell, Photographer African American Museum of Iowa Cedar Rapids, Iowa
Pg. 161	African Americans on Maui Association Maui, Hawaii

The author extends sincere appreciation to all photographs and celebration hosts who granted permission for photographs to be included in this work. The creator(s) of some photographs could not be determined. Any copyright infringement was not intended. If such occurred, a sincere apology is offered.

Cover and interior graphics by D. J. Norman-Cox

Index

Symbols

13th Amendment 7, 14, 17, 18, 25, 26, 27, 28, 131, 137, 149, 151, 160

A

Acosta, Teresa Palomo 114
African American History Memorial 154
African Methodist Episcopal Church 102
  Colored Church on Broadway 87, 102
  Reedy Chapel 87
Alabama 22, 28, 43, 86, 121, 150
  Birmingham 43
  Ft. Morgan 92
  Mobile 85
Alaska 28, 121
American Samoa 28
Arizona 28, 89, 121
  Phoenix 89
Arkansas 22, 28, 43, 121
  Pine Bluff 43
Atlanta, Georgia 36, 43, 191

B

Baldwin, William H. 95
Battle Hymn of the Republic 140
Battle of Galveston 80, 144
Battle of San Jacinto 209
Black Codes 187
Black National Anthem 139
Black Power 156
Black, William R. 212
Buffalo Soldiers 90, 91, 174

C

California
  San Diego 128
  San Francisco 108
Captain Renshaw 145
Cavenaugh, Alex Pearce Howard 105
Civil Rights Act of 1964 201
Civil Rights Act of 1968 201
Clapp, William H. 162
Clark, George W. 95, 99
Clements, Bill 150
Coleman, Bessie 153
Collins III, Samuel 135
Colorado 10, 28, 121, 154
Colored Church 87, 102
Colored People Day 200
Confederate 14, 61, 80, 88, 94, 144, 145, 147
  Heroes Day 147
Connecticut 28, 121
Cotham, Ed 81
Cruz, Ted 160

D

Delaware 21, 22, 28, 121, 151
Doubleday, Abner 204
Douglass, Frederick 149
Downs, Gregory 54
DuCongé, Oscar 201
Durham, Jami 81
Dwight, Ed 154

E

Ebony Magazine 161
Edwards, Al 120, 150, 153, 154
Ellis, Rodney 154
Emancipation
  Compensated 13
  Day 106, 120, 123, 124, 126, 147, 150, 175, 191, 192, 193, 194, 195, 201
  Park 148, 200

Proclamation 5, 9, 13, 21, 22, 23, 27, 31, 33, 37, 39, 45, 46, 47, 52, 54, 55, 56, 62, 63, 86, 87, 95, 101, 102, 115, 120, 122, 123, 124, 127, 129, 144, 149, 151, 153, 156, 157, 159, 161, 162, 186, 187, 189, 197, 202
   Preliminary 4, 39, 50, 144, 148
   Universal 62
Emery, F. W. 27, 85, 86
Epperson, D. H. 152
Estevanico 189
Evans, Robert J. 153

F

Ferguson, Miriam "Ma" 147
Flake's Journal 111
Florida 22, 28, 122, 129, 139
Fox News 161
Freedmen's Press 200
Freedom Day 102, 106, 107, 111, 121, 122, 123, 124, 125, 126, 127, 131, 132, 133, 153, 156, 158, 162, 174, 201

G

Gardiner, Richard 61
Gates, Henry Louis, Jr. 160
General Orders
   Clark
      No. 3 99
   Granger 86–87, 93
      No. 1 85, 86
      No. 2 78
      No. 3 13, 68, 76, 80, 81, 91, 98, 99, 102, 121, 156, 158, 187
      No. 4 78
      No. 5 78
Georgia 22, 27, 28, 36, 43, 122, 191
   Atlanta
      Atlanta Constitution 191
      Atlanta Journal-Constitution 157
      Television Show 184
Granger, Gordon 9, 12, 13, 68, 72, 78, 81, 82, 85, 86, 87, 88, 91, 93, 95, 96, 97, 98, 144, 147, 161, 191, 218
Gregory, Daniel 105

Guam 28

H

Hawaii 28, 127
   Maui 173
Herron, Francis J. 5, 13, 75, 78, 79, 87, 162
Houston, Sam 54, 209
Howe, Julia Ward 140
HuffPost 159

I

Idaho 28, 122
Illinois 27, 28, 29, 95, 122
Indiana 28, 29, 122, 123
Indianola 95, 191
Iowa 28, 95, 123, 164
   Cedar Rapids 164

J

Jackson, Stonewall 43, 88, 168, 169
James Byrd Jr. Hate Crimes Act 201
Jim Crow 112
John Brown's Body 102, 140
Johnson, Andrew 27
Juneteenth
   Advertisements 176–185
   Bunk Busting 188–189
   Celebration Names 148
   Celebrations 68, 97, 102, 114, 147, 175, 191
      Dates 148
   Flag 148
   Historical Marker 87
   Independence Day 129
   Legislation
      Congressional 167–172
      State 121–127
   National Holiday 123, 126, 128–129, 129
   News 192–196
   Origin 11, 81, 98, 101, 153, 197
      Origin of the word 106–107
      Origin of wrongs 174, 186–187

233

Statistics 186
Pardons 147
Photos 10, 19, 30, 35, 36, 44, 51, 69, 89, 108, 113, 143, 146, 164, 173
Recognition Legislation 121
Stamp 153
State Memorial 154
Textbooks 187
Juneteenth Independence Day 121, 123, 125, 126, 129, 132, 136, 165, 167, 168, 169, 170, 171, 172
   Act 135

K

Kansas 28, 123, 142, 192
Karankawa 159
Kelly, John H. 95
Kentucky 21, 22, 28, 88, 123, 151, 186

L

Lee, Robert E. 201
Leonard, Charles H. 99, 204
Lift Every Voice and Sing 138
Lincoln, Abraham 4, 13, 25, 75, 132
Livingston, Lindsay 18
Logan, Thomas 95
Lott, Trent 167, 172
Louisiana 9, 21, 22, 28, 43, 123, 162, 209
   Grambling 51
   Monroe 43
   New Orleans 22, 85, 86, 92, 151, 199
   Shreveport 162

M

Maine 28, 123
Mariana Islands 25, 28, 29
Martin Luther King, Jr. Day 201
Maryland 21, 22, 28, 123, 186
Massachusetts 28, 123, 140
McDonald, W. J. 152
Methodist Episcopal Church 204
Mexico 9, 29, 87, 88, 125, 149, 151, 159, 197, 209
Michigan 28, 29, 124
Military
   Mexico 209
   United States
      Buffalo Soldiers 90, 174
      Freedmen's Bureau 12, 202–207, 206
      Military Telegraph Corps 46–47
      Navy 12, 91, 152, 201
      Ships, Union
         U.S.S. Clinton 85, 95
         U.S.S. Corinthian 85, 95
         U.S.S. Crescent 85, 86, 95
         U.S.S. Exact 85, 95
         U.S.S. Fort Jackson 71
         U.S.S. Montauk 85, 95
         U.S.S. Nightingale 85, 95
         U.S.S. Prometheus 85, 95
         U.S.S. Rice 85, 86, 94, 95
         U.S.S. Westfield 145
         U.S.S. William Kennedy 85, 95
         U.S.S. Wilmington 85, 95
      Troops
         9th Calvary 91
         10th Calvary 91
         12th Regiment Massachusetts Volunteer Infantry 140
         13th Army Corps 95
         24th Infantry 91
         25th Infantry 91
         25th Union Army Corps 92
         28th Indiana Colored Infantry 95
         29th Illinois Colored Infantry 95
         31st New York Colored Infantry 95
         34th Iowa Infantry 95
         62nd Missouri Colored Infantry Regiment 91
         83rd Ohio Volunteer Infantry 94
         83rd Ohio Volunteer Infantry Regiment 95
         94th Illinois regiment 95
Miller, Dorie 201
Mississippi 22, 29, 43, 92
Miss Juneteenth - Movie 153
Missouri 21, 22, 29, 91, 124, 186
Moore, Frederick W. 95

Morton, Azie 201
Murrah, Pendleton 87
Myers, Sr., Ronald 136

N

NAACP 200
National Association of Juneteenth Lineage 167
National Freedom Day 130, 201
Negro Chamber of Commerce 201
Negro Peace Officers Association 201
Nelson, Richard 109
Nevada 29, 113, 125
  Las Vegas 113
Newsweek 157
New York 29, 32, 54, 88, 125
  Buffalo 69
North Carolina 22, 29, 43, 126, 128, 133
  Charlotte 43

O

Okeson, J. B. 95
Oregon 29, 126
Overstreet, Morris 201

P

Patton, William W. 141, 142
Pennsylvania 29, 116, 126, 131
Pittsburg Courier 192
Politico 156
Poll tax 200
Prairie View A & M University
  Alta Vista A&M College of Texas 200
  Prairie View Normal School 200

R

Ranchero 56
Reconstruction 200
Republic of Texas 54, 151, 197, 209
Royce, Clark E. 95

S

Sands, Benjamin 12, 73
  Sands, B. F. 71
Sheridan, Philip 75, 86
  Sheridan 75, 78, 85, 86, 192
Simpson, Alex 202
Slavery 7, 11, 12, 29, 39, 120
Slave Sale, final 152
Smith, Chelsi 201
Smith, Kirby 78
Smothers, Claiborne Washington "Clay" 150
South Carolina 22, 29, 43, 126
  Charleston 43
Standard work agreement 208
Supreme Court 18, 189, 200, 201
Symbols
  13th Amendment 26
    Thirteenth Amendment 26, 29, 125, 132

T

Telegraph Corp 47
  Signal Corps 46
Telford, Pearlie 147
Tennessee 22, 29, 126
  Knoxville 43
  Memphis 146
Texas
  Abilene
    Abilene Reporter-News 195
  Amarillo Globe-Times 194
  Aransas Pass 93
  Austin 51, 53, 54, 56, 57, 99, 154, 157, 158, 191, 194, 195
    American Statesman 191
    Austin American 194, 195
    Austin Statesman 194
    State Gazette 54, 56, 57, 99
    Texas Almanac Extra 53, 56
    Weekly State Gazette 99
  Baytown Sun 185
    Beaumont 195, 201
    Bellville Countryman 55, 57

Brenham 147
  Brenham Banner 192
  Brenham Daily Banner 107, 211
Brownwood Daily Bulletin 191, 211
Bryan 195
Calwell News 185
Carbon News 174
Cass County Sun 192
Central Committee of Colored Men 200
Clarksville
  The Standard 13, 56, 63
Colored Baseball League 200
Constitution 187
Corpus Christi 56, 93
  Corpus Christi Caller 194
Corsicana Daily Sun 194
Dallas 43, 55, 150, 152, 177, 192, 195, 200, 201
Dallas County 152
Dallas Herald 55
Denison Daily Cresset 157
El Campo Citizen 211
El Paso 43, 200
  El Paso Times 182
Fort Worth
  Fort Worth Daily Democrat 192
Galveston
  Ashton Villa 80–83, 83, 87, 174
  Battle of Galveston 80, 144–145
  Celebration 98, 102, 104–105, 140, 195
  Confederate 80, 94
  Flake's Daily Bulletin 85, 102, 104, 105
  Flake's Weekly Bulletin 87
  Galveston County 13
  Galveston County Daily News 81
  Galveston Daily News 180, 184, 191, 192, 193, 198, 199
  Galveston Historical Foundation 81, 85, 87
  Occupation 12, 27
  Osterman Building 81, 85, 87
  Troop arrival 86, 87–88, 94, 95, 187
Gonzales 193
Grimes County 208
Hallettsville 180

Harlingen Valley Morning Star 194, 195
Henderson Times 55
Houston 13, 14, 54, 55, 57, 59, 62, 83, 85, 86, 87, 99, 102, 106, 107, 148, 151, 153, 158, 174, 178, 183, 201, 206, 207, 209, 211
  Daily Post 192
  Houston Informer 177
  Houston Post 194
  Police 200
  Telegraph Suppliment 60
  Tri-weekly Telegraph 50
  Tri-Weekly Telegraph 5
LaGrange Journal 211
Lampasas Daily Leader 175
Longview 200
  Longview News-Journal 182
Laredo Weekly Times 194
Lubbock 195
  Lubbock Evening Journal 195
Mansville High School 201
Marshall
  Marshall Messenger 183, 185
  Marshall News Messenger 194
McAllen 195
Weimar Mercury 195
Negro Peace Officers Association 201
Negro Tax 153
Palestine 200
  Palestine Daily Herald 211
Palmito Ranch 27, 61
Paris 200
Paul Quinn College 200
Rockdale Reporter and Messenger 211
San Antonio 193
  San Antonio Express 177, 211
  San Antonio Register 179, 180, 184
  Semi-Weekly News 56
Schulenburg
  Schulenburg Sticker 211
Slave Sale 152
  State Fair 200
  Supreme Court 18, 189, 200

Taylor Daily Press 195
Temple Daily Telegram 211
Texas Almanac 53, 56, 57, 150
Texas Education Agency 186
Texas Emancipation Day 120, 153
Texas General Land Office 12
Texas History (textbooks) 187
Texas Monthly magazine 150
Texas Revolutionary War 209
Texas State Historical Association 114
Texas State Library and Archives Commission 157
The Eagle 195
The Monitor 195
The Representative 109, 111
The Tribune 180
Tyler Morning Telegraph 182, 195
Van Zandt 193
   Van Zandler 193
Victoria 191
   Victoria Advocate 191
Waco News-Tribune 194
Washington 68
Washington County 87, 192
Waxahachie Daily Light 194
Weatherford Weekly Herald 193
Weimar 195
Texas State University for Negroes 201
Time 161
Translations 15, 25, 26, 32, 33, 46, 68, 133

U

Underground Railroad 149
United States
   Constitution
      13th Amendment 14, 25, 27, 28, 131, 149, 151, 160
      15th Amendment 200
      19th Amendment 112, 200
   Department of State 158
   House of Representatives 167
   Library of Congress 172
   President
      Biden, Joseph 134

Ford, Gerald 29
Grant, Ulysses S. 88, 92
Kennedy, John F. 188
Obama, Barack 201
Truman, Harry 131, 132, 133, 201
Trump, Donald J. 163
Senate 167
University of Texas 152, 157, 158
University of Texas at San Antonio 157
Utah 29, 126

V

Van Anda, S. G. 79
Vermont 29, 127, 158
Virginia 21, 22, 29, 43, 127, 148, 151, 189
   Charlottesville 148
   Richmond 43
Virgin Islands 29

W

Wallace, George 150
Ward, Henry 95
Washington 109, 127, 150
   Spokane 143
Washington, D. C. 29, 43, 54, 122, 140
Watch Night 9, 54, 101, 144, 162, 217, 224
Watermelon 148, 210–213
Weekly Telegraph 5, 54, 55, 57, 59, 60, 62, 83, 86, 87, 99
Weitzel, Godfrey 85, 86, 95
West, Emily 209
West Virginia 22, 29, 86, 127
Wisconsin 29, 30, 127
Wood, T. J. 88
Wyoming 29, 127, 186

Y

Yellow Rose of Texas 209

237

Juneteenth 101

Lest We Forget

NEGRO WOMAN AND CHILD FOR SALE.
FOR SALE, a young and likely negro woman and child, for Confederate money. Apply to
o28-tf   L. FELLMAN.

(Above) Classified advertisement from:
The Texas Almanac -- "Extra."
Vol. 1, No. 9, Ed. 1, Oct. 30, 1862.

(Right) Photo of Mary Ann Patterson.
Former slave, Fort Worth, Texas
Depository: Library of Congress.

238

Made in the USA
Columbia, SC
19 April 2025